S0-DFG-603

ENDORSEMENTS

Steve Wisniewski wasn't just a great football player who went to eight Pro Bowls and set a physical tone for the Oakland Raiders. He's a great man who found Christ and is setting a tone carrying his message off the field. This is a must- read book from a man you just have to meet. He's a difference maker and so is his message.

—JON GRUDEN
Super Bowl Winning NFL
head coach for the Tampa Bay Buccaneers,
and *Monday Night Football* Commentator
and analyst for ESPN, Former Head Coach
of the Oakland Raiders.

I can think of no finer man, who represented the National Football League while prioritizing Faith and Family than Steve Wisniewski. There are those who pontificate, Steve has lived it. Through this well written book he has shared with others the balance of Faith, Family and Football with those who have not had the luxury to have witnessed first hand as I and many have. I'm forever proud of Steve and consider him a life long friend.

—JIM HARBAUGH
Head Football Coach at the University of Michigan,
former Head Coach of the San Francisco Forty-Niners,
Stanford University and University of San Diego.

When our son Kyle was about to begin his career as an offensive lineman in the NFL, Steve was one of the guys that I told Kyle to watch on film. He played the game the way it was supposed to be played. But the biggest compliment that I can pay to Steve is that I told Kyle to emulate him as a person, because as great a player as Steve was, he's an even better person.

—HOWIE LONG
NFL Hall of Fame Defensive Tackle

Steve Wisniewski was one of the fiercest competitors that ever stepped foot on the NFL gridiron. A faithful Christian friend, husband and father, Wiz is STILL COMPETING, as he challenges men to follow God's call in their life. Wiz offers spectacular stories, insights, and biblical truths that apply directly to men's lives. These stories of football and faith will leave you wanting more, as you feel the excitement and determination in Steve's words. He has transitioned admirably from competing for championships, to competing to win men to Jesus. I am honored to call him a good friend!

—BRENT JONES
Former San Francisco Forty-Niner player
and Principal of Northgate Capital

"Wiz" is a Hall of Fame contender both on and off the field. Through this masterful work Steve explores what it means to finish well and finish strong. Using football as a metaphor he opens the door of God's locker room and places you in the holy huddle to learn how to live out your faith. This is a must read for anyone who wishes to become stronger in their Christian walk and character while better understanding God's playbook—the Bible.

—DR. JIM GRASSI
Author and Former NFL Chaplain
Founder/President Men's Ministry Catalyst

Steve Wisniewski is a great role model for people to follow. Every task that God has given him to do, Steve has done with all of his might: from being a physical and intimidating All-Pro offensive linemen, to being a caring God-following husband and father. I'm proud to be one of the many people who are blessed to know him.

—DAVID SHAW
Head Football Coach, Stanford University

Quiet, modest, unassuming...the 'Wiz' has always been a make-it-happen guy on the field, a true warrior. Fortunately for you and me, he has penned this powerful book to share his insight, faith, and wisdom...and wow...it's impactful! If you are searching for your purpose in life, or just want to learn from Wiz's life's lessons, this book is for you. Wiz, thank you for sharing!

—RANDY WILLIAMS
Founder and CEO of the Keiretsu Forum—
worldwide angel investing network

Steve Wisniewski is someone who I admire as a football player but even more so as a man of God. He has a passion for helping other men reach their full potential in Jesus Christ."

—BRUCE MATTHEWS
NFL Hall of Famer
former Tennessee Titan Offensive
Lineman and Coach

I have been blessed to call Steve my friend since his rookie year with the Raiders and will forever be grateful for his friendship and dedication to serving God that was instrumental in my salvation.

Many people will remember Steve as a tenacious player who was always looking for someone to hit on the football field, and he was, but it was his off-field demeanor that I found most attractive. Whether in the locker room engaging teammates, with his family or in the community, sometimes inviting a homeless person to share an impromptu meal, he has always led from the front and inspired others to follow his example. I am excited for Steve to share his lifetime of experiences which I am sure will challenge us to live a more purposeful life.

—JOHN C. GESEK
Partner, Fusion Capital Management

HAND ON THE LINE

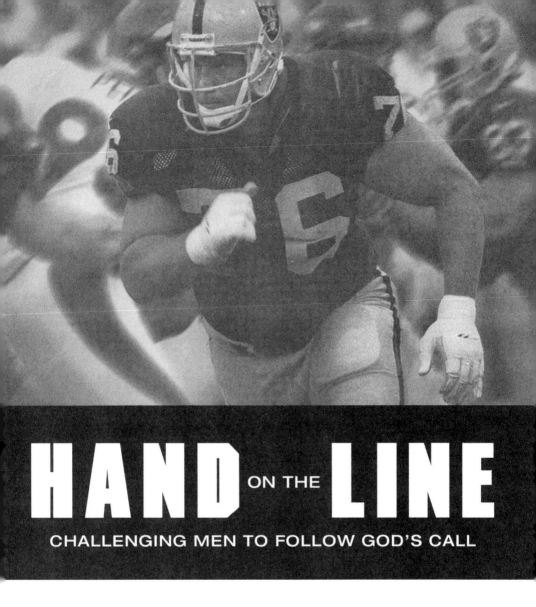

HAND ON THE LINE

CHALLENGING MEN TO FOLLOW GOD'S CALL

STEVE WISNIEWSKI

WITH JEFF ROSTOCIL

© Copyright 2015—Steve Wisniewski

All rights reserved. This book is protected by the copyright laws of the United States of America. This book may not be copied or reprinted for commercial gain or profit. The use of short quotations or occasional page copying for personal or group study is permitted and encouraged. Permission will be granted upon request. Unless otherwise identified, Scripture quotations are taken from the HOLY BIBLE, NEW INTERNA-TIONAL VERSION®, Copyright © 1973, 1978, 1984 International Bible Society. Used by permission of Zondervan. All rights reserved. Scripture quotations marked MSG are taken from The Message. Copyright © 1993, 1994, 1995, 1996, 2000, 2001, 2002. Used by permission of NavPress Publishing Group. Scripture quotations marked NKJV are taken from the New King James Version. Copyright © 1982 by Thomas Nelson, Inc. Used by permission. All rights reserved. Scripture quotations marked NLT are taken from the Holy Bible, New Living Translation, copyright 1996, 2004. Used by permission of Tyndale House Publishers., Wheaton, Illinois 60189. All rights reserved. Scripture quotations marked ESV are from The Holy Bible, English Standard Version®, copyright © 2001 by Crossway, a publishing ministry of Good News Publishers. Used by permission. All rights reserved. Scripture quotations marked KJV taken from the King James Version. All emphasis within Scripture quotations is the author's own.

DESTINY IMAGE® PUBLISHERS, INC.

P.O. Box 310, Shippensburg, PA 17257-0310

"Promoting Inspired Lives."

This book and all other Destiny Image and Destiny Image Fiction books are available at Christian bookstores and distributors worldwide.

Cover design by Eileen Rockwell

Photos used by permission of Oakland Raiders

For more information on foreign distributors, call 717-532-3040.

Or reach us on the Internet: www.destinyimage.com

ISBN 13: TP 978-0-7684-0806-5

ISBN 13 EBook: 978-0-7684-0807-2

For Worldwide Distribution, Printed in the U.S.A.

1 2 3 4 5 6 7 8 9 10 11 /17 16 15

ACKNOWLEDGMENTS

I would like to give thanks to my Lord and Savior Jesus Christ, who considered me worthy to write this book. It was an assignment I did not want and that I did not ask for. But in yielding myself to it, it broke me, and I am a better man for it. I was nothing but a disobedient sinner, but I am now redeemed by the grace of God. I praise God who remained so faithful and patient with me even when I wallowed in my own excuses.

I would like to thank my incredible wife, who never gave up on me or her vision, support, and encouragement for this book project. When I was ready to quit on this book, she encouraged me to press on and follow God's call at all costs. To my three amazing kids who inspired me in so many ways and always believed this message was worth sharing with others.

I would like to thank my spiritual brother, Jeff Rostocil, for his years of love, support, and his gifted writing and editorial skills. He and his family were a huge blessing and catalyst to bringing this story to print. He is incredibly gifted and an amazing servant of the Lord.

A godly heritage is a blessing from the Lord. I would like to thank my mother, Valia, and father, Jim, who never lived long enough to see the completion of this book, but whose inspiration and Christian examples were indelible. Thanks to my sisters

Mary, Diane, and Sharon, and my brothers Vince and Leo, who always encouraged me that I had a message to share.

Disciples aren't born. They are made by the loving investment of other believers. I would like to thank my former teammate and pastor, Napoleon Kaufman, and all members and staff of the Well Christian Community in Livermore, California. Pastor Napoleon's patience in answering many years' worth of questions and his tireless support in my personal discipleship was a major catalyst to my growth.

"As irons sharpens iron, so one man sharpens another" (Prov. 27:17). I want to thank all the other godly men who have taught me life lessons and inspired me in the things of God. I was blessed to learn from selfless pastors such as Steve Madson, Ron Pinkston, Jim Grassi, Loren Heath, and Dave Slotje, as well as team chaplains Adam Ybarra and Ron Seroto. Thank you to all my coaches, teammates, and good friends over the years who impacted my life and loved me like a brother. I am a better man today for what each of you taught me. Special thanks to my bros: Chester, Danny, JYD, Biek, The Clarkster, Hoss, Mosey, Gogs, Brent, Kohn, "The Wiz Zone," and the men of Ruby Hill. You have deposited far more in me than I in you.

CONTENTS

INTRODUCTION

In our Christian faith, we're either running to God or running away from Him; we're either drawing closer to Him and to His purposes for our life, or we are drawing farther away from what He has planned for us. Like an athlete in training, there can be no middle ground.

I may be best known for my football career, as I spent thirteen seasons playing offensive guard in the NFL as an Oakland Raider. I embraced my role as an aggressive and tenacious player who proudly wore the silver and black, a team captain, and an eight-time Pro Bowler. I roamed from sideline to sideline looking for someone to hit, a teammate to support, or a fight to finish. *Sports Illustrated* named me the NFL's "dirtiest player" of the year in 1997,[1] and one website has me ranked as the twelfth dirtiest player in league history.[2] Perhaps it was deserved.

But God reached out to me and began to touch my heart and draw me closer to Him. As He often enjoys, God chooses the unlikeliest of characters to begin a Christ-centered transformation. I was the proverbial ugly duckling of a child, crippled by an auto accident, but slowly transformed into an All-Pro football player. I went from being a mean competitor to a minister of the gospel of Jesus Christ. I came from a divorced home only to become a committed husband and father. Intensely shy and inwardly focused as a child, I now find myself as a public speaker who bares his soul to strangers. I was dyslexic as a boy and disliked school, but somehow I managed to become a college graduate and a reluctant author.

At times I hungered after God, and for a time I ran from the tasks He assigned me. Yet in those seasons when I was faithless, God always remained faithful to His purposes for me. He never gave up on me, and He hasn't given up on you either. He has a plan and a purpose for your life, just as He has a plan and purpose for mine.

I pray this book will be a catalyst for your spiritual growth. I have not written it to be a sermon, but life lessons learned the hard way. May these stories become helpful resources that stimulate discussion and reflection deep in your heart. In my disobedience, I wasted many years in a spiritually dry place. I don't want that for you. I hope these simple truths speak to your own doubts and struggles and inspire you to fully commit to God, advance your faith, and hunger for more of Christ's presence in your life. Please share it with others as it is written to be a study guide to facilitate discussion with other unlikely candidates of God's grace.

If you hate to read, doubt your calling, struggle with your faith, or just haven't fully committed your life to the Lord, then this book is for you. You may not realize it now, but you're not in this alone. Take your time to read each chapter and ponder the questions at the end. Let God do what He does best—stir thoughts in your spirit and draw you closer to Him. I am praying that you would respond to the voice of God in your life.

Endnotes

1. *Sports Illustrated*, http://sportsillustrated.cnn.com/events/1997/ nflpreview/FEATURES/nasty.html, accessed February 17, 2015.

2 This information is taken from http://www.ranker.com/list/ dirtiest-nfl-players-of-all-time/prosportsextra, accessed February 17, 2015.

CHAPTER 1

A GENTLE WHISPER

What you do in this life echoes in eternity.

—GLADIATOR

Great moments don't always seem great in the moment. It is not until after we look back on them that we tend to realize they were the catalyst that catapulted us in a certain direction, and propelled us past the point of no return. Mine came January 19, 2002, on a football field in Foxboro, Massachusetts.

Tom Brady, a talented second-year quarterback out of the University of Michigan, stood on the sidelines next to his offensive coordinator. Down 13–10 in blizzard-like conditions, with less than two minutes to play in the fourth quarter, he and the New England Patriots were trying to advance the ball down the field and advance beyond this AFC divisional playoff game. To do so, however, they would have to go through the teeth of a gritty and seasoned Oakland Raider defense.

On most days the hype and excitement of the game overshadows the weather. On this night, however, the forces of nature dominated the event. An arctic storm had settled in over New England with game-time temperatures dipping down into the teens. Sleet followed by steady snow blanketed the field with as much as five inches of powder, making the field markings virtually indistinguishable. During commercial breaks, the maintenance crew provided cosmetic and comic relief as they slipped and sputtered across the field, trying to push snow blowers. We used the longest spiked cleats the league would allow, but finding any kind of solid footing on this frozen turf was next to impossible.

And to make matters worse, the crowd was just as unpredictable as the weather. Over 60,000 juiced-up Patriot fans shook the grandstands like rolling claps of thunder. Night games in the NFL always draw a more raucous and inebriated crowd, but this was something for the ages—a nationally televised playoff game in a driving snowstorm on the final game to be played at Foxboro Stadium. The fans hoped to steal a victory, a goal post, or perhaps even the seat they sat on as they exited the ballpark in celebration. They sensed they had something special in this team and in their young quarterback, and they were hungry to witness their first championship.

Propane heaters were positioned along the sidelines for the players, and as our guys tried to stay loose by stretching and throwing footballs, some fans did their best to distract us by hurling snowballs, insults, and taunts of every unmentionable kind. Over the course of my career, I have been hit with batteries, beer bottles, cups of urine, and chunks of ice, so in comparison the Pats fans were quite mild. In fact, I loved playing in hostile environments, as I always could respect passion and fan hatred for the opposing side. It actually fueled me and motivated me to further embarrass and defeat their beloved team.

From the outset, this game had all the elements of a truly epic football game—the weather, the talent, the playoff atmosphere, and the crowd. It was a roller coaster of a game, and every player was physically and emotionally invested in it from start to finish. This was NFL playoff football at its finest, and football like it was meant to be played—demanding, unforgiving, unrelenting, and unpredictable.

"Hey, we should go three-by-one and throw the slant backside," Brady relayed to his coach.

In the chaos of the moment, neither Coach Weiss nor Brady noticed six-time Pro Bowl Raider cornerback Eric Allen stationed stealthily along the sidelines. Stealing signals in the NFL has long been refined to an art form, and no one did it better than our opportunistic defense. As players hustled back to their respective sidelines, Allen simply followed the pack of Patriots as though he was part of the team. Kneeling down as if to tie his shoe, the fourteen-year veteran stood directly behind the official's down marker and inconspicuously crept to within earshot of the Patriot signal caller.

Like a fox stalking the hen house, he overheard the offensive play call, and raced back to the Raider huddle to set up the defense. It wasn't too difficult to decipher the play, as both teams ran similar offenses, and many of the offensive terms in the league were widely used. "Hey, they're gonna go with a three-by-one formation, so linebackers make sure you're in that first throwing window."

Little did we know this would prove to be the biggest play of the game in the biggest game of the season for our team. And, in particular, this would be the biggest play for me as well.

Planning to Retire

I had intentions of retiring the previous offseason in 2000. I informed management of my plans early in preseason so they could prepare for it by signing or drafting a replacement for me. But owner Al Davis and general manager Bruce Allen didn't want me to retire and simply wouldn't take no for an answer. A few days into training camp that year, Bruce and Head Coach Jon Gruden showed up at my doorstep unexpectedly saying the team missed my leadership on the offensive line and needed me to come back for one more season. So, of course, I did.

This year, however, there was no recanting my retirement plans. I had announced my retirement before the season began, so this was potentially the last game of my professional career. After thirteen full-throttle seasons as an offensive guard in the NFL, my body was feeling the effects from countless collisions, concussions, and contusions. Starting with my head and working my way down to my ankles, Monday mornings were usually a very slow process of assessing the pain level and mobility in my body. Something each week was bound to hurt, and my body never seemed to have enough time to fully heal before I went out and injured myself again the following Sunday.

Practice and weight training only furthered to aggravate old injuries. Football players learn to live with the stiffness and swelling of the previous game, as adrenaline, ice, painkillers, and anti-inflammatory drugs can only carry you along for so long. As my career progressed, the season evolved into a seven-month marathon of pain management, physical treatment, and emotional swings from narrow victories and bitter defeats.

When it came to retirement, I had always admired players who walked away from football at the top of their game. They refused to whimper and hang onto one more season, even if they could still perform at a high level. I admired men of strength, conviction, and character, like former Raider teammates Matt Millen, Howie Long, Jeff Hostetler, Don Mosebar, and Bo Jackson. They were proud to wear the silver and black and were men who could be trusted and counted on when the game, or, for that matter, my life, was on the line. From early on I sought to model my career, my actions on the field, and my style of leadership after these guys, and I hoped that perhaps I could instill something positive into those who came after me.

The Raider organization had been wonderful to my family and me, and deep down I was disappointed that I was never apart of a Raider team that won a Super Bowl. At 33, I was getting old for an NFL player, and inwardly I doubted that I was physically up to the challenge of another season. Football is a young man's sport, but I reasoned that I owed them one more season if they felt so strongly that I could be of help. They agreed with that logic and said, "Pack your clothes. It's time to report to camp." With that I was off.

The week prior to the Patriot game, Coach Gruden gave a fiery speech to the team, laying out the wild-card scenario and how we were going to defend home turf against the New York Jets. Gruden was a brilliant offensive coach and is now an excellent commentator. He is a true competitor, always outspoken, and has the heart of a lion. He made it fun for us veteran players, and his energy and confidence were contagious, sometimes even comical with his coarse language and exaggerated facial expressions. Needless to say, I loved playing for Gruden, as did the rest of the team. He was able to take an average group of guys, some past their prime and with limited ability, and convince us that we could be champions. He expected us to win and helped us believe that we would win every time we stepped onto the field.

I had no intention of going out a loser, so I meticulously prepared myself for this contest with the New England Patriots. I had an exacting pregame routine, and I stuck to it religiously. I arrived at the stadium on the early bus, which gave me nearly four hours to prepare prior to kick off. I laid out my uniform, socks, and several pairs of shoes. I stretched my stiff, cold body, and taped down my jersey and shoulder pads with double-sided tape. It took me nearly forty-five minutes just to make sure my jersey wouldn't have any creases or extra material a defender could grab. Athletic trainer Scott Touchet then taped my ankles, wrists, knuckles, and eventually my cleats once they were fully laced up. It was a process scripted to the smallest detail, which is typical for any player in the NFL. Every player has their own routine on game day, and coaches learn to give guys their space in the locker room as they prepare.

Every game I saw myself as a warrior going into battle with my teammates at my side. Like a boy with a Superman cape, I felt invincible. "The field is my playground," I would say to myself. It was a phrase I had coined early in my career, and I would regularly repeat it to my teammates. Sometimes I quoted Psalm 23 to myself to bring additional comfort as I walked through the haze and noise of fan ridicule.

As was my custom, I reviewed my assignments, my playbook, and my personal goals for the game. The night before each game, Coach Gruden detailed the first fifteen opening plays with us as an offense, and I would make it a point to memorize my list. On the handout, I also wrote down my personal goals, tips to look for during the game, and my favorite motivational Scriptures. My paper always included Psalm 28:7 and Psalm 91:2.

The mental aspect of professional sports is something that cannot be overlooked. Athleticism only carries you so far, but great champions in every sport tend to be mentally strong. Mentally strong people are not fazed by adversity and trials. People like to label Christians as weak and timid. But I hate this stereotype, as there is no weakness found in the Man Jesus Christ. His spirit is unshakable, and with Him we have no one or nothing to fear. Christians should not apologize for boldly standing their ground for truth and righteousness.

In order to play at a high level, I had learned to tune everything out during a game—to completely focus my thoughts inward, control my heart rate, and breathe slowly while maintaining awareness of all that was going on around me. Before games I would sit at my locker in silence, eyes closed and mind focused as I visualized my blocks and the scenes of the opening plays. I was determined to play with all of my heart and to be there to support my teammates through thick and thin. If there was a fight, I wanted to be in the middle of it. When our ball carriers were tackled, I wanted to be there to help them up. If there was an interception, I wanted to make the tackle. Like a gladiator in the coliseum fighting for his life, I felt I owed it to my teammates to lead them out of the arena victoriously.

The Biggest Play of the Game

After three hours of preparation, I was taped up, tapped into the Spirit, and in full battle mode a good twenty minutes before the coin toss. In all my twenty-four years of playing organized football, I never felt more prepared for a game than this one. Win or lose, I was determined to spill my guts onto the gridiron that night, and from the first snap to the final play I did. I flew over every pile of bodies, sprinted out every play until the echo of the whistle, and competed with reckless abandon for four quarters.

As the game progressed, stinging wind and ice relentlessly punished my face. At one point I looked down at my uniform, stained with grass and dirt—my body was covered in sweat as blood oozed from a recurrent gash on my forehead. My team-mates were equally as focused and driven. I remember seeing wide receiver Jerry Rice's uniform looking weather-beaten, soaked and twisted on his shoulder pads. Without a word I reached across the huddle, pulled the collar of his jersey back over his pads, and lightly slapped the side of his helmet releasing several inches of packed snow from his facemask. Not a word needed to be spoken because he too was oblivious to the surroundings.

When Brady dropped back to pass, little did we know that we were participating in arguably the most controversial play in all of

NFL history. Anticipating the slant, Charles Woodson got a good break from the line and got to the quarterback on a blitz. Brady lost the ball. Greg Biekert dove on it and recovered the fumble on the forty-seven yard line. With 1:43 remaining in the fourth quarter, a victory and a birth in the AFC championship game was all but secured. The Raider sideline instantly exploded in celebration, as the Patriots sideline and their fans recoiled. There was no mistaking what had just happened. The tide of momentum had clearly swung for the Raiders to seal a victory.

Action shot from that evening in Foxboro as the snow started to accumulate.

Just as our offense lined up to snap the ball and run out the clock, the referees waved their arms and blew their whistles. They made their trot over to the replay booth. The play was under review. "Review?" we questioned one another. "What is there to review?" It was clearly a fumble. Even by witnessing Tom Brady's reaction after the play, he clearly knew it was a fumble too. He didn't even question the referee's call or raise an argument in displaying his dismay. Dejected, he immediately put his head down and walked over to the sidelines.

Players and fans alike never want the officials to decide a game because of a bad call, and the longer they looked at the play the more nervous we grew. We all felt a knot in our gut when head referee Walt Coleman returned to the field and signaled incomplete pass. He explained that the ball was moving forward at the time it was dropped, thus declaring it a dead ball. The obvious fumble was overturned, and the ball was returned to the Patriots. Both teams appeared shocked and momentarily stunned in disbelief. Instead of the Raiders gaining possession on our own forty-seven yard line, the call kept the Patriots' drive alive.[1]

The Patriots took advantage of their new life. Facing strong winds and driving snow, placekicker Adam Vinatieri sent an explosion of snow up into the air as he drilled the ball through the uprights from forty-five yards out. With twenty-seven seconds remaining in regulation, his line-drive field goal tied the game at 13–13 and sent it to overtime. In the overtime period, we never got the ball back. The Patriots won the coin toss and drove sixty-one yards in fifteen plays, winning it on a Vinatieri twenty-three-yard field goal. New England would advance to the AFC championship game against the Pittsburgh Steelers, and eventually defeat the St. Louis Rams to win Super Bowl XXXVI.

This game went down as one of the most watched football games in all NFL history. It is commonly referred to as the "Tuck Rule Game" or the "Snow Bowl." To Raiders fans, however, it is dubbed the "Snow Job," as replays showed the tuck call was a dubious matter of interpretation at best. After the game, Charles Woodson described the play as he saw it: "He pumped the ball, brought it back down. Maybe he wanted to bring it back up, but the ball came out. Game over. It kind of took the air out of a lot of guys. We knew the game was over. We were all celebrating." He was right.

Two Plays Before

For me, however, the play of the game came two plays before the controversial tuck rule play, before the Patriots had even taken possession of the football. With only a couple of minutes remaining on the clock, we had the ball at midfield. It was fourth and one, and instead of punting the decision was made to go for it. We needed just one yard to get a first down and seal the victory.

14 BLAST

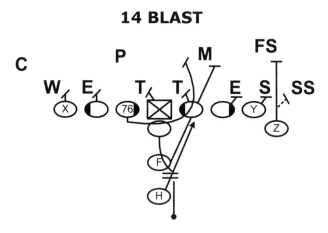

The play came in as 14 Blast. I loved the call. It was just like Jon Gruden. It was bold, it was risky, and it showed that he had full faith and trust in his offensive unit. The play came into the huddle as our old faithful "Fourteen Blast." This was our number one go-to short yardage and goal line play. Our coaches preached for years that this play is unstoppable even if the entire stadium knows you're running it. Sadly, that night, I think the entire stadium did know we were running it. In theory, the play requires simple execution and should gain at least one yard or more on every attempt.

On this play, the center and right guard are trained to block any defender in the gap to their left. The left guard (which is my position) pulls around to the play side "A" gap, and the fullback and I act as lead blockers for the tailback. It should result in a mass of bodies running the ball right over the original alignment of the right guard. We had practiced it hundreds of times over the years, and even ran it successfully dozens of times in previous games.

I grabbed my dirt-covered mouthpiece that I taped to my facemask, and bit down hard on the frozen and brittle plastic. Quarterback Rich Gannon called the play. We broke the huddle and sprinted to take our positions on the line of scrimmage. This was it. We could win the game right now, all on our own. We only needed one yard, and this was the play to get us that yard.

I sunk my hand into the snow and attempted to dig my cleats into the frozen turf. With my hand on the line, I kept my eyes up to scan the defenders' locations. I saw Patriots linebacker Teddy Bruschi inching forward as Gannon started his cadence. Blitzing defenders just can't help themselves. Like predators stalking their prey, their body posture and demeanor almost always give them away. Just as anxious as I was to gain a yard and get a first down, so he was equally determined to make a big play and stop us for no gain.

When the center flexed his bicep to snap the ball, Bruschi sprinted to the play side "A" gap over our right guard. He watched film too and was well coached. Before our right guard could take his first step, Bruschi was in his gap, causing penetration and a pileup of bodies. As I pulled out of my stance, the fullback and I tripped on the surge of defenders. In an instant there was a plume of snow, dirt, cleats, and a pile of bodies that looked like the scene of a small avalanche.

When the whistle had been repeatedly blown, the referees began pulling players off the pile only to reveal the ball carrier was stopped an inch or two short of the first down. I felt sick to my stomach like I had personally failed my coaches and my team-mates. If I had done a better job, maybe we would have gotten that first down. That play still haunts me to this day. The Patriots took possession of the ball on downs. Had we converted, the tuck rule play would have never happened.

The Best Is Yet to Come

After the game, however, there was an intense outburst of emotion from both teams. The Patriots and their fans celebrated wildly while we were shell-shocked and in utter disbelief. Some of my teammates quickly sprinted off the field surrounded by security guards as the crowd erupted into a Mardi Gras-like pandemonium. Others slowly filed off the field and into the locker room. Tears were streaming down grown men's faces while others vented a tirade of profanities. Most of my teammates felt the officials cheated us out of victory. Jerry Rice summed it up best when he said to reporters in the locker room: "I feel like we had the game stolen from us."

After the game I joined a small group of players from both teams at midfield to kneel in prayer, which is a time-honored NFL player-led custom since the early 1990s. In an act of Christian unity seldom covered by the media, a member of the home team leads in a brief prayer of thanks and praise. My mind was already being flooded with a sea of thoughts, so I'm not exactly sure what was prayed that night. I thought about the many unplanned and unscripted events of my career, the gut-wrenching losses, the miraculous come-from-behind victories, the many failures and successes I had experienced over the course of my twenty-three years in organized football.

I recalled my teammates, some of whom had suffered devastating injuries. I thought of center Don Mosebar who lost the use of his eye in a preseason scrimmage in Dallas, and Napoleon McCallum whose knee was dislocated and turned around backward right in front of me at a game in San Francisco. I remembered fun times and adventures with my teammates, the joy I felt when named team captain, and the pride I took in representing my team in the Pro Bowl.

Despite being utterly crushed and disgusted with myself that we lost the game, an inexplicable wave of peace came over me as I neared the end zone. Limping off the field, I found myself involuntarily singing the tune of a children's Sunday school song:

> *The Lord is good to me,*
> *And so I thank the Lord*
> *For giving me the things I need,*
> *The sun and rain and an apple seed.*
> *Yes, the Lord's been good to me.*

"What a ridiculous song to come to mind," I thought to myself, yet I couldn't stop singing it to myself. In that moment, any thought of looking back with sadness or regret vanished and all that remained was the grace of God. A huge smile came to my face, and it felt like a mountain of frustration lifted off my back. I didn't hear any audible voice from heaven, nor did I see any visions from above, but I had a strong impression that the Holy Spirit was whispering something to my soul: "The best is not behind you. The best is yet to come. I've called you to do more then just play football."

If anyone around me was watching, they must have thought I had gone loony. We had just lost the biggest game of the season, and we did it in devastating fashion. We had fallen short of our goal of reaching the Super Bowl, and to make matters worse, this was the last game of my NFL career. This is not the way I wanted to go out, and normally I was disappointed and very critical of myself after a loss. But in the midst of an angry, volatile locker room, I was smiling, hugging teammates, and mumbling a happy little children's tune that simply wouldn't get out of my head.

Sensing a Call from God

I had sensed the call of God on my life over the final years of my NFL career. I followed whatever play was called by the quarterback for twenty-three years of organized football. I never questioned it, faithfully executing my assignment each and every time. But would I be willing to follow the call of God?

I thought at one time maybe God was leading me into full-time ministry, yet that didn't seem appealing. I would be bored out of my mind working in a church. I inwardly hungered to learn more about God though, so I read a slew of Christian books when we traveled as a team and began a more disciplined study of reading through the Bible. I spent more time in prayer and in fellowship with other believers, and somehow I felt there was something more for me than just a life in the world of football.

I read an account in the Old Testament about how God revealed Himself to the prophet Elijah. He had Elijah go up to a mountain, and a great wind ripped through the mountain. After that, an earthquake violently shook the rock, and finally a blazing fire swept across the mountain. Each time it states that the Lord was not present in those events. He certainly had a hand in causing them, but He did not speak through those events. It states that after all that chaos, the Lord revealed Himself to Elijah through a gentle whisper (see 1 Kings 19:10-13).

That resonated with me—*a gentle whisper.* At different times throughout my life, I went through violent mountain top experiences, but God didn't necessarily speak through them. As the storms cleared in my life, however, and especially now at the tail end of my professional career, I could sense a gentle whisper coming from the heart of God. I believe it was God drawing me in, revealing Himself to me, and giving me an assignment.

The Raiders would have welcomed me back for another season, but I felt it was the right time to step away. The reality of God in me was becoming greater than the desire to pursue the glamour of the lifestyle that surrounded me. For most, retirement is the end, but for me it was just the beginning, the start of my journey toward answering the call of God for my life.

Chalk Talk

1. How do you currently handle times of stress, hardship, disappointment, or personal failure?

2. Does God care who wins a football game? Is anything really too big or too small to bring to Him?

3. Have you ever tried to invite God into your workspace? Do you turn to Him in prayer when life's pressures are on you, or do you try to carry the burden alone?

4. Do you sense any kind of calling or gentle whisper from God in your life? What's He saying to you?

5. Do you sense it is time to move into a new season for your life spiritually, emotionally, or physically? How might you do that?

Endnote

1   In later interviews, Coleman cited an obscure rule known as the "tuck rule." This little-known rule stated that when an offensive player is holding the ball to make a forward pass, any intentional forward movement of his arm starts a forward pass, even if the player loses possession of the ball as he is attempting to tuck it back to his body. In his opinion, this rule applied to the play, making the reversal of the call on the field "easy."

CHAPTER 2

THE CALL

*To each there comes in their lifetime a special moment
when they are figuratively tapped on the shoulder and
offered the chance to do a very special thing, unique
to them and fitted to their talents. What a tragedy if
that moment finds them unprepared or unqualified
for that which could have been their finest hour.*
—WINSTON CHURCHILL[1]

With my football career now over, I look back amazed that it ever
became a reality. At the age of 3, I was nearly killed in a freak
accident when I was struck by a car and dragged across the pave-
ment at the edge of our suburban front yard in upstate New York.
I was pinned under the chassis of the vehicle in a pool of blood.
It was a life-threatening situation that required emergency care, a
prolonged hospital stay, numerous skin grafts, and intensive reha-
bilitation. Both my legs were shattered from the accident, and I
was left with permanent nerve damage and significant scars. I had
to relearn to walk, and still today I feel the effects of that accident.

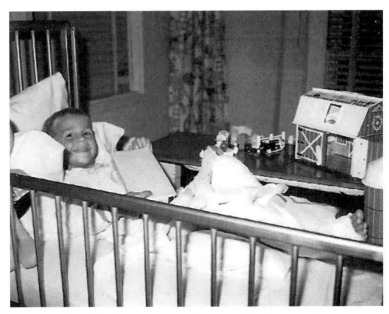

All smiles during my extended hospital stay as a child

In grade school I was that pudgy kid who was usually picked last for football and basketball games. I still can't sink a basket if my life depended on it. It was also discovered early on that I had dyslexia, which required several years of special education classes and tutoring. The special education classes were fun for me because they rewarded us with candy at the end of the week for good behavior, so I didn't mind it too much. I worked hard, and by middle school I eventually learned to read on par with my class-mates. I'm not sure if it was the candy that motivated me to read or if it was all those classes that gave me a sweet tooth, but still today I have an enduring love for both.

I was a sophomore in high school when my parents divorced after thirty-one years of marriage. Being the youngest of six kids, I was the only one still at home so I went to live with my mom in a small two bedroom apartment. Because of my background and perceived shortcomings, I tended to be shy, especially disliking public speaking. The awkward separation from my father at that age also fostered in me a sense of rejection and a lack of trust in my relationships.

No one who knew me then would have ever guessed that I would one day become a professional football player. Who would have thought the kid who struggled to read would go on to earn a four-year business degree from a major university? Only in a Disney movie does an unathletic kid who walks with a slight limp earn a scholarship, become a two-time All-American, and an eight-time Pro Bowl football player. I didn't even see in myself that I could become a vocal team captain in both college and the pros. But that's God for you. He redeems and He sees in us what we don't even know is there. Only God could have known what He had encoded into my DNA.

There are over 7 billion people in the world today, and, with the exception of identical twins, each one of us has a unique DNA fingerprint. Like an actual fingerprint, our genetic fingerprint serves as a DNA profiler used to identify us as distinct individuals. DNA is the blueprint of life. It is in all living things and can be found in almost every cell of your body, but are you aware that the amount of genetic information in you is so vast that your entire DNA sequence would fill two hundred 1,000-page New York City telephone directories? If you were to unwrap the entire DNA in your body, it would reach the moon 6,000 times.[2] We are indeed incredibly complex and unquestionably unique (see Ps. 139:13-14; Eccles. 3:11).

It should come as no surprise that the inventor of DNA has an eternal blueprint for each of our lives and has encoded His DNA onto our hearts. King David writes, *"Your eyes saw my unformed body; all the days ordained for me were written in Your book before one of them came to be"* (Ps. 139:16). This means that even before you were born, heaven had a playbook drawn up for your life, one with your name on it and written exclusively for you. In it is what you are created to do and who you are designed to become.

The single greatest thing a man will ever do in his life is follow God's blueprint, as it is for this reason we were created. It is not accidental or coincidental that we have been born in this time and in this place. No one else can fulfill your call for you, and your assignment is critical to this hour of history. God made you for a specific purpose. Now it's time to walk in it.

Draft Day

I'll never forget the anticipation I felt the day I was drafted. It was an unseasonably mild spring morning in 1989. My fiancée, and I hustled back from church to the musty two-bedroom apartment I shared with three of my teammates on the campus of Penn State University. We were in search of a quiet and somewhat private place to hide where I could nervously watch the draft and await "the call" that might forever change the course of my life.

Draft day in professional sports is a surreal event, unlike anything else in life. It's when a young and relatively naïve student athlete with only a few dollars to his name watches helplessly as his future is decided by some unseen sports executive. This random decision determines where an athlete will work, where they will live, and ultimately what they will initially earn. Teams spend several months on thorough predraft analysis, yet every year the draft produces surprising sleepers and outright blunders. Both the players and the teams themselves never know quite how it will all play out.

At the time I was a senior finishing up my degree in marketing at Penn State. Having completed four seasons of football, I had been named a team captain and was a two-time All-American offensive guard. As a three-year starter, I had the privilege of being a member of a national championship team in 1986, and competed in the Hula Bowl and Japan Bowl, two postseason all-star games. I had also put up some good numbers at the NFL scouting combine in Indianapolis, running a 4.9 forty-yard dash while bench-pressing 225 pounds thirty-three times. At 6'3" and 285 pounds, I was a bit on the small side for a lineman, but as an aggressive, strong, and athletic player I was told I was a good prospect as a pulling guard in the NFL.

As I walked up to the Nittany Lion Apartments that day, I saw a mass of bodies overflowing from my unit and pouring out into the common area. I commented, "Oh great, just what we need." Much to my dismay, my supportive roommates had invited several dozen people over for an impromptu draft party. I thought, "Who are some of these people, and where did they all come from?"

As I walked closer to my apartment, someone offered me what looked like a half-drunken beer in a plastic cup. "No, thanks," I muttered. We finally worked our way through the door and squeezed past the wall-to-wall bodies to my bedroom where I could quietly contemplate my future. The only television we had was in the living room, and unfortunately I couldn't see it as the sea of people blocked the screen. Every few minutes someone would have to go into the living room and press his or her face to the set to report the name of the player being selected.

As the first round came to a close and the network went to commercials, we all collectively let out mumbled sighs of disappointment. I had no exact idea where I might fall in the selection process. Some scouts said as early as mid-first round or early second round, but players usually have no way of knowing for sure. What was especially disappointing was seeing players selected later in the first round that I personally knew were not as talented or motivated as I was. With each passing pick, there were also financial repercussions at stake. The salary of NFL rookies is largely determined by draft round and position, so to fall out of the first round means a big reduction in potential earnings.

After the commercial break, the broadcasters were in the midst of recapping the first round when the second round opened. Along the bottom of the screen the scrolling tape stated that with the first pick of the second round, which was the twenty-ninth pick overall, the Dallas Cowboys selected guard Steve Wisniewski from Penn State. With this realization, the apartment cut loose with loud shouts and whistles as the place turned into a jubilant celebration. We all danced around and hugged one another like it was New Years Eve in Times Square.

I had some NFL apparel given to me from various teams, so I fished around in my closet and put on a Dallas Cowboy hat. My fiancé and I embraced. Both of our families lived in Houston, so we were especially overjoyed to be so close to them. In the Lone Star State, the Cowboys are bigger than life, and playing for Dallas would give us the opportunity to be relatively close to home.

In the midst of the celebration, however, I was a bit puzzled that I hadn't received any phone calls from the Cowboys front office. It was customary for a team to call the player just prior to making the selection to let them know what was about to happen. I shrugged it off, knowing the television results couldn't be wrong. A few minutes later, however, the phone did ring and a hush broke out over the apartment. All eyes were on me, as everyone wanted to hear who was calling and what was being said. I stepped over several people to reach the phone and picked it up on the third ring.

Clearing my throat, I answered in my low voice: "Hello, this is Steve." Between the chaos in my apartment and the background noise on the other end, I couldn't quite make out what the man was saying. Strangely, the voice on the line sounded just like my friend and teammate Roger Duffy. Having noticed that Roger was strangely absent from the apartment at the time, I thought he was playing a joke on me. I said, "Roger, get off the phone, man. Someone might be calling me." And I promptly hung up.

Within thirty seconds the phone rang again. I picked it up, and this time it was a different but more stern voice, saying, "Don't hang up on me!" He identified himself as Head Coach

Mike Shanahan of the Los Angeles Raiders, and explained that the Raiders had just completed a trade with the Cowboys for my rights. I was now a Los Angeles Raider. Apparently, time was running out on the draft pick, so Raider owner Al Davis asked his good friend Jerry Jones to select me, and they worked the trade details out after the selection was in.

A brief look of bewilderment spread across the faces of everyone in the apartment, and then suddenly a new chorus of laughter and cheers fired up: "Raiders! Raiders! Raiders!" In the course of a few short minutes, I had already been traded and was now on my second NFL team. I promptly threw the Cowboys hat to the floor, went to my dresser, and put on a Raider T-shirt that said, "Real men wear black!"

That's the NFL for you, completely unpredictable. It didn't matter to me, I was ready and willing to go anywhere on a moments notice. I had never been to Los Angeles previously, nor did I know they had any interest in me. I gladly loaded up everything I owned in a few shabby bags and I was off with a smile, never to return. I was with the Raiders my entire thirteen-year career.

Tap on the Shoulder Pad

The phone call I received that Sunday to play professional football redirected the course of my life and set my future in motion. Although it was unexpected for me, God was not surprised by where I ended up. Before I was born, He knew that day would come, and He knew what awaited me in Los Angeles. It was very similar to the call from God each of us receives in life.

We all set out to learn, grow, and be a productive member of society. With our future uncertain yet full of optimism, we launch out, not knowing exactly what to expect or where we will end up. Along the way, however, God intervenes and reveals Himself to us. He imparts to us a call for a higher purpose. His calling may not be as well defined as a single phone call, but it will give us direction for our life all the same. This newfound purpose and direction for our life is *the* call of God on our lives—the destiny and the purpose for our very existence. Despite the many distractions and voices calling out for our time and attention, God will make it clear when He is on the other line. We can't miss it if we are expecting to receive it.

There comes a point in your life when your Creator taps you on the shoulder, calls you by name, and gives you an assignment to do for His kingdom. How you respond to this call will ultimately determine the level of success and effectiveness you find in that calling. Jim McDonald, who founded a ministry called Meeting God in Missions, once told me, "When God speaks to you, what you do next tells Him what you truly think of Him."

On draft day I was completely and wholeheartedly willing to go anywhere and do anything asked of me in order to play professional football. I was hungry for the opportunity to prove myself in the NFL. It wasn't so much about gaining fame or fortune; rather, in those days the salaries were good but not like they are today. I wanted the chance to go on to a higher stage, to continue my athletic career, and to step out into a bold new world of challenges. Had I been traded again and again, it wouldn't have mattered to me. Any NFL team would have elicited the same joyous and zealous celebration from me. I was just ready to answer the call no matter where it led me.

In the same way, the call of God should elicit a wholehearted and willing response on our part. Following God's call is thrilling and adventurous, not something dreadful or debilitating. Our heavenly Father has traded His Son's life in exchange for the right to ours, and we are now drafted to be apart of His victorious team. It matters not where or to whom that call may lead us. Instead, we simply consider ourselves fortunate to even be in a position to hear and answer that call.

I was so incredibly eager to serve man with something as inconsequential as a game whose purpose was to run or pass a leather bag filled with air over a painted strip of grass. How much more should I desire to respond to something as monumental as the Creator's master plan for my existence? Life is much bigger than sports, and much more important than school, jobs, or bank accounts. We're talking about eternity here. Be encouraged to know that whether it comes in stages, or whether it comes in childhood or in the golden years of your life, your call from God will come. And it is not too late to answer it today.

The Play Caller

As a player, and later as an assistant coach, I was blessed to have worked with some brilliant men. Coaches have a tireless and sometimes thankless job, often working eighty to ninety hours per week studying film, recognizing tendencies, and making preparations for the next practice and game. Most people are unaware of all that goes into a coach's preparation for a game or of the level of expertise necessary to be a coordinator at the NFL level. For this reason, coaches teach their players to never question the call of the quarterback in the huddle. Players are paid to play the game, and coaches are paid to coach. Players must learn to trust each other, work as a team, and be sure to handle their own assignments on any given play.

When Jon Gruden called "Fourteen Blast" on fourth and one with the game on the line, not one of us questioned the call. Why? Because we trusted him. He was smart, he worked hard, he believed in us, and he loved us as his team. And the same is true with God. He loves us, believes in us, and is altogether wise, knowing the end of our days as well as the beginning. We can trust His play calls too.

One time my faith in a coach's decision was put to the test while playing a game in San Diego. We had a relatively new offensive coordinator, Ray Perkins, whom we didn't know much about other than that he was a former head coach at the University of Alabama. Facing a very talented Charger defense led by line-backer Junior Seau, Perkins opened the game by calling twelve straight offensive pass plays.

Offensive linemen usually only get noticed when they do something wrong, like give up a sack or commit a penalty. For this reason, most linemen prefer run plays. Pass blocking puts a great deal of stress on an offensive lineman, especially when backed up against your own goal line. A sack or a holding call when the quarterback is standing in the end zone is an automatic safety, and no lineman wants their mistake to show up on replays and cost his team two points. They'd prefer they make the ESPN highlight reel for other reasons, or to not make it at all.

In the huddle that night, guys began to grumble and curse as the quarterback called pass after pass after pass. We ran twelve straight pass plays to begin the game before our first run. I told the guys to shut their mouths, dig in, and get the job done. Inwardly, however, I was just as bewildered as anyone else. We usually prided ourselves in establishing the run game early on as a team, and we would all have appreciated some advance notice because it didn't make sense at the time to have such a one-sided offensive attack. But it worked. We went on to win the game 38–13.

When it comes to following the call of God on our lives, it is best to not question His play selection. He knows what He is doing on each and every play. Like a good coach, God likes to break some of our old tendencies. Like football, some instructions are not going to make sense to us at the time, but there is usually a good reason for the call. The central question is, do we trust Him with the play He has called?

God is a master strategist, and He knows how to condition your heart and direct your decisions. To the casual observer, His directives may not make sense at the time, but often the details don't come into focus until later on in life. It is only then that we come to appreciate the ways of God and the wisdom of Scripture. When we stand before God someday, those who sought to follow God's directives will stand in amazement as we are allowed to see the many times and ways that God directly interceded on our behalf. God's hands keep us off the path of destruction and on the road of righteousness. We may think we know what to do or what decisions to make in any given situation, but we can only move according to the instructions and rules of the game. When God directs us through the Word and by His Spirit, He has the big picture in mind, and it is ultimately for our good. He has the ability to set many pieces in motion at once to better our outcome and see us to victory.

Once in your stance as a lineman, you have a very limited view of the game. Even the quarterback cannot clearly see the entire field like their coaches can or like viewers watching from their living rooms. At least four coaches sit high above the field in the press box with binoculars at every game and are in constant communication with sideline personnel relating their observations. They record and report such things as the personnel group that comes on the field each play, the spot of the football, the alignment of the defenders, and blitzes run by the opposing team. Each box also has several television monitors so coaches know when to challenge a referee's call based on replay footage. We fans like to sit comfortably in our favorite recliners munching on chips and playing armchair quarterback while we complain about the referees and scold our team for what they should have done with the game on the line. Between the lines and in real time, however, the game is not so easy or simple.

Trusting God with our hearts and decisions, and glorifying Him is the goal of our life, yet it is not so easy either. Too often reason and our own desires get in the way of simple faith. If we would allow our heavenly Father to call the plays and direct our lives, we would discover that no obstacle is too great and no opponent too daunting for our God. The Lord has the advantage of watching it all from an aerial view (see Isa. 55:8-9). He sits high above the field of our lives and outside the bounds of time. He is able to see through the fog and knows vastly more than any human being ever could.

Our perspective of life is very restricted, but God's is unobstructed. Our resources are limited, but His are infinite. We can't even say with certainty what will happen tomorrow, but God knows what will happen for a millennium. It all comes down to being able to trust Him as our Head Coach, believing that He has the ability and desire to make us victorious, and that He has our best interests in mind.

Trusting God is the essence of true faith. What trips us up the most is when we are uncertain if He is trustworthy. Too often we decide to take matters into our own hands. Regrettably, we have all gone down that path, myself included. But God assures us that when we trust in Him with all of our hearts, leaning not on our own understanding, acknowledging Him in all our ways, then He will direct our paths (see Prov. 3:5-6). We don't have to call the plays or spend countless hours devising our own game plan. He is the Coach, and we are simply His players. If we will do our part in trusting Him, He will do His part in leading us.

If you are having a difficult time letting go and trusting God with your life, try getting to know the character of God as it is revealed in the Bible; not through the rules of religion, but through the person you read about in Jesus Christ. We often do not and cannot trust Him because we don't know Him well enough to trust Him.

I'm often amazed by Raiders fans who seemingly know more about the team than I do. Perhaps it's due to the popularity of fantasy football today, or to the plethora of statistics available on the Internet, but some fans know a player's height, weight, college, and hometown from memory. They remember every win and loss and can cite strange facts and obscure information about their favorite players. When I was a coaching with the Raiders, friends would often call and ask me about personnel moves they saw reported on Twitter. Nine out of ten times I hadn't even heard about it even though I was working inside the Raider facility at that exact moment. These people are die-hards and think of their team as family. The problem is that while they know a great deal *about* the team, they don't actually know anyone *on* the team.

There is a vast difference between knowing about someone and really knowing that person. It is one thing to know facts *about* God, and it is quite another to know Him experientially. But this is how He wants to reveal Himself to us. There are plenty of people who know a great deal about God—they can recite Bible stories, church history, and have a Scripture verse handy for any circumstance they may find themselves in. They may even sit in church pews and attend Bible studies on a weekly basis. Those are all great things, but none of it translates into knowing and trusting God personally.

The truth is that those who have not made a decision to receive Christ into their life, upon their death they will have to acknowledge that they have rejected Him and His sacrifice. There is no middle ground when it comes to what we say about Christ: we either sought God's Spirit to lead our lives or we didn't. Only you and God know where you stand, and it's clear to Him based on how you live your life.

Christ died for us long before we knew we needed His sacrifice. He chose us first; we didn't choose Him (see Eph. 1:4-14). But like any gift, it too can be rejected. There are many reasons people come up with to reject the amazing gift that our heavenly Father has given us, which usually revolves around some kind of false belief structure they've created in their mind. Regardless of the reason, when we reject Christ in this life, we ultimately reject

Him in the life that is to come. Heaven and hell are real places. Heaven is a place where we enjoy the presence and fellowship of God for all of eternity, while hell is the full embodiment of a complete separation from God. The Lord doesn't sentence us to hell so much as we choose it ourselves when we choose to live apart from Him in this life.

God is a perfect gentleman—He will not force Himself upon you. If you choose to pull away or not follow Him, He will reluctantly oblige. But it will not be without disappointment, both for Him and for you. The tragedy of walking away from truth is that you are denying the very reason for your existence. No amount of fame or fortune, and no great advances in medicine, business, or athletics can compare to the single greatest mystery of knowing, loving, and communicating with the Creator of the universe. He is the only One who knows all your secrets and still loves you perfectly.

The Extra Point

When you purchase a new product, it often comes with instructions and an owner's manual that explains in detail the purpose and proper use of the equipment. The manufacturer is responsible for knowing what the item is made of, what it was designed for, and what it is capable of. The manufacturer is the sole expert on how to use the product properly and safely.

God is the designer of your life and the manufacturer of your heart. He knows your blueprint, and He knows how to help you achieve your purpose in life. He has given you the Bible as an owner's manual to instruct you and train you for greatness, and only He has the right to define you. Why? Because He is the One who invented you, who made you.

Ultimately, God Himself is our highest calling and our purpose for existence in this life. We are called to Him first and foremost. In the next chapter you will discover how He reveals Himself to you is usually an indication of who you are called to become. He is the One who wired your DNA and created you for a specific plan and purpose—one that only you can fulfill.

Chalk Talk

1. On a scale of one to ten, how much do you really trust God? Based on your answer, would you say that you are fully committed and submitted to His plan for your life?

2. Do you believe God know what's best for your life, or do you believe you can handle your future better yourself? Have you been complaining like a disgruntled player about the changes He's trying to make in you?

3. An athlete knows they are either improving or giving up ground. Do you feel you are moving toward God and His call upon your life, or moving further away from Him? Explain.

4. What is the key to finding God's plan for your life? If you've already said no to that which He has asked you to do, do you think that God will continue to reveal His plan for your life?

5. When God has prompted you to act in the past, how did you respond to it? What did you learn from the experience about yourself and Him? Was it a setback or a step forward?

Endnotes

1. This quote was accessed from GoodReads, http://www.goodreads
    .com/quotes/67420-to-each-there-comes-in-their-lifetime-a
    -special-moment, accessed February 17, 2015.

2. This information is taken from http://dnafacts.net/, accessed
    February 17, 2015.

CHAPTER 3

THE ASSIGNMENT

When God allows or even invites us to wrestle with
Him, His constant goal is to make us overcomers.
Even when God appears to be against us, He is for us.
—BETH MOORE

Several months after my NFL retirement, I was in Nashville to take in a Titans football game with two good friends, Peter Hunt and Robert Jenkins. Former teammate Gennero DiNapoli was playing for the Tennessee Titans at the time, and he told me great things about the area and about the real estate market in Tennessee. I still didn't know exactly where I wanted to sink my roots or what I wanted to do with my post-football life, so I invited my buddies to accompany me to go check it out.

After renting a car, we roamed around downtown Nashville, ate some barbeque, and checked into our budget hotel. Wanting to go cheap, I made the rookie mistake of opting to share a room among the three of us. Anyone who knows Robert Jenkins will tell you he is an imposing mountain of a man with a heart of gold. I absolutely love the guy, but he snores like a jackhammer with an unnatural ability to shake the curtains. I roomed with him at training camp one year and learned that without earplugs, an iPod, and a curled pillow over my head, insanity settles in after only a couple of days of sleeplessness.

As the travel planner, I caught the hail of jokes regarding our accommodations and sparse luxuries. Peter was regularly getting up to turn off the air conditioning because he was cold. Robert and I, the two walruses, were constantly turning it back on high. To make matters even worse, the room reeked of musty socks and unclaimed farts due to the beans, barbeque, and hours spent walking downtown. I'm not sure how we ever fell asleep under those conditions, but after a long conversation about God's will for our lives and saying a collective prayer for each other and our families, we did. After much tossing and turning, I eventually fell asleep around 1:00 a.m. Little did I know that God would answer our prayers so quickly, making His next assignment clear to me that very night.

The Assignment

It seemed like I had finally just shut my eyes and drifted off to sleep when I was physically shaken by what seemed like a dream in extreme high definition. This was the most realistic dream of my life, and my best attempts to describe it fall well short of the magnitude of the experience. Like suddenly being dropped into a Hollywood sound stage, I awoke in an expansive field of what appeared to be wheat gently swaying in a slight breeze. The field spread out as far as the eye could see in all directions. It was a beautiful backdrop, bright and pleasant, and the sky was a majestic shade of blue. I remember the captivating color and depth of the sky being so astonishing, yet I can't accurately describe it or find its exact shade on a color wheel. There was an indescribable sense of peace and comfort that came from being in the presence of God.

In that moment I felt fully alive and awake, and I had a great sense of awe and wonder. Yet I was without fear. It was as though I was loved, welcomed, and fully accepted for who I was. I had a conversation, if I dare call it that, because I can't say that I heard an audible voice speaking to me. It was like I received a file-share of information that I interacted with. I remember verbally speaking back, but I didn't see a specific face or figure. There was only a warm and inviting presence of light. At the same time, the conversation was clear yet surprising. I had this distinct knowing that I was to write a book, and the title was to be called *Hand on the Line*.

What came next was an incredible influx of thoughts, titles, and chapter ideas for this book. I really don't consider myself a creative, imaginative, or inventive person. But like one computer transferring files to another, it was as if God downloaded a book full of His thoughts into my mind in a matter of mere seconds. I remember speaking back, "A book? Me? *Hand on the Line*?" This revelation was astonishing to me, because I never had a desire to write a book. It wasn't like I was thinking of doing this project anyway and was praying for some kind of confirmation. No one had proposed the idea to me or told me it might be a good thing to do.

I awoke with a startle, sat up, and looked quickly to my right and left. I said out loud, "Robert! Peter! Did you guys hear that?" It was obvious they were both sound asleep, as they didn't react. I stood up, walked closer to them, and stared at each of them in the face to make sure they were not awake and playing some kind of practical joke on me. I could feel that my face and skin were flush as if I had just experienced a surge of energy, like I had just completed an intense workout.

I knew I couldn't possibly go back to sleep, so I grabbed my notepad, tiptoed past the suitcases to the small bathroom, and closed the door so as not to wake the guys. Immediately, I examined myself in the mirror to confirm I really was awake and that this was really happening to me. It all seemed so surreal. I literally pinched myself hard in the cheek just to see if I would wake up. I splashed some water on my face, dried myself with a towel, lowered the toilet seat cover, and sat down and began to write about what had just happened to me. I wrote quickly, filling seven large pages with notes, thoughts, and impressions. I was simply filling the page like a stenographer taking dictation. God dumped this information into my brain, and I was merely transcribing it to paper. I remember being awestruck at the time, as I didn't have to strain or scratch my head for ideas. God gave me great recall of a number of sermons, analogies, and Bible studies, some of which I had created in the past. Like a free-flowing river of words, it was amazing to see how God weaved it all together.

I have never experienced anything like this before or since that time. To this day it remains the most clear, most realistic communication I have ever had with God. To be clear, I don't put much stock in personal experiences people share like this with me, nor do I want you to either. God still does speak using dreams and visions today, just as He has done many times throughout history, but dreams and visions too easily can be influenced by outside forces.

This dream occurred in the fall of 2002. I wish I could tell you that I immediately went home, hammered out each chapter, ironed out the book, and released it later that same year. But that didn't happen. I picked up this book project and set it down so many times over the years I risked developing carpal tunnel syndrome from my vacillation. It wasn't until 2012 that I finally committed to writing this book, and it wasn't finished until 2015. A project that could have been completed in a few months took me nearly thirteen years to write because of my disobedience and self doubts.

The subtitle *Challenging Men to Follow God's Call* is not just for your sake but mine, as this book relates my own personal struggle to obey the call of God that is upon my life. For nearly thirteen years, I wallowed in some level of self-doubt, procrastination, and disobedience regarding the task God had given me to do. I fought myself, and in doing so I fought God. And let me tell you, when you wrestle with God, there is no peace, no grace, and no clear direction evident within you. Somehow, I think you know what I'm talking about.

In many ways I have stubbornly wasted over a decade of my life sidetracked from the purpose God had for me. This separation from God took its toll on me, and also those closest to me. I kick myself now because in one fit of rage I even shredded the original seven pages of notes I transcribed that night. What an idiot I was. I guess I thought that would somehow release me from the conviction of the task God assigned me. Because of my stupidity, the finished version you hold in your hands now is not the same book God instructed me to write. My delay has caused me to forget some details of the original vision.

God's Holy Spirit was likely saddened by that act of belligerence, but He didn't lose His faithfulness or patience with me. I know now that I have missed numerous opportunities intended for this book and for my life, and for this I have asked forgiveness from the Lord. Not a single person may ever read this book, but that's okay with me. At this point, it's about me being faithful to complete the task I was assigned to do. I am asking God to put back the pieces I have scattered of my life.

You can bet that I have paid a heavy price personally wallowing in a spiritual wilderness of sorts. I look back on it now and realize that wandering from God's path not only caused a great deal of pain and anxiety for me and my family, but it also led to spiritual resistance and oppression from the enemy. I had to do some painful soul searching as the material in this book first and foremost confronted and convicted me.

I may have experienced a small dose of what the children of Israel must have had to endure as they wandered around the desert for forty years because of their refusal to follow the leadings of God after their exodus from Egypt. With the exception of Joshua and Caleb, all of that unbelieving generation passed away, having never accomplished their God-given destiny. That task was punted to the next generation, as the responsibility of conquering the Promised Land would rest squarely on the shoulders of their children and grandchildren. Imagine living out of a tent and out of the will of God as a nomad for forty years in the desert, having missed their lot in life. I don't want that any longer for my life. Yet this was the consequence for Israel's refusal to follow the call of God. But just as God did not give up on the children of Israel, neither has He given up on me—He hasn't given up on you either.

Maybe you have been in a wilderness yourself for thirteen years, or maybe it has been forty years like the Israelites? Perhaps you've doubted God's call, procrastinated away your youth, squandered your inheritance, and disobeyed the last thing God told you to do. Sometimes one setback in life leaves us wallowing in shame, battling ourselves, and beating ourselves up over our failures. Now is not the time to blame-shift, but to acknowledge you have been fighting against God. Now is the time to bust out of your wilderness, and it is God's will that you do. There is no better time for repentance than today.

GODISNOWHERE

Depending on your perspective, you can read the statement listed above in one of two ways: "God is nowhere" or "God is now here." How you see it depends on your vantage point and what you think about God. What do you believe about God? Is He nowhere or is He now here?

I have noticed in my life and throughout Scripture that God tends to speak to me at moments of His choosing, not necessarily mine. Significant moments with God usually come at unpredictable times and in somewhat unexpected places. At times I felt like He was nowhere to be found, yet at other times His presence would show up unexpectedly and He would feel so near. Perhaps this is so that my response to His call would bypass my mind and reveal where my heart allegiance really lies.

Living in the Bay Area, I made it a point to wave to fellow commuters who displayed a Raider bumper sticker or silver and black license plate frames when making the thirty-five-minute drive to and from work. I never wanted to lose focus that it was the fans who paid my salary, and I have always enjoyed showing them my appreciation. The ironic thing is that ninety-nine times out of a hundred they looked at me like I was crazy. Sometimes while standing at the checkout line at the grocery store, or working out at the gym, I would join in conversations with others talking about the Raiders. They had no idea who I was or that I was a team captain. I discovered that at those moments they were so preoccupied with other tasks they weren't expecting a professional football player from their favorite team to drop in on their day. They missed it because they were caught unaware. But how many times have we done that with God and His voice?

Peter was a simple fisherman who wasn't expecting the Savior of the world to drop in on his daily grind. One night he had a particularly hard and frustrating evening fishing on the Sea of Galilee. It was morning and he still hadn't caught one single fish to show for all his efforts. He was exhausted and hungry, his hands dirty and sweaty from a long night of work and failure. He just wanted to get home for some much-needed rest when Jesus appeared and asked him to put out on the lake. He did, and from Peter's boat, Jesus taught the crowds gathering on the shore. Jesus then asked him to press out into deeper water to let down his nets again for a catch. It made no sense in the natural, because he had already struggled all night without success. Little did Peter know that this one encounter would change the course of his life forever (see Luke 5:1-11).

Years later, Saul was probably lost in deep thought riding a feeble old donkey on a dusty trail to Damascus. His hatred fueled his intentions of locating, questioning, and imprisoning every Christian he could find. That is precisely when a piercing light knocked him off his mount and onto the ground, leaving him blinded. The resurrected Christ spoke to him and laid out His game plan for the rest of Saul's life. Saul wasn't in a church building or at a confessional booth when he encountered the risen Christ, yet God was more than able to get Paul's attention and redirect the course of his life instantly (see Acts 9).

God-moments are defining moments, but often they come unplanned and unexpected. It is our response to them that is most telling to God and to us. When God speaks to us, what we do next tells God what we really think of Him. You and I are really no different from the men who highlight the pages of the Bible in our doubts, struggles, weaknesses, and strengths. Peter was a mighty man of faith who walked with Jesus; he once even stepped out of the boat and walked on water with Christ (see Matt. 14:22-33). Yet he was also the one who denied our Lord three times in front of a campfire when his life was on the line. Saul was a man trained in Scriptures from a young age and surpassed his peers in knowledge and education, yet he persecuted the church and consented when Stephen was being martyred.

Peter and Saul were ordinary men like you and me, but they repented and surrendered all to follow Jesus. It is because of their obedience and faithfulness that we have had the good news passed on to us today. Peter the fisherman became one of Jesus's chief disciples. He was the first to proclaim the risen Christ to the Jewish and Gentile communities after Jesus ascended back to heaven, and he is responsible for sharing his eyewitness accounts with Mark, the writer of the first gospel. The renegade Saul, also known as Paul, brought the gospel to the then-known world, and as an apostle penned almost half of the New Testament. His answer to the call of God changed the course of modern history forever.

Your obedience and faithfulness may not seem critical to you now. You may feel that you are not hurting anyone else by wasting away your life and avoiding your true calling, but look at the potential ripple effect that a life fully surrendered to God can make. Your future family, your children, and your grandchildren are looking up to you—they are your teammates. The generations who follow you are counting on you to rise up and fight for all you were designed to become. God chose you because He knows you. If He couldn't use you He wouldn't choose you. He believes in you, but do you believe in Him?

We each make significant decisions of faith on a daily basis. The chair we're sitting in, the brakes on our vehicle, the driver of the taxi we hailed last week, and the bank we deposit our money in all involve an aspect of faith. We consistently and blindly place our trust in people we have never met and know nothing about, people like pilots, surgeons, and mail carriers. Even atheists have some type of faith—they believe in themselves and place their faith in humanity. Faith only differs in who or in what we place our trust.

If our faith is in others, then we are at their mercy. If our faith is in our abilities only, then we are limited by our own limitations. If our faith is simply intellectual, there will be no heart-commitment to it. It is up to us to decide to whom we will entrust our lives to and to what extent.

We often think we need more faith, but all we really need is to have more boldness in the faith we already possess. God has given each of us a measure of faith, and you and I have enough faith in us to respond to God's call upon our lives. Some balk, saying, "Why should I trust God?" and my response is, "Why not trust Him?" It always amazes me that we as broken people can quickly entrust our heart to another person whom we have only known for a short time. Yet we have such trouble entrusting our life to a God who is perfect, infinite, and who created the heavens and the earth. People worship at the feet of politicians, celebrities, and even their favorite sports personalities, yet they won't give honor to the One who willed these people into existence.

Paul wrote, *"The only thing that counts is faith expressing itself through love"* (Gal. 5:6). Faith has an expression, and it must express itself in order to be useful. Saving faith is active trust and it produces action. Our faith in God activates the flow of God in our lives. James put it this way: *"Faith without deeds is dead"* (2:26). It is paramount to our salvation, but faith must be put into action in order to release its power. A faith that is not exercised is meaningless and useless.

As important as it is to have faith, I have found that faith is usually not the issue when it comes to following Christ. The issue is our wills. Ask yourself, can my faith be proved in my actions? This is the litmus test of your faith.

I recently spoke to a group of men on the topic of faith producing actions. I told them that faith is not an emotion, a decision, a belief system, or an ideology; rather, it is a catalyst that produces action in our daily lives. Hebrews 11 is often referred to as the great hall of *faith* as it details some of the heroics of men and women throughout biblical history. Twenty times in that chapter it prefaces each story with the phrase "by faith"—they did, they conquered, they obeyed, or they were made victorious. It was their faith, not their inactivity, that proceeded and provoked God-inspired exploits.

I especially love Hebrews 11:34: *"Whose weakness was turned to strength."* This reinforces and reassures me that God uses everyday people to accomplish extraordinary tasks for His glory. We all have faults and doubts at times, but the God we serve is even bigger than our shortcomings. He can give strength to our feeble frames and even turn our personal weaknesses into strengths for His glory.

A Name-Changing Wrestling Match

There is a story told in Scripture about a man named Jacob. Born grasping at the heel of his red, hairy twin brother, Esau, Jacob had fallen short of being the firstborn and securing his father's prized inheritance by a matter of seconds. And in ancient cultures, the birthright of the firstborn meant everything. He must have viewed himself as second rate, because he lived his life seemingly trying to make up for his shortcomings. He conned Esau into selling him his birthright for a bowl of stew (see Gen. 25:27-34), he deceptively stole his nearly blind father's blessing by dressing up as his brother (see Gen. 27), and he even duped his father-in-law out of cattle and livestock (see Gen. 30). Jacob became what his name meant—a con artist.

In one moment, however, everything changed. In what is one of the Bible's most mysterious narratives, Jacob wrestles with a man all night until the breaking of dawn (see Gen. 32:22-32). When the man realized he could not overpower Jacob, the man touched the socket of Jacob's hip and injured him. He then said to Jacob, "Let me go, for it is daybreak."

Jacob responded, "I will not let you go unless you bless me."

The man asked, "What is your name?"

"Jacob," he answered.

Then the man declared, "Your name will no longer be Jacob but Israel, because you have struggled with God and with man and have overcome."

From that day on, Jacob was a new man. He was Israel, and Israel walked with a limp.

There must be more to this story than what we are initially told. Who was this man, and why did he change Jacob's name? Hosea helps us out a little bit, revealing that the man Jacob wrestled with was an angel (see Hos. 12:4). Many Bible scholars believe this was "the angel of the Lord," who is often identified with the God Himself in the Old Testament. This heavenly being changed Jacob's name to Israel, which means "prince with God," "he strives with God," or "may God preserve." This angel allowed Jacob to prevail, but he purposefully injured Jacob's hip socket. It was a reminder that he should no longer walk in his own strength but must walk in dependence upon God.

We can only assume the angel knew Jacob's name all along. So why did he ask him his name? It seems he wanted Jacob to admit who he was—a deceiver. He knew that if he could get Jacob to willingly acknowledge his weakness, he could get him to look beyond it and change his mentality. This was a necessary step in Jacob's transformation. This one God-encounter changed Jacob from thinking of himself as a con artist to realizing he was an overcomer.

Similarly, you and I are coming out of some old patterns and into new ones, out of an old identity and into a newborn identity, and a time of wrestling with God may be needed. There is a place for contending with God in our time of need. Jacob was chosen to inherit the promises of his father Isaac and grandfather Abraham, and he would settle for nothing less than his full inheritance. He knew God wanted to bless him, and his contending mentality allowed him to prevail.

The issue that Jacob had to overcome, however, was his self-image. God saw Jacob as victorious long before Jacob ever saw himself that way, so He changed his identity first in order to change Jacob's course in life. For Jacob, God was not only a name-changer but a game-changer too.

A. W. Tozer was an uneducated Baptist who lived in the early 1900s, and he went on to pastor and write over thirty Christian books. He wrote in one of his books:

Man is a cobbler. When He wants a thing to be better He goes to work to improve it. He improves cattle by careful breeding; cars and planes by streamlining; health by diet, vitamins and surgery; plants by grafting; people by education. But God will have none of this cobbling. He makes a man better by making him a new man. He imparts a higher order of life and sets to work to destroy the old.[1]

Like me in that hotel room that night, one genuine encounter with God has the profound ability to alter our course in life and change our identity. Peter was a sinner, Saul was a persecutor, Jacob was a swindler, and I was the dirtiest player in the NFL. It's only through God-encounters that we develop a reliable self-image and find out who we truly are and who God sees us to be. Though we may see ourselves as second rate, He treats us like we're first class. While we see weakness, He sees strength. Why are you settling for so much less when He will give you so much more? God wants to bless you, but you must be willing to fight for what He has secured for you.

Hand on the Line

The line of scrimmage is the pivotal point of conflict in football. It is ground zero, the meeting and clashing of two opposing wills. Coaches, players, and fans all agree that this is where the game is either won or lost. The team that controls the line of scrimmage controls the game. Fittingly, you want your biggest, strongest, and nastiest players on your line. Like a Sumo wrestler, a football player begins every play by first getting in a powerful and balanced stance. In the huddle, the quarterback quickly gives instructions by calling the play as relayed to him by the coach. Players clap in unison to "break" the huddle, and as a unit purposefully sprint up to the line to get set.

The ball isn't snapped until all eleven players are in their proper positions. As an offensive lineman, I would squat down, lower my shoulders, dig my cleats in, and place my hand on the line. With my eyes up and back flat, I was prepared for the mayhem that was about to ensue. When my hand is placed on the line of scrimmage, there was no turning back. I'm committed at that point. I can't pick it up again until the ball is snapped or it would be a penalty. I'm all in and fully invested for that play. The outcome is not certain, but I know what my objective is. I may get my butt kicked, I could get knocked unconscious or bloodied, or I could return feeling victorious from a great block or a big play. The outcome of that play is only decided when the official blows his whistle, ending the play, but virtually anything can happen up until that point.

In life it's no different. To move forward in your walk with God, it will require struggle and conflict, a clash of two wills— yours and God's. The devil, who is your opponent, has no intention of giving up ground to you, so he too will fight you at the line of scrimmage. To survive in this arena, it will require a confrontation with the forces of evil and a resolve to never back down. You must enter this arena fully committed or not at all.

Theodore Roosevelt once said,

> "It is not the critic who counts; not the man who points out how the strong man stumbles, or where the doer of deeds could have done them better. The credit belongs to the man who is actually in the arena, whose face is marred by dust and sweat and blood; who strives valiantly; who errs, who comes short again and again, because there is no effort without error and shortcoming; but who does actually strive

to do the deeds; who knows great enthusiasms, the great devotions; who spends himself in a worthy cause; who at the bestknows in the end the triumph of high achievement, and who at the worst, if he fails, at least fails while daring greatly, so that his place shall never be with those cold and timid souls who neither know victory nor defeat."[2]

As fathers, husbands, and sons, every day we must put ourselves into position to fight that which seeks to steal our faith, kill our dreams, and destroy our families. We are left with only two options: to quit or to engage our faith. Will you retreat in cowardice or press on to confrontation? Your decision will determine your destiny.

Hand on the line and committed to the next play

The Extra Point

In God's Book, the greatest moment in history is when He sent His Son to the line of scrimmage on our behalf. Beaten, bruised, betrayed, and spit upon, He took the punishment of our sins and carried it away. He lowered His shoulders and knocked the devil off the playing field. This is His story.

The question we must all ask ourselves is, which side of the field are we on? Are we on the side of the victorious or on the side of the defeated? Even if you feel you are losing at the game of life, you can still come out a winner. Jesus said, *"For whoever desires to save his life will lose it, but whoever loses his life for My sake will save it. For what profit is it to a man if he gains the whole world, and is himself destroyed or lost?"* (Luke 9:24-25 NKJV).

Losers become winners when they join God's team, and God is calling you to enter the field and get your life aligned with the cross. His team is the winning team. You can cover your ears if you want to; you can attempt to drown out this call with headphones or by maintaining a hectic pace of life; but you cannot escape His voice calling you to surrender to Him. His love and His call are relentless. All of heaven is watching, waiting to see what you will do. Your future and the destiny of your loved ones hinges on your response to this call.

Committing your ways to God will not be easy. You can count on trials and tribulations, you can be certain there will be setbacks and failures, and you may even have to walk through the wilderness only to fight for your God-given inheritance. But what you get for your struggle is not half as valuable as what you will become. There will be no growth without being pushed beyond your comfort level, and Christ will see to it that He personally walks the narrow road with you. He put His life on the line for you. Will you put your hand on the line for Him?

Chalk Talk

1. Do you believe that God is still capable of speaking through dreams and visions? If so, why is it important to compare any such idea we receive with Scripture before acting on it?

2. Have you ever felt like you've wrestled with God over a specific matter? Can you ever find peace if you are at odds with God and His will for your life? How do you remedy this situation?

3. Where is your faith placed (in yourself, in humanity, in the government, or in God)? Do you need more faith in God or more boldness in the faith you already possess?

4. Why do you think people often received a name change when they came to Christ? What does it mean to be a new creation in Christ?

5. What life experiences have helped to develop your faith and trust in God? What has caused you to doubt God?

6. What does it mean to put your "hand on the line" for Christ?

7. Have you ever felt inspired or instructed by God to do something? What held you back from the task? What propelled you forward to obedience?

Endnote

1.   A. W. Tozer, *That Incredible Christian* (Christian Publications, 1964), 30.

2.   http://www.theodore-roosevelt.com/trsorbonnespeech.html

DISCIPLINE

CHAPTER 4

FORWARD PROGRESS

One man fully committed is better than
ninety-nine with an interest.

A young rookie, Tim Kohn, who was an offensive lineman out of Iowa State, walked up to me during training camp one day, and asked, "Hey, Wiz, can I workout with you?"

"Sure, but you may not like it," I said, smiling. "Just try to do what I do."

Professional football is extremely competitive. NFL teams bring in over eighty players to training camp each year to fill fifty-three roster spots. Usually sixteen offensive linemen are invited to camp, nine are kept on the active roster, and only seven are in uniform on game day. Teams are always searching for replacement players who can replicate the same production for less money. With new players every year looking to make the roster, some guys are not so eager to help out rookies. Their mentality is, why would I want to help another guy take my job?

I can understand this attitude, but it was not the one I had. I had great coaches and teammates who helped me become a better player, and I was happy to help rookies or veterans who asked for it. I considered it my duty to make the weakest guy stronger so that we could all improve as a unit. I even felt I should be willing to give away my position if need be. If I was no longer one of the best nine offensive linemen on our team, then I shouldn't be on the squad.

Pumping iron after a long practice

During training camp, I made it a habit to put in some extra work before and after each practice to run, stretch, take pass sets, and work out with weights. Before dinner I'd go for long jogs around the surrounding neighborhood of Napa. I found that jogging a few miles through the normalcy of a local subdivision was just as much a mental release as a physical one. The sight of kids riding their bikes, men cutting their lawn, or youth football practice at the local middle school was a welcome distraction from the drudgery of training camp.

After grueling two-a-day practices, Tim and I did some extra work on the field and then changed into our running clothes. We started our jog at the gates of the facility and ran through the neighborhood.

That evening after a quick shower and dinner, we hustled off to team meetings. At each meeting coaches take attendance, and Tim was found missing. After breaking up into position meetings, there was still no sign of Tim. It's not uncommon for rookies to unexpectedly quit during training camp, but this surprised me. One of the coaches asked, "Has anyone seen that rookie, Tim Kohn?"

I spoke up, "Yes. He went for a run with me today." The entire room burst into laughter. Just moments later, athletic trainer Rod Martin came in to inform the coach that Tim was in the hospital with severe dehydration. He cramped up at dinner and required immediate medical attention. This was not the first time something like this happened with someone who trained with me. Thankfully, Tim did recover, and we became good friends. He had a strong soul and a great work ethic. Through our friendship and through a number of late night conversations, Tim received Christ and was later baptized with me in the Raider hot tub at our training facility in Alameda.

Although our time together with the Raiders was short, Tim has gone on to have a fantastic career in the financial services industry and has generously shared his passion and love for Christ with a great many people. One man building a relationship with another in Christ is what the gospel is all about. None of us has all the answers, but we can encourage one another as we press on to take hold of what God has for our life. (Phil 3:13-14).

The Cost of Following Christ

The Gospels recount the story of a young ruler who walked up to Jesus and asked, "What must I do to inherit eternal life?" Jesus answered him simply enough: "You know the commandments— do not commit adultery, do not murder, do not steal, do not give false testimony, and honor your father and mother." The man responded, "All these I have kept since I was a boy." Giving us a glimpse into His heart, Jesus looked at him and loved him:

> *"One thing you lack," He said. "Go, sell everything you have and give to the poor, and you will have treasure in heaven. Then come, follow Me." At this the man's face fell. He went away sad, because he had great wealth* (Mark 10:21-22).

The rich young ruler had a lot going for him, which turned out to be the problem. He was young, wealthy, and powerful, but he was not prepared for what Jesus asked of him. He was interested in eternal life, but the road to heaven was much more demanding than what he expected. He may have been prepared to follow Jesus, but he was not prepared for what it would cost him.

There is a cost to following Christ. Just as a man counts the cost of marriage, or a soldier counts the cost of going to war, so we must count the cost of pursuing the call of God in our lives. The high life is not for the faint of heart. For the rich young ruler, it would cost him everything—his riches, his identity, his comfortable lifestyle, and perhaps even his very life.

Following the call of God is not some fad diet that we do one day only to give up the next. It isn't a fitness regimen or a New Year's resolution. You have probably tried budgets and health plans and discovered that the success you achieve in those pursuits is directly related to the level of commitment you give to the venture. We essentially get out of them what we put into them. When it comes to the call of God, however, our greatest return on our investment comes when we go all-in.

Each of us are no different from the rich young ruler: We want eternal rewards. We have wealth, and we each have something to gain, something to lose, and something to give. Money, prestige, power, and strength may promise us a comfortable lifestyle, but they cannot buy us freedom from sin or rewards beyond the grave. Are you prepared for what Jesus might ask of you?

Too often men test the waters of Christianity only to walk away sorrowful at the price they are asked to pay. The cost is simply too great for them; the commitment is too demanding. They walk away from eternal riches for the same reasons some men walk away from their marriages—the demand placed on them is just too high. At the time it seemed to be what they wanted, but it turned out to not be as glamorous or as convenient as they once expected. When the cost seemed to be higher than the benefit, they bounced and settled for inauthentic relationships.

Inauthentic relationships require very little from us. They are one-sided and shallow, benefiting mostly us and costing very little in return. These kinds of relationships enable us to hide from our hurts, avoid genuine communication, and effectively give others the emotional stiff-arm when they get too close. Though they seem safe, they silently cost us our souls.

It makes sense that when we talk about having a relationship with God, we must define what kind of relationship we mean. Heaven is not calling us to a shallow or cold business arrangement. God prefers loving, heartfelt, mutual devotion and authenticity. He calls us to make ourselves vulnerable. He promises to love us and not bail out when things get dicey. He has even put His hand and His heart on the line for us, and He is asking for ours in return.

Is it risky? You bet it is. But then again, love is risky. But when God chose to love us, He took a risk as well—we could reject Him and choose to love other things or other people instead of Him. But it is precisely the risk of being rejected that makes love so valuable, and for God we are a risk was worth taking. He knows there is something far worse than unreciprocated love—it's to never love at all. The risk of rejection didn't stop Him from choosing to love us, and it shouldn't stop us either.

In our efforts to reciprocate the love God has shown us, we must remember that there is no such thing as love without commitment. Jesus requires this of us, because He demonstrated this for us. To be worth something of value, true love always costs us something, and that cost is total commitment.

Perhaps you've heard of the conversation that took place between the chicken and the pig. One morning the pig asked the chicken, "What should we eat for breakfast?"

The chicken suggested, "Let's have ham and eggs."

The pig answered, "What? Oh no, not ham!"

The chicken replied, "Why not? I'll furnish the eggs and you supply the ham."

The pig balked, "For you it's just involvement, but for me it's total commitment!"

Welcome to total commitment. Lou Holtz once said, "If you don't make a total commitment to whatever you are doing, then you start looking to bail out the first time the boat starts sinking." Commitment is not something to fear, men. It is something to celebrate, which is why we celebrate weddings. In the same way, heaven throws a party when one person repents. So get ready for the adventure of your life.

Diving In

When I lived in Los Angeles, the Raiders' practice facility was located in the beach community of El Segundo. After workouts, some of us would make the short mile-and-a-half drive down to the beach to relax. The water and the ocean breeze were invigorating after hard workouts on the practice field.

Most of us had special edition, custom-made XXXL size boogie boards, and we had a blast riding the towering waves together. Imagine the sight of blubbery, white flesh hitting the waves in a pair of droopy, Raider-issued workout shorts. Wait... maybe you don't need to imagine that! On more than one occasion the pounding of the incoming surf launched me, my board, and my shorts all in different directions, effectively mooning anyone who might have been watching. I can assure you, it was an ugly sight.

I cherish those memories with my teammates, but they would not have happened had I not been willing to endure the initial shock of the Pacific Ocean's chilly waters. On the first few visits, I limped my tired body across the beach and into the cold surf only to turn around and retreat to the warmth of my beach towel. The guys laughed at me, calling me a wimp (and a few unprintable names). They said, "You'll never get in that way. You've got to just run, dive in, get wet, and start swimming. You'll warm up, and soon you'll feel great." How right they were.

And how right Jesus was as well when He essentially told the rich young ruler to run and dive in with both feet. Adventure awaited him as it awaits you in your walk with Christ, but only when you are willing to launch out from shore, endure the initial shock of the water, and start swimming. You will get wet, but you'll warm up to it if you go all the way in. We cannot dip our toes in this water and expect to be able to walk on it. Perhaps this is why God instituted water baptism as a sign that we were committed to Him.

The way to experience the full benefits of Christianity is by plunging fully into the pursuit of God with reckless ambition. No athlete ever boasts after the game, "We gave seventy percent out there today." No one ever sings, "I surrender ninety-five percent." Only when we are willing to fully and wholly give all of ourselves to God is God willing to fully and wholly give all of Himself to us. He has given all that He is to us so that we can give all that we are to Him.

The Few

From the response of the rich young ruler, we can gather that not everyone who sought Jesus came for the same reasons. Some came to be fed, while others came out of curiosity. Some wanted to see miracles, while others wanted to experience one. The prostitute was in search of mercy, the religious wanted to find fault with Him, and the soldier sought healing for his sick daughter.

As word spread about the carpenter's son who spoke with unmatched authority and power, Jesus resisted the temptation to water down His message or pander to the audience. He was neither politically correct nor especially polite. He was a God-pleaser, not a man-pleaser. He confronted the hypocrisy of the leaders, called sinners to repentance, and gave mercy to the humble. He simply preached the unadulterated truth of God's Word with conviction and without compromise.

Looking at the swelling crowds around Him, Jesus had a growing problem: He was too popular. Too many people wanted to follow Him—many for all the wrong reasons. At times it seemed He purposely chased away the masses in hopes of finding those whose hearts were in it. Today, Jesus is still popular, but not everyone is coming to Him for the purest reasons. Some come to see miracles; others to appear spiritual. Some come to offer thanks out of duty or tradition, while others come to get from Him something they desire.

While Jesus preached to the masses, His message was only accepted by a few. He promised His followers that they would be hated, persecuted, and face hardships at every turn (see Matt. 24:9). It was a straight road and a narrow path, not nearly wide enough to accommodate the in-crowd. The herd was traveling in a different direction, far too busy with life and with too much going on and too much to lose. Although many were called, few choose to step forward and accept the call.

Those who did step up found honor and glory in the narrow road. They became world-shaking, history-making, city-taking, stronghold-breaking, nation-quaking legends. Through the power of the living God, they toppled kingdoms, worked righteousness, routed enemy armies, shut the mouths of lions, trampled the fire of violence, shattered the walls of tradition, destroyed the works of the devil, and obtained the promises of God. They possessed a passion that could not be quenched and a power that could not be equaled (see Heb. 11). This world was not worthy of them. The only way to stop them was to kill them or to imprison them, but that did not intimidate them in the least. They knew it would be far better to be a prisoner of the Lord for a few years than to be a prisoner of regret for eternity.

The call to be a disciple of Christ is the call to abandonment, to spill out our guts for the glory of heaven. It is a life lived on purpose, for a purpose, by a God of purpose. In our pursuit of it, we would do well to *give it up*, *take it up*, *bring it in*, and *give it out*.

Give It Up

Jesus asked the rich young ruler to give it all up for Him. In our modern vernacular, give it up is used in several ways. It is a way to offer appreciation and support to someone through applause. The television host may say, "Give it up for..." as the crowd cheers the next guest coming on. We also use this phrase to convey letting go of something that is not working. When a person gives it up, they abandon a futile effort or mindset for something more productive or healthy.

The rich young ruler was asked to give it up—to give up his riches in exchange for the applause of heaven. God never asks us to give up something that He Himself has not first given up for us. He bankrupted all of heaven when He sacrificed His Son for our sin, and He demonstrated to the world what it means to give it up for the ones you love. Earthly riches were a small sacrifice compared

DISCIPLINE

to the heavenly treasures that Jesus Himself gave up and promised to give to the rich young ruler.

Whenever God asks us to give up something, He will always give us something greater in return. In this way we leave heaven's table richer than when we first arrived. Like any good father would do, our heavenly Father makes sure that we walk away with the better end of the bargain.

Giving it up for God can be likened to a fighter who is outmatched and is forced to tap out. In mixed martial arts, fighters can take a brutal beating—broken limbs, cracked clavicles, hyperextended knees, and shoulders ripped out of their socket. If a fighter is put into a potentially injurious position, they can "tap out" and end the contest by slapping the mat three times. When a fighter taps out, they are publically surrendering to their opponent and admitting defeat. For many years I wrestled with God. In my stubbornness I was too proud to tap out, and I somehow convinced myself that defiance was preferable to admitting defeat. Unbeknownst to me, however, I was only setting myself up for anguish and injury.

Perhaps you are wrestling with God as well. Life's circumstances have put you in a headlock, and you're faced with only one logical decision—surrender to God. Like the rich young ruler, it may require giving up riches or the pursuit of wealth. It most likely will involve sacrifice, hard work, and humility, but consider what it would cost you to not tap out. The blessings that you currently enjoy, when not devoted to God, will eventually become a curse. But when given over to God, those blessings come back stronger, and God turns the curse into a blessing.

Take It Up

Jesus asked the rich young ruler to take up his cross and follow Him. It is not enough to *give it up*; we must also be willing to *take it up*. Following Christ is not only about what we walk away from, but about what we embrace as we walk away. Freedom is found in what we embrace—in this case, embracing the cross.

The path to salvation always runs through the cross, for it is the ultimate emancipation from self, the great exchange where we give up on those things that brought us down and *take up* those things that lift us up. It is the place where we renounce the right to life and surrender the claim we have to our own souls.

Cross bearing is part of being a disciple of Jesus. His first followers did not shrink from martyrdom, and all true Christians have a martyr-spirit. This means we have the ability to endure what is brought upon us, whether that is suffering, shame, or even death itself. While the loss of life may not be literal as it was for Jesus and the first-century church, it is spiritual, and we should be willing to pay the ultimate sacrifice if need be.

Jesus was not singling out the rich young ruler with this talk of radical commitment. He taught something similar to His disciples as well: *"If anyone would come after Me, he must deny himself and take up his cross and follow Me. For whoever wants to save his life will lose it, but whoever loses his life for Me will find it"* (Matt. 16:24-25). Notice that if a man is to follow Christ, it must be voluntary. This is not a draft, and no one can force another person into it. It is self-enrollment and self-surrender. It must be by choice and of your own free will, because without love and desire there will be no growth or perseverance in this walk.

"Whoever wants to save his life will lose it, but whoever loses his life for Me will find it." With this statement, Jesus uncovers one of the great paradoxes of life: self-seeking is self-losing, and self-losing is self-finding. In other words, eternal life is found only through self-denial, which is quite the opposite of some commonly taught humanistic philosophies of loving yourself or finding God in you. William Wallace said in *Braveheart*, "Every man dies. Not every man really lives."[1]

It is impossible to give oneself to Christ without suffering some kind of loss. Taking it up means voluntarily letting go of everything that might hinder our discipleship to Christ, starting with our will. Living our lives on our own terms will ultimately result in losing the life we worked so hard to preserve. The man who denies Christ for his own convenience impoverishes his own nature and lowers his self-worth. Living our lives on God's terms, however, results in receiving it back with His blessing.

From a Wimp to a Warrior

If you knew me before my football career, you might think I was a bit of a wimpy kid. I had more fat than muscle with hardly a speck of athletic ability. When I entered junior high, I had a pear-shaped body and couldn't even do ten push-ups. I made the seventh grade football team only because there were no cuts. I was just another kid on the team and certainly nothing special. As the seasons passed, I progressed from awful to mediocre to just okay. By my junior year in high school I was pretty solid, and by my senior year I looked like I might have some promise.

Even though I was pudgy, overweight, and unathletic, that is not what made me weak. I became weak when I lost my life at the cross and found strength at the empty tomb. In God's economy, the weak are made strong and wimps often become the warriors. When Paul was asking God to remove the thorn in the flesh he had suffered with for quite some time, God finally said to him, *"My grace is sufficient for you, for My power is made perfect in weakness"* (2 Cor. 12:9). Paul went on to say:

> *Therefore I will boast all the more gladly about my weaknesses, so that Christ's power may rest on me. That is why, for Christ's sake, I delight in weaknesses, in insults, in hardships, in persecutions, in difficulties. For when I am weak, then I am strong* (2 Corinthians 12:10-11).

The world is full of unsuspecting down-and-outers who eventually find great success. The Wright brothers never graduated high school, Eli Whitney was laughed at when he showed people his cotton gin, and Michael Jordan was cut from his junior high basketball team. Samuel Morse had to plead before ten congresses before they would even look at his telegraph. The first sewing machine was smashed to pieces by a Boston mob. It took Alexander Graham Bell eleven years to invent the telephone, and only after 8,000 failed attempts did Thomas Edison invent the light bulb. He even had to install it free of charge for anyone to be interested in it.[2]

The Bible is full of once weak and wimpy people who were given great favor and strength. God loves to demonstrate His provision by doing the impossible and using and blessing the improbable. Moses was a murderer and a stutterer. He was so insecure that he asked God to choose someone else to deliver Israel. When he finally did surrender to the call of God on his life, Moses became one of the greatest prophets of all time (see Exod. 2–3).

Joseph was sold into slavery by his jealous brothers, wrongly accused of rape, and thrown into a dungeon for a crime he did not commit. But God helped this dreamer save his family and an entire nation. He went from the pit to the prison to the palace on his way to becoming the second-in-command in Egypt (see Gen. 37–39). Gideon was insecure, insignificant, and descended from the weakest clan in Israel. He was the least in his family and the runt of the litter. After an encounter with God, however, he stood up to tyranny and oppression and became a mighty man of valor (see Judg. 6). And Zacchaeus was a short, thieving tax collector who was despised even by his own countrymen. But when Jesus called out to him, this weasel climbed down a tree, changed his ways, and became a friend of Jesus (see Luke 19:1-10).

Peter was full of fear and denied Jesus three times in front of a campfire (see Mark 14:66-72). After being filled with the Holy

Spirit, however, this once fleeing and terror-filled man became one of the pillars of the church, ultimately laying down his life for Christ. Church history recounts that Peter was indeed crucified just as Jesus had predicted, but he was crucified upside down at his own request. He insisted that he was not worthy to be crucified as his Master was. Truly, it is through Christ that we are made strong, and this should be the trademark of a Christian man.

Heaven is full of weak, doubting, and wimpy people who become warriors for Christ. They exchanged their weaknesses, doubts, and fears for Christ-empowered strength. They allowed Jesus to redeem them, and in doing so they traded in their malfunctioning lives for the life they were always meant to live. Some men refuse to commit to Christ for fear of becoming a wimpy man who has no life. The ironic truth is that coming to Christ is exactly the opposite. He gives us our strength, boldness, and passion for living. The next time someone tells you to get a life, inform them that you already have one in Christ, and it rocks.

It was Jim Elliot, a missionary who was killed in 1956 at the hands of the people he loved and served in Ecuador, that profoundly said, "He is no fool who gives what he cannot keep to gain that which he cannot lose."

Bring It In

The two most common questions I get asked most about my football career are, "Do you miss it?" and "What do you miss the most about it?" Yes, I do miss it. Every player I know misses it to some extent. We miss the competition, the adulation from the fans, the feeling of accomplishment after a big victory, and, of course, the financial compensation for playing a game we love.

Without a doubt, though, the single biggest thing I miss is the camaraderie. The sense of brotherhood and community is something men crave but don't easily find. I shared a special bond with my teammates, regardless of their race, background, social status, or religious faith. We were a family. If they wore the silver and black, I had their back. And for guys who were true Raiders, I knew they had my back too. We could rib one another and play brutal practical jokes on each other, but when the game was on the line, I knew I could trust them. You can't put a price tag on that kind of friendship.

Without a doubt the most underrated ingredient of any championship team is chemistry. The best teams in professional sports seldom have the highest payrolls, but usually possess a great team chemistry. It's so invaluable that coaching staffs are intentional about holding training camps in distant locations for the sole purpose of forcing players to interact with one another. Former Raider coach Art Shell even paid for wings and pizza every Thursday night throughout the season just so we could hang out and socialize as a team. It was a mandatory weekly team event. If a guy skipped out for no good reason, he was likely to receive a brotherly attitude adjustment the next day.

It's not just sports teams that value camaraderie either. Soldiers, policemen, and fire fighters do as well, and so does Christ. That special bond of brotherhood, the feeling of belonging to a family and a community, is what Jesus had in mind for His disciples. The church is designed to be an ethnically diverse family of believers who genuinely love God and one another. Our sense of unity comes from our shared devotion to God and our mutual faith in Christ. Christian meetings should be a safe place to laugh, learn, love, fail, grow, bear one another's burdens, and be strengthened by the Lord and one another.

Are there any men like that in your life? Men you can huddle up with, learn from, confess your sins to, and hold one another accountable? God created the church to fill our need for community, and only in community can genuine discipleship take place. You will not grow in Christ without having others support and encourage you. In sports, bring it in means to huddle up, come together, and unite for a common goal. And this is precisely what every Christian man needs in his life. We all need each other to learn from, lean on, and lift up. As my brother Leo often tells the men in his ministry "Locking Arms", the Christian life is a team sport, don't go it alone.

One-on-One Isolation

Why is it that men like to drink beer together? It's the camaraderie. Most men are so out of touch emotionally that they have to have a few drinks in them before they can get real and raw with other guys. The alcohol wears down their defenses and gets them to loosen up and puts them in touch with their feelings. It's a sad statement when men have to be hammered in order to be honest with their friends.

It's my experience that most men aren't the least bit transparent in churches either. We often put our church face on and go through the motions. We likely, park in the same parking spot, sit in the same seat, clap our hands and give the appropriate responses all the while looking at our watch or thinking about our things to do that day. We may even state some Christian catch phrase like, "I'm too blessed to be stressed" when in reality we're dying inside. We don't want others to think poorly of us if we were to truly open up and confess our sins, shame, doubts and the personal demons that haunt us. That stuff is messy, and we'd rather not go there or be around those who do. For example, even as I volunteered as a minister, No one would know by looking at me that at times I was struggling to find my niche professionally or fighting depression, or doubting God's call on my life. We have brothers all around us battling disease, fighting addictions, spiritually and financially bankrupt, dying in their marriages and more times than not, we are completely unaware.

By nature men don't like to appear weak or vulnerable, and opening up about their lives is unorthodox and uncomfortable.

As an NFL player I always respected men of strength. To me as a player I strived to intimidate my opponents and never wanted to show any signs of weakness. Sadly, I carried this into my personal life and I didn't realize at that time that vulnerability is not weakness. In fact it takes courage to be real, speak truth and be emotionally transparent with others. It's the glue that builds meaningful relationships. I am striving to do this now. I recently discovered some great material on vulnerability written by Dr. Brene Brown. I highly recommend you read her book "Daring Greatly" or at least watch her short videos available on the Internet. It challenges me to let my guard down and be vulnerable and genuine in all my relationships but especially with those closest to me.

Because men don't naturally open up to others, discipleship does not come naturally to us. We are either too busy or too prideful to admit when we need a hand. I'll be honest with you: I am the last person to stop and ask for directions, and I often struggle with a problem far too long before admitting I need help. That's not healthy, because the enemy lies to us all, especially when we are isolated.

I have found the best way to grow in faith with my Christian brothers is to get out and do something together. Hunting, fishing, boating, going for a hike, shooting a round of golf, or serving a person in need are great ways to develop camaraderie and connect with other guys. Discipleship does not mean we sit around and talk about our inner feelings over a cup of tea. That may work for some people, but not for me. The best moments of discipleship I've shared have always been outside the walls of the church, which is what Jesus modeled. He did teach in the temple and synagogues, but some of Jesus's best sermons were out in the open. He mentored His disciples by doing things together and by being together in the great outdoors.

If you are serious about growing in your Christian faith, find some godly men who are going in the direction you want to head. In addition, get involved in a local Bible-believing church where you can submit yourself to godly teaching and worship. It is through communities of faith that we become spiritually fed, inspired, and equipped. If you do not know where to go, pray and ask the Holy Spirit to lead you.

You can be confident in this: with the call of God also comes the provision of godly fellowship. God has a church, Bible study, or group of men waiting to help encourage you in the right direction and advance your faith. If there is not one available, start your own and *bring it in.* Just know that you cannot make it in this Christian walk alone.

Give It Out

Every football team practices the two-minute drill. Down by a few points with the clock winding down, the two-minute drill simulates any scenario that involves marching down the field in the final seconds of the game. A team's execution must be perfect, and with the game on the line communication is critical. The quarterback and the coach cannot afford to waste words discussing what must take place in order to get the next play off quickly. They must be of one mind. Like a man on his deathbed whose life is slipping away, there is no time for meaningless words or idle chatter.

Jesus knew that His time was short. The clock was running out, as He would be leaving His disciples to go be with the Father once again. There was no time for meaningless words or idle chatter. Communication was critical to executing His next move. Jesus and His disciples knew they must be of one mind, and in His parting words He declared to them:

> *All authority in heaven and on earth has been given*
> *to Me. Therefore go and make disciples of all nations,*
> *baptizing them in the name of the Father and of the*

Son and of the Holy Spirit, and teaching them to obey everything I have commanded you. And surely I am with you always, to the very end of the age (Matthew 28:18-20).

Known as the Great Commission, this famous statement is often considered the mission statement of the Christian faith, and in it we find this instruction: "Go and make disciples." Once we have *given it up, taken it up,* and *brought it in,* it is time to *give it out.* Following Christ includes becoming disciples *and* making disciples. In this way we are both the tutored and the ones doing the tutoring.

Young Jewish men of the first century received their spiritual training from well-respected rabbis. Well-versed in the Scriptures, these mentors would attract students and instruct them in the way of life. These disciples would live with their rabbi, learn from him, study with him, serve under him, and eventually take on his philosophies and mannerisms. This was the model that Jesus used with His followers as well, as He lived with them, laughed with them, and did life together with them.

This style of education was not limited to spiritual training. In ancient times, virtually every profession involved an apprenticeship of some kind. Medicine, law, art, trade, music, and soldiering were all learned through mentorship and one-on-one instruction. Often, deep and meaningful relationships developed as the students learned from their teachers and worked alongside their peers.

This is how I learned to play football. I would watch and imitate those who knew the game better than me. I refined my play as an offensive guard by studying hours of film on former Penn State guard Mike Munchak, who became a Hall of Fame player with the Houston Oilers. I developed toughness and tenacity by emulating guys like Raiders linebacker Matt Millen and defensive tackle Howie Long. I learned consistency and competitiveness by copying center Don Mosebar and quarterback Jeff Hostetler. Most of these guys didn't even play my position, but we can learn a great deal from people in many different walks of life.

Joe Bugal was one of my all-time favorite offensive line coaches. He's best known for his years with the Washington Redskins and his Super Bowl champion offensive line, the hogs, but he also coached in Houston, Oakland, Arizona, and San Diego. He was a fiery, in-your-face kind of guy who spoke with a strong Pittsburgh accent. Everyday was a workday to Joe, as he was blue collar through and through. He wanted "snot blowers" for linemen, men who rolled up their sleeves and brought their lunch pails to the gridiron every Sunday.

Joe truly cared for his players and was passionate about what he did. He had no interest in fame or fortune. He was happy just to watch his players develop, succeed, and become the best they could possibly be. He was demanding but also loving and fair. It was not uncommon for Joe to approach you with a huge smile and hug when you came off the field after a big play or a devastating block. He knew that not every player was going to be a Pro Bowler, but he treated every player like they could be. If you bought into his philosophy, he would always stick his neck out for you, and you could trust that you would improve as a player.

Joe was the first coach to tell me he loved me, and I knew he really meant it. Because we all knew how much Joe cared for us, we would break our backs not to let him down. When we lost a game, I felt like I had let Joe down. He fostered camaraderie and the idea of believing in one another and keeping each other accountable. He demanded that we never back down from a challenge and believed that the offensive line set the standard of work ethic for the rest of the team.

Joe discipled me not just in football but in life. I still apply his wisdom today. He believed in me and saw something special in me. That is what all great teachers do. They see the promise in their pupils even when the student doesn't know it exists, and they know how to draw it out.

After surrendering to Christ, our highest call is to invest ourselves in the lives of others. Jesus didn't build a religion; He built relationships. He didn't buy real estate, construct ornate synagogues, hire publicists, or drive a fleet of high-priced chariots. He invested in people. He took the time to walk and talk and pray with those He was called to love. Because of this, Jesus is the perfect model of a coach. He taught His disciples, mentored them, led by example, and set the standard by His own behavior. I imagine there was much laughter and tears and deep discussions as they ate together, joked with each other, and colabored for the kingdom. Jesus poured His expertise and wisdom into their lives so that when He departed they could do the same.

This kind of interactive discipleship is not easily found today. It has become apparent to me that discipleship is the neglected daughter of the church. The American church has done some amazing things over the past 200 years. We have helped fund mission endeavors and deliver relief assistance all over the world. We have created libraries of written theology, founded Christian universities, printed countless Bibles, and created amazing music. We do a great job with offering media resources through the Internet, television, radio, and podcast programs. We have online search engines, prayer chains, quotes of the day, ring tones, and even Christian dating sites.

But what we still don't do well is create true disciples. This is in part because it takes true relationship to form a disciple. Most Christian men today go either undiscipled or are discipled using the assembly line approach. Mass discipleship is not nearly as effective as personal discipleship, and Sunday schools and Bible studies cannot do what one-on-one relationship can.

Paul writes to the Corinthians, *"For though you might have ten thousand instructors in Christ, yet you do not have many fathers; for in Christ Jesus I have begotten you through the gospel"* (1 Cor. 4:15 NKJV). We have many instructors today, but may I encourage you to be a spiritual father to someone you know? It starts with finding someone whom you respect and who will meet with you for your personal growth. Then, in turn, you pay it forward by taking someone under your wing and imparting to them what you know.

Every man could use a Paul, a Barnabas, and a Timothy in their lives. Pauls are spiritual fathers, ones who are more mature and can teach us how to walk in Christ; Barnabases are peer-level friends, ones we can encourage and be encouraged by; and Timothys are spiritual sons, those who are younger than us, people we can coach and mentor.

Paul instructed Timothy, *"And the things you have heard me say in the presence of many witnesses entrust to reliable men who will also be qualified to teach others"* (2 Tim. 2:2). Notice Paul's strategy for discipleship: entrust your time and energy to reliable men who are willing to teach others. Do you see the layers of discipleship woven throughout this verse? Paul instructed Timothy, who in turn taught trustworthy men, who could then tutor others. From Paul to Timothy to reliable men to others—that's four generations of spiritual instruction.

As we seek to disciple others, we can't forget that we first need to be living examples of men surrendered to Christ before we can be examples of it to others. Only a true disciple of Christ can make another genuine disciple. Let's walk the walk *and* talk the talk.

Do you remember what I said to Tim when he came up to me during training camp? I told him, "Just try to do what I do." Discipleship is as simple as that. Invite the disciple into your life and allow them to observe how you live. Eat, walk, jog, workout, pray, and study the Bible together. Find a book like this one and go through it together. Let these Scriptures and stories ignite your own discussions of faith. The reason I've included questions at the end of each chapter is to facilitate additional discussions. Take what you know and pass it on to someone else. Let your lifestyle be your discipleship. Your life may be the only Bible someone ever reads.

The Extra Point

Discipline comes from *disciple*. Whether it's art, music, or martial arts, if you desire to grow in any discipline, you must first become a disciple of it. Remove disciple and there is no discipline. The same is true for our discipleship to Christ. To grow spiritually, we must be disciplined and dedicate ourselves to the task at hand. If you are serious about following Christ, then it's time to bring the heat. If your commitment to Christ does not become your first priority, it will eventually become your last.

My brother Leo was an all-state heavyweight wrestler and football player in high school. He was seven years older than me, and at 6'2" and 230 pounds, he was a beast. I remember countless times when he would latch onto my arm, drive my head into the carpet, and test out his latest wrestling move on me. He'd always say, "You control the head, you control the body," as he twisted me in another painful position. I'd do my best to fight back, but the episode usually ended with me crying or squealing, "Mom!"

When we place Jesus at the head of our life, we can trust that He will steer us in the right direction. Like a skilled life coach, He is a proven expert and knows how to tap into our potential.

I played six years of football before earning a scholarship to Penn State, and even then I was not a nationally prized recruit. It was a slow, painful process of development that included many bumps and bruises along the way. Know that your path to righteousness will be no different. Don't be discouraged if you are not progressing as fast as you first envisioned. Spiritual growth takes time to develop. The Christian life is not a sprint; it is a marathon. No one just wakes up one morning and discovers they are

DISCIPLINE

a scholar, a world-class athlete, or an accomplished businessman. Success at any level takes focus, commitment, and sacrifice.

If you're like me, you're still a work in progress, but by God's Spirit He will transform you into the man He wants you to be. And like the rich young ruler, eternal rewards await you. Your trials and challenges today will be tomorrow's triumph and glory. We may not yet be who we want to be, but thank God we are not who we used to be.

Chalk Talk

1. What does it mean to count the cost of following Jesus? What are the costs?

2. If Jesus already carried the cross, how do we carry our cross daily?

3. What does it mean to be a true disciple of Jesus? What does it take on our part?

4. What does give it up, take it up, bring it in, and give it out mean to you?

5. What do you fear most about making yourself vulnerable with other men and those you love most? Will they reject you? Would Christ reject you?

6. Have you ever allowed shame to isolate you from others? In those times, what caused you to pull away? What can you do when you see other Christians pull away in isolation?

7. Whose life are you investing in? Who is your Paul, Barnabas, and Timothy? If you don't have any candidates, are you willing to pray right now that God would bring some to you?

Endnotes

1. This quote is from the movie *Braveheart*, http://www. quotesquotations .com/quotes/william-wallace-quotes.htm #ixzz34BbszFQt, accessed February 17, 2015.

2. John Mason, *You Were Born an Original, Don't Die a Copy* (Grand Rapids, MI: Revell, 1993), 59.

PRAYER

CHAPTER 5

THE MISSING LINK

No man fears to kneel before the God he trusts.
—KING ARTHUR TO SIR LANCELOT
(King Arthur, 2004)

There is no substitute for prayer. No amount of study or worship or sacrifice can compensate for time spent alone with God in prayer. It is an indispensable transaction, an irreplaceable commodity, and a force to be reckoned with. It is the highest law of the universe, having the ability to suspend all other laws of science by sanctioning God's intervention. To call upon the Most High is the most privileged, creative, intense, passionate, assertive, and aggressive action available to man.

E. M. Bounds writes,

> God shapes the world by prayer. The more praying there is in the world the better the world will be, the mightier the forces against darkness. The prayers of God's saints are the capital stock of heaven by which

God carries about His great work upon earth. God conditions the very life and prosperity of His cause on prayer.[1]

Prayer is the lifeblood of the believer, and the vehicle by which we establish, develop, and maintain our life and position in Christ. Vance Havner used to say, "I don't understand all about electricity, but I'm not going to sit around in the dark till I do."[2] Prayer is much like electricity—it keeps things going. Though we may not always see it in action, we can observe its dramatic effects upon our circumstances.

I recently purchased a state-of-the-art notebook computer. It was not your standard laptop that is sold at Wal-Mart. This was an ultimate computing machine. It came equipped with a lightning quick processor, ridiculous amounts of memory, and all the latest graphics and gaming capabilities it could handle. Ten years ago tech geeks only dreamed of gadgets like this all wrapped up in a notebook. Needless to say, it also came with a high price tag.

I quickly learned that of all its sophisticated features, none was more important than the standard $20 power cable included in the box. Unless the computer was plugged in, it was no more valuable than a colorful paperweight. Expensive machine or not, it still needed to be charged up frequently in order to function, and without the necessary power all its features were rendered useless. In fact, the more applications running at once, the quicker the battery drained.

Like any electronic device, our spiritual mechanisms are ineffective unless we are plugged in and charged up. The skill and power to process life is available to us in the Spirit, but we must be properly connected in order to access it. The more you have going on in your life, the quicker you will fade to dark and quit if you don't frequently charge your battery. Prayer is our way to get empowered, and without prayer we are nothing more than a paperweight. You may be gifted, but if you are not praying you are only pretending. God doesn't need us or want us to move in our own power, He wants us to move in His power and authority.

Appealing to a Higher Authority

When God gave Adam dominion over the earth, he was appointed as keeper, manager, and protector of creation (see Gen. 1:26-28; 2:15; Ps. 8:3-8; 115:16). Adam was installed as the guardian over the earth and was given dominion over the plants, animals, and environment. The condition of Adam's world was his responsibility, and his alone. Heaven would neither usurp nor undermine Adam's God-given position of authority.

This does not mean God would not or could not intervene in the midst of His creation. What it means is that God did not intervene unless man asked Him to do so. From the beginning, the Creator's plan was to work with people and *through* people, not independent of them. This is why prayer is a necessary exercise. God seeks a body that will cooperate with Him in order to see His will done on the earth.

Saint Augustine wrote, "Without God we cannot; without us, God will not." In other words, we need the Almighty to accomplish through us what He wants to accomplish for us. He has chosen humanity to bring about His plan for the earth, and in this way God does nothing on earth unless invited to do so. He simply waits to be invoked.

Andrew Murray writes,

> Prayer still remains what it would have been if man had never fallen: the proof of man's Godlikeness, the vehicle of his intercourse with the Infinite Unseen One, the power that is allowed to hold the hand that holds the destinies of the universe. Prayer is not merely the cry of the suppliant for mercy; it is the highest forth putting of his will by man, knowing himself to be of

Divine origin, created for and capable of being, in king-like liberty, the executor of the counsel of the Eternal. God's giving is inseparably connected with our asking. Only by intercession can that power be brought down from heaven which will enable the Church to conquer the world.[3]

In light of this, perhaps we've been too casual in our approach to prayer. We're probably all guilty of underestimating its power and purpose. The condition of the world, the condition of *your* world, is your responsibility, and one of the ways you govern it is through prayer. Through prayer you can shape your world and bring about the will of God in and around you.

Prayer not only invites God to intervene in our affairs, but it's also an admission that we need a power greater than ourselves to accomplish a mission higher than ourselves. In the midst of the Civil War, Abraham Lincoln admitted, "I have been driven many times to my knees by the overwhelming conviction that I had nowhere else to go. My own wisdom and that of all about me seemed insufficient for the day."[4]

God is eager to gain access into your world through your prayers. Too often we blame Him when things are not as they should be. We assume He is too busy or uninterested or absent. In reality, however, if justice and goodness are being withheld, it is we who should assume responsibility, not God. Collectively, we are allowing the injustice to occur by not appealing to a higher authority and by not petitioning God's intervention on our behalf.

God is not disinterested or ambivalent to your circumstances. He wants to be intimately involved in every activity of your life, but it is your job to invite Him into your life, your relationships, and your decisions. If you will not, then He will not. He is a true gentleman in that He doesn't force His will on anyone. It's not that He doesn't care about you or see your plight, but He waits to be wanted.

When my kids were young, I loved the sight and sounds they made eating meals in their high chair. They would often grunt, groan, or slurp and give a hand gesture that they wanted something from the table. As they grew older, we made them verbalize their requests and say please and thank you. In doing so, they learned to be polite and appreciative for the blessings of their daily meals. We call that love.

Ronald Dunn wrote the book called *Don't Just Stand There, Pray Something.* In it he wrote,

> We carelessly say, "Well, whatever happens is God's will. If God wants me to have this, I will get it. If it was meant to be, it will be." That is only partially true. The words of Jesus, "If you ask, I will do," carry the obvious implication that if we do not ask, Jesus will not act. James says it plainly enough: "You do not have because you do not ask" (James 4:2).[5]

Just as Jesus embodied the will of God here on earth, so now you and I are the expression and extension of His body here on earth. What an honor that God has chosen to work through humans, even at the price of becoming one.

Prayer in the NFL

Prayer and football have this in common: they both strive to achieve forward progress. Prayer is not just for the overzealous fan rooting, wishing, and even pleading with God for their favorite team to win each Sunday. Prayer is for the players too. Before each game, most of my Raider teammates, coaches, and I would link hands and say a prayer with our team chaplain. Like warriors preparing for battle, we understood that God was the giver and sustainer of our abilities. Only He possessed the power to help us achieve our goals and keep us from injury. People marvel that after thirteen years of professional football, and ten more years in the sport leading up to that, I never had a serious injury. I attribute that to God's blessing and the power of prayer.

If you've ever attended an NFL game, you will notice that after the game many players from both teams meet at midfield to form a prayer circle. In a voluntary act of sportsmanship and unity, it's a postgame tradition that most television networks don't cover. It may surprise you, but prayer is just as common in the football arena on Sundays as it is in church buildings. In fact, it was Coach Gruden himself who would lead us in the Lord's Prayer in the locker room after each game. Win or lose, elated or dejected, he did this prior to making any postgame comments to the team as a whole.

We can pray in all places and at any time throughout the day. The Bible records people praying while standing (see 1 Kings 8:22; Neh. 9:4-5), sitting (see 1 Chron. 17:16; Luke 10:13), kneeling (see Ezra 9:5; Dan. 6:10; Acts 20:36), bowing (see Exod. 34:8; Ps. 95:6), lying on the ground (see 2 Sam. 12:16; Matt. 26:39), in their beds (see Ps. 63:6), and lifting up hands to heaven (see Ps. 28:2; Isa. 1:15; 1 Tim. 2:8). So why not while playing football? I often prayed quietly to myself in the huddle and even as I walked up to the scrimmage line. Still today, I find myself praying at the gym, in the car, in the shower, while on runs, while mowing the lawn, and at my kids' soccer practices.

Prayer can be silent or loud (see 1 Sam. 1:13; Neh. 9:4; Ezek. 11:13), with our minds or with the Spirit (see 1 Cor. 14:14-18), with words, with Scripture, with song, or even with utterances too deep for human words (see Ps. 92:1-2; Eph. 5:19-20; Col. 3:16; Rom. 8:26). When it comes to prayer, let God out of your preconceived religious notions. Think of prayer as a long and continual conversation with God that stretches over the course of your life and spills over into eternity. It's an all-the-time occurrence, not just a single event.

The beautiful thing about prayer is that anyone can do it—children, adults, men, women, rich, poor, the uneducated, the handicapped, or the outcast. It is appropriate anywhere at any time for any reason by any person. Prayer is an equal opportunity resource made available to all who are interested. Age, appearance, and social status make no difference to the Lord when it comes to prayer. It is for the parent concerned for their child, for the manager responsible for important business decisions, and for the college student walking into a final exam. It's just as appropriate for football players huddled together in a locker room as it is for elderly women huddled in a circle at a Bible study. Prayer is the language of heaven. It does not take talent. It takes heart.

The condition of our hearts is the single most important factor to effective prayer. When we come before God we should be humble and sincere in our requests, thankful and joyful for what God has already given us, submissive and obedient to His will, faithful that He will hear and answer our prayer, and lastly, real, truthful, and genuine before God. If you have sin, doubts, fears, or frustrations, confess it and bring it to God through prayer.

When I was dating my wife, it was not a chore to spend countless hours talking on the phone with her. Just to hear her sweet voice telling me about the details of her day and to know she was on the other end of the line opened me up to share about my day and my struggles. This happened because my heart was in it. Prayer is no different. Getting to know God's character, recognizing His voice, and growing in your commitment to Him are all kept alive through times of vibrant prayer. Through this kind of personal interaction, His desires become our desires, and we become more in-tune with His purposes for our lives.

Do you want to know and love God better? Prayer is the fast track toward achieving it. Sir Isaac Newton once said, "I can take my telescope and look millions of miles into space but I can go away to my room and in prayer get nearer to God in heaven than

I can when assisted by all the telescopes in the world."[6] In prayer, we develop a bond and a history with the living God that pulls us closer to His heart and gives us favor with Him. It's through a lot of kneeling that we are kept in good standing with God.

Don't get me wrong: prayer is not easy. It is a discipline and a perishable skill. At times it is hard work because it requires focus and devotion. Much like working out at the gym, there are immediate rewards to praying, but long-term gains are secured through determination and consistency. The way to learn how to pray is by simply praying. Like any activity, prayer is most beneficial when exercised and practiced.

Prayer is not designed to change God. Rather, it changes us. It changes our attitudes, our demeanor, and our perspective. It's only when we are on our knees that we're tall enough to reach heaven. One man put it this way: "The man on his knees has a better view of things than the world has on its tiptoes."

It's important to know that the goal of prayer is not to get what you want; rather, it is to help God get what He wants. It's less about asking God to help you and more about asking how you can help Him. That's a radical paradigm shift, I know, but once this is realized, prayer becomes so much more God-centric. Don't think of prayer as overcoming God's reluctance or twisting His arm to get Him to do something for you. Prayer is simply cooperating with His willingness. Do this, and you will see your prayers answered more often. Trying to convince God to give you something you think you need never seems to end well. Trust me, if God doesn't want it for you, you don't want it anyway.

How Should We Pray?

Plenty of great books have been written about prayer, but I refer back to what Jesus taught. I encourage you to read Matthew 6:5-13, where Jesus teaches His followers about prayer. This is the passage in Scripture where we find a common prayer referred to as the Lord's Prayer, or the Our Father. More than just a single prayer to be memorized and repeated, I believe this passage lays out for us a great model of *how* we should pray. I've found the acronym ACTS to be useful: Adoration, Confession, Thanksgiving, and Supplication.

Adoration means praising God simply for who He is and what He has done on our behalf. This is the most important aspect of our prayer time. God wants us to love Him just for who He is and what He has done—not just for what He can do for us. He is the Creator, the Sustainer, and the Almighty One. He is our righteous and faithful God. As we focus on and proclaim how big our God is, it will help us to see how small our problems are to Him.

After spending time adoring God, we need to then *confess* and repent of our sins, doubts, frustrations, anger, and apathy. Be transparent and genuine because the intentions of your heart are not hidden from Him anyhow. If you have no desire to read the Bible or spend time in prayer, admit it to God. If you are struggling with lust, envy, jealously, anger, or any sin in particular, tell Him. Christ is our intercessor and He already knows what we are going through. There is nothing we can hide from Him (see Matt. 27:51). When we openly confess our sins and our need for help, it removes the roadblocks and barriers the enemy has tried to place between God and us. Then when we make our confession to those we have wronged and ask for their forgiveness, it opens the door to spiritual healing.

Next, we are to *thank* God for specific things He has done for us. You may want to start by thanking Him for your salvation, your health, your employment, your marriage, your children, His Word, and all things both big and small. Thank God for what He has done for you, and what is He doing in your life today. When we give thanks with a humble heart, it motivates Him to continue to bless us. We need to cultivate thankful hearts while in God's presence.

Supplication simply means praying for the specific needs of the day. This is your "daily bread," so to speak. The Bible teaches us to make our needs known to God, and to seek Him with persistence and tenacity. If you have a need, by all means ask God to meet it. If you have a question, need wisdom, or guidance, then seek it through prayer. If your child had a critical need and you had the resources to fulfill it, wouldn't you want them to seek you out and make their need known to you?

The Challenges Ahead

The national championship of 1986 was the greatest single sports memory of my life, and also one of my biggest personal challenges. As the hard winter in State College blasted us with cold weather during bowl practices, it also knocked me to my knees with a case of pneumonia in both my lungs. The team arrived in sunny Tempe, Arizona, the week prior to take on the University of Miami, and I was sent back to my hotel to rest. Other than practice, I only remember the fevers, hacking, wheezing, and chills of my sweat-covered sheets in that hotel room. I tried my best to hide the severity of my condition from the coaches, but I had to fight just to stay upright at practice and in meetings. A few hours before kick off, I weighed myself in a locker room, and the scale read 242 pounds—I had lost twenty-three pounds! I was already undersized as an offensive guard at 265 pounds prior to my illness, but this was now unacceptably lighter than any defenders I would be facing during the game. It was almost laughable to think I would start and play a football game that night.

I remember crying out to God that week, especially the night of the game. To honor my mother who passed away prior to that season, I was not going to let anything or anyone keep me off that field. As players lined the field and the national anthem played that night, I had a few tears streak down my face. I had serious doubts that I was even capable of playing at all, let alone playing well that night. In that moment, I suddenly felt a wave of peace pass through my body. It was as if God whispered, "Be still and know that I am God."

I repeated those words over and over. With that touch from God, I felt His strength as I proceeded to play one of the best games of my life. Hacking, coughing, and light-headed at times, yet I was able to persevere and push through to help my team achieve a great upset in our 14–10 victory. It wasn't the prettiest win ever, but we remained undefeated and were named the undisputed national champions of college football.

I often feel we do a disservice to young Christians by not equipping them properly for the challenges they will surely face as new believers. When we stand up for Christ, we can be assured that unwanted invaders will creep into our world. Some challenges may be spiritual or educational, and we can be assured that our enemy will not sit idly by as we are led to the cross and set free. We are like prisoners from hell's kingdom who escaped with the keys to the prison doors and with a vision to set other captives free.

As a Christian man, you can expect challenges, hardships, and persecution as you follow the call of God for your life. I know personally four faithful Christians with life-threatening cancers who are fighting and believing God just to see another day. The good news is that God promises to be faithful as He will never leave us nor forsake us. His strength and peace will sustain us, even in the face of such adversity.

When you experience difficulties in life, don't allow them to cause you to run away from God. Rather, let them drive you to your knees in prayer. Like water, don't follow the path of least resistance. Rivers and streams often snake wildly across the landscape because water is a blind force that, as it pushes forward, follows the path of least resistance. God wants us to not

PRAYER

follow the easy path—He wants us on *His* path. Problems and resistance should drive us to pray, because it is only through prayer that we can tap into His Spirit and push through the barriers in our path.

Years ago, my wife and I were served with a significant lawsuit that we felt was unjust. The moment after being served the lawsuit, we laid hands on the stack of papers and gave it to God. In the name of Jesus, we claimed victory over that lawsuit. It was painful and costly, but a year and a half later, and after ten days in court, we were victorious. The struggle with injustice as a by-product caused us as a family to lean into God and into each other to see it through. Looking back, I can see now how God used it and how He was glorified through it. We all tend to wonder why life is so challenging at times. Treat those challenges as an invitation to pray. As we do, God solves them for us and in the process shows Himself to be altogether trustworthy.

It should be no surprise to us that God often uses trials in order to bring about spiritual growth in our lives. A blacksmith must first turn up the heat in order to mold the steel. A gardener prunes the plant in order to promote growth. In the same way, challenges produce a good thing in us—our dependence on God. This is why James wrote:

> *Consider it pure joy, my brothers, whenever you face trials of many kinds, because you know that the testing of your faith develops perseverance. Perseverance must finish its work so that you may be mature and complete, not lacking anything. If any of you lacks wisdom, he should ask God, who gives generously to all without finding fault, and it will be given to him* (James 1:2-5).

A Voice Out of Silence

It's no shock that prayer is a chore for most men. If you find praying as uncomfortable and unenjoyable as a trip to the dentist, know that you are not alone. Because men are visual, staring at a wall in silence or closing our eyes to focus on something unseen for long periods of time might be an exercise more conducive to taking a nap than praying. It's because prayer is an all-out assault on our flesh and an affront to our pride. Our sinful nature does not want us praying. Of course, the enemy doesn't want us praying either, so he'll throw every distraction possible our way the moment we bow our heads.

When you invoke God you will provoke the devil, but this is a battle worth fighting if you want to take ground in the Spirit. The devil only resists what he is intimidated by, so you must be into something good when you pray. If you can press through the frontlines of lethargy, distraction, and your screaming flesh, you will gain access to a power that is otherworldly.

I have learned that prayer becomes more thrilling and interactive the more I do it. In fact, prayer is where all the action is. As I close my eyes, things come to light. As I vocalize my concerns, stress leaves my body. As I mediate on God's Word, I walk away with wisdom beyond my years.

But we must remember that prayer is not a monologue; it is a dialogue. Jesus said, *"My sheep listen to My voice; I know them, and they follow Me"* (John 10:27). Hearing the voice of the Shepherd should be normative in the life of the sheep. It is the basic right of every child of God to hear their heavenly Father speak to them. It is our source of wisdom and our voice of navigation. If you feel you have never heard God speak to you, then think again. You are likely just not recognizing His voice when He does speak to you. In fact, every Christian has already heard God's voice. You would not have been compelled to follow Christ unless you had heard the call of Christ to come follow Him in the first place. It was God Himself who drew you to repentance, salvation, and faith.

We sometimes wonder why God is so silent. The more we pray, however, the more we realize that God is anything but silent. His Word is alive and His Spirit is active. Prayer is God's way of keeping the communication lines open. Too many times we're not hearing His voice because He does not hear our voice in prayer. Like fine-tuning a radio, God uses prayer to transmit His signals to us and dial us into His whispers.

The Cherokee and the Cricket

There's a story told of a Cherokee Native American who was walking with a friend in downtown New York City one day. Suddenly, he said to his companion, "I hear a cricket."

"Oh, you're crazy," his friend replied.

"No, I hear a cricket. I'm sure of it!" the man insisted.

His friend balked, "It's the noon hour. There are people bustling around, cars honking, taxis squealing, engines revving. How can you hear a cricket in the midst of all this city noise?"

He contended, "I hear it." He listened attentively as he walked around the corner, across the street, and found a shrub in a large cement planter. He dug beneath the leaves and found a cricket. His friend, who had accompanied him, was absolutely astounded.

The Cherokee explained, "My ears are no different from yours. It simply depends on what you are listening to. Here, let me show you." He promptly reached in his pocket, pulled out a handful of change—a few quarters, some dimes, nickels, and pennies—and dropped them on the sidewalk. Every head within a block turned. "You see what I mean?" he said as he picked up the coins. "It all depends on what you're listening for."

What are you listening for? The voice of opportunity, the voice of personal gain, or the voice of God? Silence is not our problem.

Our problem is that we are plagued by too little of it. The modern man is forced to swim through an ocean of sound bites, commotion, and noise pollution just to maintain some semblance of peace and clarity of mind, and in the process the voice of God too often gets drowned out. Still a voice speaks, and in the midst of swirling activity and surrounding distraction, those who are listening can still hear God.

Put a group of men in a room and it's easy to recognize who the leader is. Leaders monopolize the listening. A leader knows when to listen and who to listen to. When you are speaking to God, take some time to listen too. The Holy Spirit wants to direct you in what to pray and what you need to know. Remember that divine guidance is not a formula. It is an art. One skill worth developing is to learn how to talk to God so that He listens and how to listen so that He will talk to you.

Cure for the Bored Believer

Are you stagnant in your Christian walk? Then I would encourage you to try prayer. Do you have a desire to hear God speaking to you? Then pray. One of the greatest motivators for talking to God is when you discover that He is a God who talks back.

I am compelled to believe that God is speaking to you right now. The issue is not so much His reluctance to speak but our inability to discern His voice when He does speak. Expect that He will speak to you as you pray today. When you begin to hear God's voice consistently, the excitement level your faith rises to a level where heaven and hell alike take notice. Prayer then goes from being a monologue to a dialogue, from an action to an interaction. You don't ever have to be bored with prayer again.

When Elijah prayed, it was far from boring. His prayers caused rain to fall and droughts to begin, the dead to rise and widows to rejoice. Black birds brought him bread in the morning and meat in the evening. Elijah saw fire fall from heaven, rainclouds fill the sky, and chariots of fire usher him to heaven in a whirlwind of glory (see 1 Kings 17–19).

On one occasion, an angel roused him twice from a nap with food and water at his feet. Fueled by the strength of that food, he ran for forty days and nights until he reached Mount Horeb, the mountain of God. While in a cave, God's presence passed by in a strong wind. It tore into the mountain and split rocks in two, but Scripture records that God wasn't in the wind. An earthquake followed, but God wasn't in the earthquake either. Then a fire passed by, but God wasn't in the fire. Finally, a still small voice emerged—a gentle whisper. At that, Elijah tucked his face in his garment and conversed with God.

Many times we discount a spiritual experience when God's voice doesn't come to us in booming fashion. People who demand that God must first write it in the sky before they will believe wouldn't believe even if He did write it in the sky. They would still find a way to be skeptical. Hearing God's voice will always carry with it a measure of faith, and that's what makes it so fascinating to us and so debilitating to the enemy.

Without question, God does speak in spectacular ways, but His voice doesn't have to be spectacular in order to be supernatural. Figuratively speaking, He still uses fires and earthquakes to capture our attention, but He most often speaks to us through that gentle whisper. You may think it is your conscience or an inner voice, but it can be much more than that—it is often the very voice of God speaking to our hearts.

James 5:16-18 says, *"The prayer of the righteous man is powerful and effective. Elijah was a man just like us. He prayed earnestly that it would not rain, and it did not rain on the land for three and half years. Again he prayed, and the heavens gave rain and the earth produced crops."* You are no different from Elijah. Your prayers are more powerful and effective than you give them credit. Perhaps the enemy realizes this as well, which explains why he fights you at the door of your prayer closet. Don't be discouraged. Rather, rise up and contend for all God has for you.

The Extra Point

Not only is communication the backbone of our society, but it essential to the health of any relationship. In a marriage, for example, communication is the single most important factor to maintaining and sustaining a strong union. When there is a communication breakdown, oftentimes there will be an accompanied breakdown in the marriage itself. Addressing unhealthy patterns in communication is the first step toward restoring a marriage that is falling apart.

Likewise in war, communication is essential to achieving military victory. The lines of communication are the channels of life, the arteries that connect the soldiers on the frontlines to their base operations. Positioning troops, securing supply chains, replenishing numbers, and uniting an army are much more difficult without clear and unabated lines of communication.

Prayer is not as complicated as we often tend to make it. It is simply communicating with God. In the fight for our marriages, our children, and our country, we need to make it our aim to become a master communicator. In the fight for your calling, make it your aim to keep the lines of communication open with heaven. Prayer is your channel of life, the artery that connects you to your base of operations. Through it God will position you, protect you, replenish you, and give you all things needed to achieve victory.

You cannot be the man you are created to be without a vibrant prayer life. I've learned that great men with great talent have great practice behind them. This is true with prayer as well. You have great potential to be a mighty man of God, and the practice of prayer might be the only thing that separates you

PRAYER

from that greatness. So I would encourage you to set your heart to pray today.

Chalk Talk

1. Are you in the habit of allowing God to steer your path in life through prayer? Do you regularly intercede for others? When and where do you pray?

2. Do you know how to pray using the ACTS model (Adoration – Confession – Thanksgiving – Supplications)? Are you intimidated to pray in front of others? If so, what's holding you back?

3. Do you regularly lead prayer in your home or with loved ones? Name a time when God answered one of your prayers. What was it, and how did He answer it?

4. When was the first time you heard God speak to you? What did He tell you? How did you speak back to Him? With words or with actions? Describe the details.

5. Are you pushing loved ones in a direction you want them to go or the direction you feel the Lord is leading them? What are the consequences of making snap judgments instead of seeking God's wisdom and direction through prayer and the study of His Word?

6. In your communication, are you a better listener or talker? How might you improve your communication with God and those you love?

7. What current challenges are you or your loved ones facing? Are you allowing God to use these circumstances to draw you closer to Him? Are you willing to share your difficulties with others?

Endnotes

1. E.M Bounds, *Purpose in Prayer*, (Grand Rapids, MI.: Christian Classics Ethereal Library), 2.

2. Ronald Dunn, *Don't Just Stand There, Pray Something* (Nashville: Thomas Nelson, 1991), 52.

3. Rev. Andrew Murray, *In the School of Prayer*, (New York: Fleming H.Revell Company, 1895) Public Domain.

4. Roy B. Zuck, *The Speaker's Quote Book: Over 5,000 Quotations and Illustrations for All Occasions* (Grand Rapids, MI: Kregal, 1997), 300.

5. Ibid., *Don't Just Stand There*, 52.

6. Ibid., *The Speaker's Quote Book*, 298.

PRAYER

OBEDIENCE

CHAPTER 6

THANK YOU, SIR. MAY WE HAVE ANOTHER?

One act of obedience is better than
one hundred sermons.
—DIETRICH BONHEOFFER

After my late night God-encounter in Nashville, I came to the realization that my career was not yet over. In fact, it was only beginning. I was being handed a new job assignment from the Lord. God had a wild adventure awaiting me beyond football, but it would require a radical commitment to that call. The ball was now in my hands, and if you know anything about football, linemen aren't comfortable handling the ball.

Jesus tells the story of a landowner who had two sons (see Matt. 21). One day the father said to the first son, "Son, go work in the vineyard." The son answered and said, "I don't want to," but later thought better of it and went and worked. The father approached the second son, saying, "Son, go work in the vineyard." He responded, "Of course," but he never actually got around to it. Jesus then asks the question, "Which son did what his father asked?" The answer is self-evident.

God's will for your life is not overly complicated. In fact, it's just a matter of obedience. Jesus's story reveals that God the Father is less concerned about what we say we will do and more about what we actually do. Our words alone are never as powerful as our actions. Sometimes good intentions are the enemy of good deeds. While I had good intentions of writing this book for thirteen years, I could never reap the benefits of it until I actually hunkered down and finished the task at hand.

The point of the parable is that obedience pleases the heavenly Father far more than mental assent or the appearance of compliance. Too often we are guilty of placing more emphasis on saying the right thing rather than actually *doing* the right thing. While we may be able to dupe others with conciliatory words and sweet talk, we cannot fool the Almighty. Our grandiose prayers and promises are just empty words if they are not backed by responsible action. God doesn't take pleasure in seeing us make grand sacrifices and severe punishments for our disobedience. He would rather bless us through our obedience the first time around.

For the Christian there is simply no substitute for obedience to what God asks of us. It is the radical catalyst of our spiritual growth. Obedience is both the entry point and the goal of our faith, and it should be placed on the highest shelf of our reach. Do not think for one second that God is limiting you or restricting you by giving you directives. Instead, He is protecting you and proving that He truly does care about you. The one who says, "I don't need God's protection; I can take care of myself," is the very one whom the commandments are given to protect, and that protection is usually from himself.

You are called to be a man of action, a man who rolls up his sleeves and gets to work, a gladiator willing to fight and bleed for the cause, and a soldier in the trenches who is undaunted by the pressures of life. What separates you, the man, from you, the boy, is not so much your strength but rather how and when you use that strength.

I recall countless times running sprints after football practices with my teammates. The more my teammates swore, grumbled, and complained, the longer our coach would be provoked to keep running us. I decided to change tactics and thank him for the experience. After each sprint, I'd joyfully yell out, "Thank you, sir. May we have another?" Soon my teammates caught on. They enthusiastically joined in the chorus, smiling, giggling, and shouting with glee like a Cub Scout troop on their way to camp. It was just another day at the office—grown men acting like a bunch of 12-year-olds. Our coach quickly ended the conditioning when he saw this experience was no longer bothering us. We were becoming unified and were having way too much fun at his expense. I discovered early on in my athletic career that a positive attitude and change in demeanor could make any situation all the more bearable and enjoyable.

Likewise, our attitude and response to spiritual requirements determines how bearable and enjoyable life will be for us. The amount of joy we display in difficulty is an indication of the amount of faith we possess in God. C. S. Lewis put it this way: "Authority exercised with humility and obedience accepted with delight, are the very lines along which our spirits live."[1]

Rules of Engagement

Most men cringe when they hear the word *obedience*. It often carries with it unpleasant connotations. It conjures up thoughts of forced behavior, threats of punishment, and heavy-handed demands. Like a callous drill sergeant barking out commands, we tend to liken obedience to coercive measures that bend our wills and beat us into submission. Whatever images you associate in your mind with obedience, most likely they are negative.

The thought of being ruled by another is an affront to most men. It challenges our masculinity and threatens our pride. Like most people, men don't like being told what to do. We like to think of ourselves as free spirits and independent thinkers, mavericks who either play by our own set of rules or completely throw rules to the wind.

If left to ourselves, we would probably all choose to live in a world without restrictions. Imagine if there were no laws to govern our universe. Suppose the sun stopped shining or the earth ceased its gravitational pull. What if seeds refused to sprout, the ocean ignored its boundaries, and storm clouds withheld their rain? Our universe and our world would self-destruct. Now think of a society without laws. Imagine if there were no laws restricting theft or rape or murder. Envision a world devoid of justice, order, free speech, and human rights, an unruly society where people could indiscriminately seize our homes or cars or paychecks or children without cause. Anarchy is no kind of freedom. It's bedlam. We see around the world atrocities of violence, abductions, bombings, and savage brutality, and it makes us grateful we live in a country that is relatively safe.

In a lawless society, just driving to work would be hazardous. Without traffic laws to govern the roads, cars would drive at top speed in every direction and on any side of the freeway, or even on the sidewalk. A red light could mean stop or go or speed up or slow down, whatever suits one's fancy on that particular day. Stop signs would be chaotic, if they even existed. In a world without restraint, we would quickly gain a new appreciation for the laws that govern our world.

Laws are not negative. Laws are positive, and they are designed to safeguard the freedoms we enjoy. Laws intrinsically protect people's liberties, not limit them. Those who say they don't need laws are really just saying they don't want to play by any rules and don't want to be accountable for their actions. No one ever really lives without any rules. It's more a question of *which* rules they choose to live by.

The popular mantra that rules are meant to be broken may seem like a cavalier idea, but can there be true and lasting freedom without laws to protect that freedom? The honest answer is no, not in this fallen world, and surprisingly not even in a perfect world. Scripture records that *"the Lord God commanded the man"* (Gen. 2:16) to not eat from one particular tree found in the garden of Eden. Even paradise had rules and boundaries for the purpose of protecting its beauty. All creation needs boundaries, and where freedom is found so is found the need to protect that freedom.

Imagine playing sports, a board game, or a round of kick the can without any established rules. Without rules, games would be reckless and pointless. Auto racing would look like demolition derby, basketball would more resemble a game of dodge ball, and football could be mistaken as rugby. Wait, that already happens! Owning Park Place in Monopoly would be no different than owning Marvin Gardens, and eventually all these games would be forgotten due to a lack of interest and plain boredom. Rules define the game, give it an identity, protect it, and protect those who play it. Without rules there is no game to be played, and it's the rules that make the game worth playing.

We have been programmed to believe that rules are a burdensome chore, a necessary evil, an obligatory mandate. In the kingdom of God, however, nothing could be further from the truth.

My Life As an Automobile

My son and I love cars. We like to go to the auto dealerships, test drive new models, enjoy that toxic new car smell, and read about the latest innovations. My son is a walking encyclopedia of auto facts, and loves to watch his favorite auto show, *Top Gear*, to stay up on all the trends. Although we love them, we can't get carried away and spend all our money on something that was designed to provide a simple function in our lives. Cars were created for the sole purpose of providing reliable transportation. As long as we provide the fuel, they provide the function. With gas, maintenance, insurance, and frequent washes, car owners pay a price to own and operate a vehicle.

But how trustworthy would our vehicles be if they had a free will? What if your vehicle woke up cranky or was upset that you haven't shown it enough care and attention lately? What if it said to you, "No, I don't feel like taking you on this bumpy road. It's too hot or too wet and my brake pads are kind of thin." Suppose it balked, "I'd love to be of service to you, but I'm really tired, and I have a meeting at the car club later." That's ridiculous, right? Well, God created you for a purpose and with a free will. He paid a heavy price to purchase you, and He continues to provide oxygen for your lungs with each and every breath you take, fuel for your soul, and the freedom to choose between right and wrong. How many excuses have you come up with just this week to take yourself out of service? Your true function in life is to be fully yielded to your Creator and to give Him glory through all you do.

The picture of a fully yielded and submitted Christian is what Watchmen Nee wrote about in his book *The Normal Christian Life*. We are to be His property, faithful in devotion, and of service to Him. We fully trust in our Lord to steer us in the direction that is best for our lives and His glory. Anything else is not a reflection of the true Christian faith. The real test of a man's character is not when he plays the role that he wants for his life, but when he plays the role God has given him.

Love and Obedience

OBEDIENCE

Just as natural laws govern our lives, so moral laws govern our spiritual lives. And the directives of God's kingdom are not overbearing or politically driven like many laws being passed today. God's laws are liberating and wise, fair and unchanging. Our Creator has given us guidelines to live by, and when applied they bring strength to our marriages, health to our children, success to our businesses, blessings to our finances, and peace to our souls. Jesus encapsulated them into one law—the law of love.

> *"Love the Lord your God with all your heart and with all your soul and with all your mind." This is the first and greatest commandment. And the second is like it: "Love your neighbor as yourself." All the Law and the Prophets hang on these two commandments* (Matthew 22:37-40).

Jesus is neither replacing Scripture with this statement nor discounting the Ten Commandments. Rather, He is summing them up and breaking them down into their most basic value—loving God and loving others. This is the crux of the Bible and the universal will of God for every man's life.

In Christian circles, there's a lot of talk about love, and rightfully so. Love is a central theme of the Scripture, both in the Old and the New Testament (see Deut. 30:16; John 14:15,21). But what does it mean to love someone? While it may be impossible to overemphasize love, it is possible to underdefine it. Let's take a look at Scriptures that talk about loving God and others.

Joshua admonished the children of Israel when he said to them:

But be very careful to keep the commandment and the law that Moses the servant of the Lord gave you: to love the Lord your God, to walk in obedience to Him, to keep His commands, to hold fast to Him and to serve Him with all your heart and with all your

OBEDIENCE

soul. Then Joshua blessed them and sent them away, and they went to their homes (Joshua 22:5-6).

And John writes in his first letter:

> *And we can be sure that we know Him if we obey His commandments. If someone claims, "I know God," but doesn't obey God's commandments, that person is a liar and is not living in the truth. But those who obey God's word truly show how completely they love Him. That is how we know we are living in Him. Those who say they live in God should love their lives as Jesus did* (1 John 2:3-6 NLT).

> *By this we know that we love the children of God, when we love God and obey His commandments. For this is the love of God, that we keep His commandments. And His commandments are not burdensome* (1 John 5:2-3 ESV).

Notice that love for God and obedience to His commands are closely intertwined throughout Scripture. The reason for this is because our obedience to His commands best communicates our love for Him. Love cannot be properly understood outside the context of commitment and trust. Where there is no faithfulness there is no love, for love will always and ultimately compel one to please the will of another.

When my son or one of daughters chooses to obey me, I don't hesitate to reward them in any measure of ways, not always with material blessings, but often with a touch, time spent together, or a simple "I love you." I know what pleases their heart, and I take pleasure in blessing them. Among the many things they do to bring me joy, it is their obedience that best communicates their love and respect for me. Let's face it: we don't always know what's best for us, and it takes humility and maturity to admit that. When my children want to be guided by my wisdom, it demonstrates their security and trust in my love for them.

When love is forced, joy is the first to leave the relationship. Compulsory love is not love at all—it's robbery. God will never steal something from us that we would voluntarily give out of the goodness of our heart. A person who loves out of obligation only gives and does the bare minimum. They may perform their duty but never fully release their heart to it. But when a person chooses to love, they invest every ounce of their being into the relationship. No sacrifice is too great; no amount of inconvenience deters them. Perhaps this is why lovers always outwork workers. Workers may dutifully drag themselves to work every day, but lovers will always go above and beyond the call of duty.

Have you ever been to a restaurant where the server seems too bothered to wait on your table? It's almost like they are doing you a favor by serving you and taking your tip. Compare that now to my 100 percent Italian mother who was deeply offended if guests didn't sit down at the kitchen table to eat a meal or enjoy a sweet treat when they visited our home. She loved to serve and always had a kind word or some homemade baked good that was ready to eat. When guests left our home, they were most likely to leave with a hug and an arm full of food.

There's a blessing found in keeping God's commands, whether we do it cheerfully or begrudgingly, but the greater blessing is found in heartfelt devotion. God loves us by choice, not by obligation. He doesn't have to love us—He wants to. Likewise, godliness isn't obligatory behavior or mandatory compliance but voluntary sacrifice. God doesn't need our love and devotion. He deserves it. Obedience with love is the goal and satisfaction of the grateful worshiper. For the lover and follower of Christ, obedience is a delight instead of a drag. When we choose to love God not because we have to but simply because we want to, we profoundly become more like Christ.

A. W. Tozer wrote, "The secret of saintliness is not the destruction of the will but the submergence of it in the will of God."[2] There is a place in God available to you where you can find true pleasure in the will of God. Too often we assume that God is going to steal our fun or ask us to do something embarrassing or dreadful. At times His will is inconvenient and humbling, but it is always fulfilling. I have found that He takes pleasure in thrilling my heart, and, because He made me, He is the expert on knowing what truly brings me joy.

A Winning Attitude

I've had the privilege of playing on a championship team, so I've been able to observe what makes a team successful. Commentators often ask the question, what makes a great team great?

Talent might be our first answer, for it is certainly a factor, but it's a smaller factor than causal fans at first might assume. What separates a winning team from a losing team? Money? Coaching? Preparation? All of these factors contribute, but there is one ingredient every championship team possesses: unselfish players who are willing to do whatever is asked of them and play whatever role is necessary to help the team. When players buy into the team-first concept, the team can often accomplish more than the sum of its individual parts.

What coaches look for beyond talent is coaching-ability. Being teachable is an intrinsic quality that is less skill-developed and more character-driven. Athleticism is useless if you won't to listen to your coaches. Speed is negated if you refuse to hustle. Soft hands and good footwork can't make up for missed blocking assignments and sloppy, selfish play.

In the same way, those who lay down their pride and are willing to do whatever is asked of them find success in God. *"For the eyes of the Lord run to and fro throughout the whole earth, to show Himself strong on behalf of those whose heart is loyal to Him"* (2 Chron. 16:9 NKJV). God is looking for those who are fully His—coachable, humble, and willing to seek the kingdom of heaven above their own pursuits. These kinds of believers don't care how God uses them, as long as they get to be apart of the team, and, ultimately, they end up accomplishing far more in life than they would have otherwise.

Calling an Audible

Memorizing the playbook is a basic yet critical part of any football team's success. In the huddle, it is imperative that every player knows the play and knows their assignment so they can properly run the play. If one player is not listening to the play call or does not know the playbook, it can sabotage the entire play.

When the offensive unit comes to the line, it is equally important they listen to the voice of their quarterback. Every player must know the snap count and what changes the quarterback may make at the line. As he reads the defense, he may call an audible and change the play altogether. Being able to hear the play and know the playbook can be the difference between winning and losing the game, especially at a crucial point in the game.

Spiritually speaking, Christ is our quarterback and the Bible is our playbook. When we avoid huddling up with Him on a consistent basis and do not pay careful attention to His instructions, we can easily miss our God-given assignments. Taking time to study and memorize God's playbook helps us make wise choices in life, prepares us for every play call, and prevents us from sabotaging the pattern we are designed to run.

The word *listen* in the Bible is nearly equivalent to the word *obey*. The general concept of obedience in Scripture relates to hearing a higher authority, and then implementing what the higher authority said. One of the terms for obedience conveys the idea of positioning yourself under another's authority and submitting to their command. Another word in Scripture for obedience simply means *to trust*. In fact, many languages don't even have two separate words for trusting and obeying—they are often one and the same.

Jesus called an audible when He walked the shores of Galilee and beckoned Peter and John to follow Him. When they heard HIs call, they left everything behind—their boats, their careers, their livelihood, their 401Ks, and their retirement accounts. They were, in every sense of the phrase, all in.

Similarly, Christ has stepped up to your life and called an audible. Have you heard the call? You probably thought your life would play out in a certain way, but He has mapped out an alternative route for you. You are left with a choice: to trust His lead or to run your own play. Just hearing His words is not sufficient; your abandonment to that call is what demonstrates your faith in Him.

Great leaders, like great players, are also great listeners. They are quick to pay attention to the play caller. The center listens to the commands of his quarterback; the quarterback trusts the play calling of his offensive coordinator; and the coordinator follows the instructions of the head coach. Whether in football or in life, every great leader is also a great follower. In the words of J. Oswald Sanders, "Many who aspire to leadership fail because they had never learned to follow."[3]

One leader I learned a great deal from was Joe Paterno. He is best remembered for being the head football coach at Penn State for forty-six seasons. What many people don't know is that he first served as an assistant coach for sixteen years, which, in itself, is a great career for most people in the coaching profession. But Joe began learning how to be a great coach by learning how to serve others first, and the ultimate "other" is God Himself.

Out of Control

If you are an experienced skier or a snow boarder, you probably already know that black and double black diamond runs are the steepest and most intimidating runs on any mountain. But, ironically, they aren't the most dangerous. The most dangerous place on any ski mountain is the bunny slope. This is where the most inexperienced skiers are found. While the grade may be gentle and flat, beginners are most at risk to hurt themselves and others when they are out of control.

Growing up I had always wanted to learn to ski, but being from Texas and concerned that I could jeopardize my young career with an injury, I put it off until later in life. I recruited my good friend and teammate Don Mosebar to try it with me. Neither of us had ever skied before, nor had we taken lessons. "How hard could it be?" we figured. After all, we were professional athletes. Don was our center, and at 6'6" and 305 pounds, he was an opposing dude. I was not far behind at 6'4" and 295 pounds.

We drove a few hours north of Los Angeles to Big Bear Lake, parked the car at Bear Mountain Ski Resort, and began to gear up. Wouldn't you know it, but Don and I had unknowingly and independently brought identical royal blue snow pants and jackets. It was no surprise, really. When you wear size XXXL, your choices are limited. We both looked like exconvicts who had escaped from Cabela's.

The place was a beehive of activity that day, yet we slowly found our way from one line to the next. With our skis and size fifteen boots, we headed out to our first run. We got an eyeful of stares as we looked like blue circus bears on the bunny hill next to dozens of small kids in ski school. Following what others were doing, we filed into line and up on our first lift. Our rear-ends barely crammed in the double chair as we rode up the hundred-yard lift together.

I told Don, "This hill doesn't look too steep. We should be fine." As we got to the top and stood up, our ski tips and poles tangled. Six hundred pounds of bodies, ski equipment, and Gortex came crashing down and lay in a heap at the top of the chair lift. We hadn't even made it a few feet and we already held our first ski equipment yard sale. The lift attendant called to his coworkers and said, "Let's help the Blues Brothers." They stopped the lift and scrambled to help us stand up and gather our gear.

Starting down the run, I was terrified that I was going to flatten some innocent little kid who mistakenly cut in front of my path. Helplessly gaining too much speed, I yelled, "I'm behind you," as a child crossed my path. Not like that statement made any sense whatsoever, as he was a beginner himself. Rapidly approaching the crowd gathered at the ski lift, I simply threw myself to the ground to avoid plowing into a pack of kids. No one had instructed me on how to safely come to a stop.

Living without self-restraint is like a snow skier barreling down the slope recklessly and out of control. Men who cannot control their anger or their tongue or their management of stress continually put themselves and their loved ones at risk. Even though life's challenges may not appear steep or dangerous, they become unbelievably treacherous when facing them out of God's will. I've witnessed men ruin their marriages, abandon their friends, and drive away their children all because they refused to listen to sound wisdom and chose to live outside God's laws. A man out of control is a runaway train on skis.

There is an old English proverb that says, "The ship that will not obey the helm will have to obey the rocks." Raw power is much less useful than focused strength. Champions know that greatness comes through self-control, not self-indulgence. You have power. If you are a male, that is standard equipment. Harnessing that power, however, is what makes us men, and men who make a mark in history are able to channel their strength for a greater good.

Catching a Blessing

Abraham's obedience was legendary, and through it God blessed the whole earth. The descendants of Abraham multiplied as the sands of the sea, and still today many refer to him as father Abraham, both in ancestry and in faith. He became a great father because he trusted the wisdom of his heavenly Father.

God is a fantastic and brilliant Father, the kind of father you and I aspire to be and the kind of father we have always wanted. He is humble, strong, perfect, present, trustworthy, and wise, and like any good father He desires to shower us with blessings of all kinds. What separates us from those blessings, though, is when we don't allow His directives to guide our behavior and influence our decisions. We can essentially block His blessings by choosing to be willfully disobedient to His Word.

There is an art to catching the football. Savvy receivers know how to position themselves to out-maneuver and out-jump the defender to best receive the football. Then, once his hands touch the ball, he must fight and contend with the defender to hang onto it and prevent it from being stripped away. The same is true in our lives. There is an art to walking in the Spirit. God's ways put us in position to receive the blessings that He desires to throw our way. Our job is to position ourselves in the center of God's will by running the right routes and blocking out that which stands in opposition to our forward progress in Christ. Our opponent will often try to impede us and strip the blessing from our hands, but we must be resolved to catch what God is throwing our way.

Following God's will for our life is not easy. Sometimes what is required of us is very difficult, costly, and seemingly impossible. But I have discovered that no matter how hard it may be, it is always easier to obey God than face the consequences of doing my own thing. When my will is completely surrendered to His, doing His will actually comes more naturally than doing the will of my flesh. And, most importantly, God promises to give us the grace and strength to equip us for the task.

The Extra Point

Golf is a sport that I both love and hate at the same time. They say it was named golf because all the other four-letter cuss words were taken. That about sums up my game. I love the feeling of being out on a beautiful golf course walking with buddies, effortlessly hitting the ball long and straight. More often than not, however, I struggle to hit the ball with consistency, and my game lacks control with virtually every club. As an offensive lineman, consistency was always the goal and was to be praised. Perhaps this is why golf and my hopeless pursuit of it aggravates me so much.

I recently took a golf lesson from a local legend named Larry who has been teaching golf for nearly fifty years. He is now in his 70s and has coached everything from refining the swing of professionals to showing kids how to hold a club for the first time. After I loosened up, he asked me to hit a few balls with various clubs. It didn't take him long to determine that I wasn't committing to each shot, neither was I following through properly. Due to my lack of control, I was gun-shy to take a full backswing, and because of my indecision I didn't swing through the ball either.

Larry told me that if I wanted to have better control with my golf game, I either had to commit to every shot or not take the shot at all. With every club in my bag, he wanted me to swing through to extension with confidence. I laughed at myself because he had me hitting the clubs with a newfound confidence and ease in no time. Golf became fun again.

As a man and a leader, we too need to follow through with confidence on the shots that God calls for our life. He doesn't want a halfhearted or half-baked response. If you aren't ready to follow God, then don't. But in the process, I encourage you to continue to seek Him, press in to truth, and ask Him to reveal Himself to you more fully. He is faithful and will give you the ability and passion to exercise your faith.

It is my hope that you would put this book down after reading this chapter and prayerfully consider what areas of your faith you need to follow through on. From golfers to pitchers, from quarterbacks to archers, all will attest that the secret to their success is in following through. What do you need to follow through with today? Have you fully committed your life to Christ or is there some area you have been reluctant to let go of? Is it joining a church, sharing your faith, or picking up your Bible more often? Do you feel the tug on your heart to obey God through tithing or being water baptized?

If we want to play in God's league, we've got to play by His rules. When we stand before God, it is our faithfulness to His instructions that will either condemn us or reward us, and ultimately every man will be measured by how responsible they were with their charge in life.

Chalk Talk

1. How does it make you feel when your loved ones (kids, spouse, siblings, friends) walk in disobedience to what you want? How do you think it makes God feel when we disobey His will?

2. Can a loving and fair God bless those who deliberately walk in disobedience to His will? If your child was an addict, and they came to you asking for money, would you, a loving parent, give it to them?

3. Are you someone who values control and a rigid daily schedule? Are you willing to adjust your plans if God decides to call an audible and redirect your efforts? If not, what's the possible consequence?

OBEDIENCE

4. Why is it important for Christian men to live a balanced and disciplined lifestyle? Does this mean we can't have fun? Is it to our detriment or benefit to live under God's direction?

5. Does your current attitude and lifestyle bless God? Are you putting yourself in a spiritual position to allow God's blessings to flow into all areas of your life?

6. How would you sum up your attitude about money and your thoughts on tithing? Why would a God who is all-powerful ask us to give money? Is this command out-dated?

7. What areas of your life do you struggle with the most in surrendering to God and following His commands? Does a lukewarm commitment to God please Him?

Endnotes

1. This quote is taken from Christian Quotes, http://christian-quotes.ochristian.com/Obedience-Quotes/, accessed February 17, 2015.

2. A. W. Tozer, *That Incredible Christian* (Christian Publications, 1964), 28.

3. J. Oswald Sanders, *Spiritual Leadership: Principles of Excellence for Every Believer* (Moody Publishers, 2007), Chapter 8

EVANGELISM

CHAPTER 7

RAIDERS OF THE LOST

Christians are either missionaries
or are in need of one.

In 1986 I was a sophomore at Penn State and had the opportunity to play in the Fiesta Bowl against the University of Miami for the national championship. Miami and Penn State were the two top ranked teams that year, and both were undefeated. The Miami Hurricanes, known as "The U," were very talented and full of future professional players, led by quarterback and Heisman trophy winner Vinny Testaverde. This matchup was billed as "The game of the century" at that time and garnered an amazing amount of hype as both teams squared off for the national title.

Prior to the game, Athletes in Action, a Christian sports ministry, had compiled a few Christian testimonies from several players of each team and printed a small pamphlet to be distributed during the game. They planned to hand them out free of charge to people entering the stadium to serve as a Christian witness to fans from both teams.

My brother Leo, a former Penn State football player and NFL veteran himself, volunteered to pass out some of the flyers that day. He later relayed to me the mixed and sometimes comical reactions of some of the people receiving the pamphlet. Some welcomed them with a smile or a thank you, while others were not so pleasant. One guy was particularly agitated and scoffed, "What is this?" Leo briefly explained, then the man angrily erupted, "Yeah, well I'm a Christian too, but I don't have to tell anyone about it!" At that, the man crumpled up the pamphlet in Leo's face, threw it to the ground, and stormed off.

Why would anyone want to keep good news of any kind to themselves, let alone the ultimate good news? Imagine just for a moment that you just proposed to the woman of your dreams. She responds by saying, "Yes! A thousand times yes! I will marry you!" Would you expect her to keep your engagement a secret? Would you be concerned if she didn't proudly wear the diamond ring you bought her or never took the initiative to introduce you to her family and circle of friends?

Committed love is something special, which is why weddings are such celebrated events. When my wife and I got engaged, I was more than thrilled to introduce her as my fiancé to my friends and family, and to share with them the details of our upcoming wedding day. It was truly good news, and I wanted everyone to know about it because I loved her. The same should be said of our commitment to Christ. To be a Christian means that we *belong to Christ.* Could we truly belong to Christ and keep it a secret? I wonder if it's possible to claim Christ but never speak of Him. How would it make you feel if the one who has professed their love for you is embarrassed to talk about you or ashamed to speak up for you?

When a person finds Christ, they also find the answers to life's toughest questions. Who are we and why do we exist? What is the meaning of life? Is there a God? Is there life after death and justice beyond the grave? We now have come to know the One who holds the universe and has the power to alter it for our sake. Our God forgives sin, heals disease, breaks addiction, charts our destiny, gives us peace of mind, and holds the keys to eternal life. We have found the cure for the world's ills. Why *wouldn't* we let others in on the wonderful news we have found? Silence is an indication that something is amiss.

The gospel means *good news,* and the story of God's redemption through Christ is truly great news and worthy to be shared. So wonderful is the story of salvation that the angels in heaven rejoice when one sinner repents. Imagine that: through the gospel, even bad news becomes good news.

This notion that faith is a personal choice and it must be kept to ourselves is utter nonsense. Whenever Jesus called someone to follow Him, He did it publically, not privately. Our faith is personal, yes, but it is not private and was never intended to be kept a secret. This is why Jesus said:

> *You are the light of the world. A town built on a hill cannot be hidden. Neither do people light a lamp and put it under a bowl. Instead they put it on its stand, and it gives light to everyone in the house. In the same way, let your light shine before others, that they may see your good deeds and glorify your Father in heaven* (Matthew 5:14-16).

Light is not easily hidden. It has a way of influencing its surroundings. Light dominates the darkness and casts an unmistakable and indiscriminate radiance for all to enjoy. One flickering candle can be seen in a completely blacked-out stadium. In the same way, you and I cannot remain inconspicuous—we are designed to shine. Our lives should pierce the darkness, not cower from it. It's a sad day when people call themselves Christians but think they need to keep it a secret. Through our lifestyle and our words, we are called to teach others the ways of God, even those

EVANGELISM

who do not wish to hear. We must resist the temptation to detach ourselves from our belief system in the public sector. We are called to live out our faith everywhere—at home, at school, at work, and in the community.

The Wiz Zone

I'm sure you are aware that the Raider organization and their fans carry a certain renegade reputation. Late owner Al Davis was a true maverick, and he didn't care what anyone thought of him or his team. He was committed to one ideal, and it was winning football games. And he was not afraid of a fight either. Several times he sued the NFL and won when he felt they interfered with his team.

Like him, many fans of the team are tough and determined. Ask people around the league which fan base has the wildest mix of characters at home games, and the votes might favor the Oakland Raiders. While football fans can be hostile, Raider fans can be flat-out intimidating, even to other Raider fans. Some of them come to the stadium dressed in sports themed costumes such as grim reapers, zombies, or pirates clad team colors. From the patch-wearing bad-boy logo to the menacing and chaotic "Black Hole" on the south end zone side of the stadium, the Raider image is daunting to say the least. Say what you want about Raider fans though; they bleed silver and black, and there is no denying their loyalty and passion.

I was a member of the Los Angeles Raiders when the franchise moved back to Oakland in 1995, and I won't easily forget the fan frenzy in northern California as the team made its homecoming. When we emerged from the tunnel for the season opener, I noticed a homemade sign fashioned out of a bed sheet hanging in the south end of the field. It read, "The Wiz Zone #76." To my surprise, I went over and saw a few guys wearing my #76 jersey. I was taken back to see strangers taking the time to show me support, and I gave them all high fives. And no, these fans were not my relatives in disguise. They were complete strangers. Though I did wonder if my wife had paid them to sit out there and cheer me on.

I asked them to come find me outside the stadium after the game, and I thanked them all for their support. Gary, a mechanic at a Ford dealership near Sacramento, organized the group. I learned that this band of six Raider fans wanted a player they could root for and identify with when the team moved back to Oakland, and for whatever reason I became their guy.

Greeting the "Wiz Zone" pregame and my dad (center) who snuck in with the group.

Over the course of the next few games, and then the next few seasons, I got to know these guys personally. We exchanged phone numbers and got together to share a meal from time to time. These guys would go out of their way to say hello, wish me well before the game, and to offer their congratulations or condolences afterward. We began a lasting friendship, which led to me sharing my faith in Christ with them. They were receptive to hear about it and respected me for who I was and how I carried myself.

As those relationships developed over time, a few of the guys committed their lives to Christ, Gary included. When I retired from the Raiders, the group disbanded because several of them were too busy with their commitments to their local church and home to make it out to the Sunday games. Now that's truly miraculous for a football fan!

And that's also true evangelism. They had found a passion more real, and a community more satisfying than what football camaraderie could offer them. Evangelism is at its best when it's the by-product of an unforced relationship and the honest testimony of a yielded vessel. We simply introduce others to Christ and step back and allow the Holy Spirit to do what He does best—convict and convince the world of truth.

Community Pastors

Evangelism is intimidating to most people simply because we've stereotyped it. We've categorized it as street-preaching or door-to-door tract distribution. We've relegated witnessing to a pastor's job or assume that someone must be an ordained minister in order to minister or lead another individual to salvation. In reality, however, ministry is simply meeting people's needs—ultimately, their spiritual needs. We can all do this, even you. Ministry is merely a fancy word for serving, and if you are willing to work you can minister to people in a great capacity.

I once heard a message that resonated with me by a pastor named Jerry Cook. In his sermon he contended that there is no need for any more new churches in America. He said, "There is a church on nearly every street corner and most are overstaffed. We have enough." He laments that when a pastor sees a young man enthusiastic about ministry, he convinces him to leave his job, enroll in two years of seminary, and then go to work in the church. He concludes, "And what have you just done to this man? You've ruined him. Certainly God does call some people to full-time ministry, but to unplug a marketplace pastor from his work and from his community is often a mistake."

The idea here is that a person does not need to quit his job and study theology in order to be a spiritual leader in his community. Jerry advocated for more community pastors, who is just a regular person like you and me who has a heart to be a light and a dif-ference-maker in their community. These marketplace ministers may lead Bible studies in their homes and places of business, vol-unteer at the local hospital, sit on the city council, lead Boy Scouts troops, become little league coaches, big brothers, or become members of the PTA. They don't pull back into a holy huddle, but rather let their light shine through their gifts, interests, and ser-vice to their community.

Pastors who serve in the church are needed and worthy of honor, but we could sure use a lot more community-minded believers to serve in the public arena. How might you be able to minister in your community?

The Men of Ruby Hill

In 1999 I was living in a beautiful housing development named Ruby Hill in Pleasanton, California. It was a fast-growing rural community surrounded by rolling hills and picturesque vineyards. Over time we saw our neighborhood take shape as more than 700 homes were added to this golf course community. Through prayer I began to feel a strong impression that I was to start a Bible study in our home. I was reluctant to do so, because I had never led a Bible study before and had never really found one that appealed to me. But nevertheless, I shared the idea with my wife and pastor, and they were both supportive.

I hadn't a clue what to do or what to teach, so I went to the local Christian bookstore and thumbed through various books and workbooks. I was hoping to find something easy that I could grab off the shelf and instantly plug into a men's group. There were some good resources, but nothing that seemed right for me. I was perplexed. On one hand I wanted to be faithful to the call, but on the other hand I also didn't want the study to suck. I wasn't sure how to proceed.

I found myself praying, "Father God, please establish the work of my hands. Let Your will be done and Your name be glorified. Please bring this work of a Bible study to pass in Your timing, in Your grace, and through Your strength and ability." As simple as it is, a prayer like this is applicable to many areas of our life and will almost always generate an answer.

Even though I had no material, the idea of hosting a Bible study was not going away. I admit that I had temptations to guilt a few guys to come over to my house to read a Christian book or discuss the Bible together. The Holy Spirit made it clear to me, however, that this was not what He had in mind. Instead, He told me that the Bible study should be topical and that I was to invite everyone. I remember asking in prayer, "What do You mean by topical, and who exactly is everyone?"

I felt inspired to make a one-page flyer and enlist the help of my 7-year-old son to fill mailboxes throughout our community. With one hand on the steering wheel and one hand holding his feet, I drove around the neighborhood while my young son leaned out the window and stuck a flyer in each mailbox. Yes, I know, not the picture of a safety conscience loving parent. After distributing a few hundred invitations, I realized that we were not nearly finished. I had underestimated how many homes had been constructed since we had bought ours. We printed out another couple hundred flyers, distributed them all, but still came up short. I filled up the ink reservoir on the printer, blasted out one last batch of 155 additional flyers, and finished the remaining houses.

Upon completion I announced to my wife that we were done. She calmly asked how many flyers we printed out, and I answered, "Five hundred fifty-five." "Wow, that's great," she exclaimed, "I didn't know so many homes were built in the community." Then panic quickly set in. "I had never really thought it through," I said. "Five hundred and fifty-five invitations. What if they all show up? What if half of them show up? What if only one fifth of the people show up? What will we do, and where will we put them all?"

My wife remained calm as she said, "Don't sweat it. You can make it an outdoor Bible study, and if need be you can just spill out onto the golf course." I tried to act calm, but inwardly I thought, "What have I gotten myself into?"

On the first night, to my surprise, roughly twenty guys showed up. I was floored. Nearly all of them I had never met before. Many of them shared that they had just been thinking they needed to find a good Bible study, and then they discovered my flyer in their mailbox. The timing was right and the Holy Spirit drew these men.

Each week I would develop an outline for a topical study and give it to the guys so they could take notes and share it with their family. We covered topics like salvation, marriage, faith, purity, prayer, servanthood, spiritual warfare, baptism, the accuracy of the Bible, and God's purpose for our lives. Each week guys invited friends and came loaded with their Bibles and questions. We shared prayer requests, an occasional meal together, and a few men's outings to develop camaraderie. Though I prepared a detailed study with questions to encourage men to think, share, and grow in their faith, I saw myself only as the facilitator of the group. The Word of God was our teacher.

Tuesday nights quickly became a family affair. My three young kids would help set up chairs, put out loaner books from my personal library, and pray a blessing for the meeting. My wife would get drinks and often bake something for the guys. We all looked forward to the crew coming over each week. After my kids would say goodnight, my wife would help me as the late night conversations moved into the kitchen and the meeting eventually dispersed.

Over the span of that Bible study, we saw guys come to Christ and be transformed in so many different ways. We even used the pool in the backyard as a baptismal. I asked my pastor, Ron Pinkston, one day, "We did a study on water baptism and now some of these guys want to be baptized. What do I do?"

He laughed and said, "You baptize them."

I replied, "Can I do that? Am I qualified?"

He asked, "Is Jesus your Lord and Savior?"

"Yes."

"Are you willing to be used by God?" he asked.

I said, "Yes."

"Are you living right before Him?"

"Yes, I think so," I said.

He said, "Then yes. You are qualified, called, and anointed for it. And in doing so you are following the Great Commission."

The Great Commission is reference to the parting instructions Jesus gave to His disciples after His resurrection. It is a mission statement as relevant today as it was then.

Then Jesus came to them and said,

> *"All authority in heaven and on earth has been given to Me. Therefore go and **make disciples** of all nations, **baptizing them** in the name of the Father and of the Son and of the Holy Spirit, and **teaching them** to obey everything I have commanded you. And surely I am with you always, to the very end of the age"* (Matthew 28:18-20).

Discipleship. Baptism. Teaching. My little Bible study was doing exactly what Christ had commissioned His disciples to do. I look back on those years of leading that Bible study as a truly blessed and remarkable time in my life. I really didn't understand at the time what I was doing or the difference I was making, but evidently God did.

To my surprise, I discovered that the greatest work was done in my own heart—far greater than the other guys who attended the study. My knowledge of God's Word and His will increased as I studied the Bible in preparation for each Tuesday night. My faith grew as I was faithful to lead. My prayer life went into over-drive as I prayed weekly for each of them and their various prayer requests. Like exercising the body on a daily basis, I grew by leaps and bounds as I exercised my faith week after week. God truly softened my crusty old heart and gave me compassion to see these men grow in their faith.

Another surprising benefit was that it brought my young family together in unity, as it took a group effort to host such a large gathering in our home on a weekly basis. What I learned is that evangelism and discipleship are not only for the benefit of others, but for ours as well. Like anything else, God watches over our own affairs and develops our gifts as we seek first His kingdom and step out onto the waters of obedience. As we seek to bless and minister to others, God blesses and ministers to us.

What's All the Fuss about Baptism?

One of the most joyful experiences of my time as an Oakland Raider took place in the unlikeliest of locations—the training room hot tub. Late one night, our team Bible study got together for a special event. After prayer and singing some off-key Christian hymns, we followed Jesus's example in the celebration of baptism. Seven teammates and I eased into the foul smelling waters of this oversized tub we referred to as the "germ vat" to publically commit our lives to the Lord. It wasn't the Jordan River, but it would have to do.

We had recently done a study on what the Bible taught about baptism after one of my teammates asked, "What's all the fuss about baptism?" He confessed how he was slightly creeped out by people in his local church who continually asked him if he wanted to be baptized. After reading Scripture on several occasions and discussing it, many of us felt convicted that we should do it. We nominated Napoleon Kauffman to do the baptizing. Although he was not an ordained minister at the time, he was the most solid Christian on the team.

When it was my turn, Napoleon looked me in the eyes and said, "Wiz, is Jesus Christ your Lord and Savior?" I responded, "Yes, He is!" He said, "In obedience to our Lord and Savior Jesus Christ, and upon your profession of faith, I baptize you, my brother, in the name of the Father, Son, and Holy Spirit." At that he put his hand on my forehead, and two huge linemen helped lower me into the salty water and back up again. Hugs were exchanged all around and everyone in the room clapped, cheered, and praised God. It was a really special time. It is hard to put into words, but everyone could feel that an eternal bond was being created in that room, both with God and with each other.

Baptism is the outward expression of an inward work of God's grace in our heart. Going into the water symbolizes being washed and purified from our past life of sin by the Holy Spirit. Because we can't breath or sustain life under the water, baptism is also symbolic of the grave. Through this act of submersion we identify with Christ's death and burial, and when we come out of the water we identify with His resurrection. Water baptism identifies that we are born anew and made alive with Christ (see Rom. 6).

In the today's church, many pastors will ask those who wish to follow Christ to stand, raise their hand, or let their eyes meet as he pans the room. Often every head is bowed and every eye closed at the time, unless your curious like me and look around. This modern practice is well intentioned but not the method used by the early church. It was water baptism that communicated one's commitment to Christ.

In biblical times, as it is now in many countries today, following Jesus could cost you your life. At the very least you risked bringing persecution on your family and yourself for confessing Christ as your Lord. For this reason there was great urgency for believers to be baptized upon making a commitment to follow Christ Jesus. In fact, the Bible records several instances when people were baptized in the middle of the night (see Acts 2:41; 8:36; 16:33).

Baptism establishes a definitive point at which we bid farewell to our old way of life and identify ourselves with Christ and the life He desires us to live. We all have a birthday to celebrate and perhaps a wedding anniversary to commemorate. Baptism is like a birthday of sorts and marks a specific day we publically mark and profess our union with Christ (see Rom. 6:3-5).

Serving as an example for us to follow, Jesus Himself was baptized by John in the Jordan River (see Matt. 3:13-17). Although He had no sin, Jesus did this as an act of obedience to the Father, which officially marked the beginning of His public ministry. I love how the Bible states that when Jesus came up out of the water, the heavens opened up, and the Spirit of God descended upon Him like a dove. A voice from heaven said, *"This is My Son, whom I love; with Him I am well pleased"* (Matt 3:17). It was as if God Himself was present giving His approval of His Son's act of obedience.

Some churches today baptize by sprinkling water over a person's head, and I am not one to say this is wrong. But an honest look at Scripture and the traditions of the early church all indicate that baptism was a total submersion in water and a voluntary public profession of faith in Christ. Other traditions dedicate children in front of the congregation just as Jesus was dedicated in the temple, and this is beautiful as well. A dedication or confirmation at birth may hold some spiritual benefits, but our salvation can never be secured by the best intentions or desires of our loved ones. As an adult, we must all reach out in faith to receive Christ's Spirit as an act of our will, and a confirmation doesn't replace that child's need to make a personal choice to follow Christ and be baptized.

I shared this information with a friend of mine some time ago, and he became wildly defensive. He said he had been baptized as a child and therefore did not need to do it again as an adult. It was as if I offended him by even mentioning it. Remember that salvation is not *earned* through baptism or ritual. It is a free gift that is given by God. Our salvation comes through a sincere profession of faith, and baptism is merely a symbolic act of the decision we have made (see Eph. 2:8-9).

If you are serious about following Christ, I strongly suggest you consider getting water baptized if you haven't already. Even if you were baptized as an infant or went through a time when you fell away from your faith, a person can be baptized more than once if they feel they need to or if they are recommitting themselves to God. Wherever and whenever you do it, I believe God will bless the intentions of your heart. There is something powerfully beautiful about humbling ourselves and being water baptized, and I don't want you to miss out on that joy.

Starting a Bible study is not the only way to spread the gospel. Evangelism can take on many forms: sharing your life story with a coworker over coffee, explaining God's plan of salvation to a hurting friend, posting spiritual truths on social media, praying for a neighbor in need, delivering a meal to a shut-in, mowing a lawn, washing a car, coaching a youth sports team, or simply taking the time to help someone out. Sports and outdoor activities make great vehicles for sharing our faith and using the stories of the Bible to relate to others.

EVANGELISM

I recently heard a great message on relational evangelism from a pastor in Colorado. He spoke to the large congregation wearing jeans, a plain T-shirt, and Crocs, which was his custom. His tattooed arms and shaved head were evident to all, and his language was frank and direct. His message was about being transparent and genuine, something he obviously modeled. He emphasized the need to share Christ with anyone the Lord leads us to, even the really scary and screwed-up ones. God loves to use our humor, gifts, personalities, and our own messed-up backgrounds to reach people, and by doing so we allow Christ to minister to them in their place of need. In that moment it's not about fixing them or telling them how they should live, where they should go, or whom they should serve. It's about introducing them to Jesus.

What Do I Say?

If you are new to this, sharing your faith for the first few times can be awkward. Here are some tips, however, to get you started.

Focus less on what to say and more on how you say it. Being the right witness is far more important than saying the right things when witnessing. Sometimes we think we have to present a well-thought-out logical response to every argument presented. This is certainly beneficial, but most people don't come to Christ as a result of losing a debate with a Christian. Truth can defend itself. Speak the truth simply, respectfully, enthusiastically, and with love.

Share a few important Scripture verses. When people ask valid questions, answer them by turning to God's Word. It's helpful to be able to explain and defend your faith, but that doesn't mean you have all the answers. If you don't know the answer, tell them so and research the Word of God together.

Share the story of your conversion. How you came to know Christ is a powerful witness in and of itself. While opponents may disagree with your opinions, they cannot deny your experience.

Be able to communicate different angles of your testimony so that your story is relatable to people in all walks of life. Sometimes just being able to relate what God has done in your life is all that is needed in that moment. God will never waste a scar if you're willing to give the experience to Him. Maybe you've had a struggle with disease, the loss of a loved one, overcoming an addiction or abuse in your past—share how God has brought you through that difficulty.

Talk to God about people before you attempt to talk to people about God. Pray for those who are spiritually lost, and make a holy "hit list" and target your loved ones in prayer first. Fast for them and allow the Holy Spirit to speak to them and soften their hearts. Ask God to give you favor, opportunities, and a burden for the condition of their soul. Likewise, pray for your neighbors, coworkers, teammates, and friends. You may be shocked at the conversations that open up as God creates the atmosphere to allow you to share His message.

Be ready to speak up. Expect that God will give you divine appointments and witnessing opportunities once you begin praying for the people He has placed in your path. He is faithful to put you in the right place and prompt you at the right time. Remember that success is measured not by conversion but whether or not the person has been brought closer to making a decision for Christ. It's good to be a silent witness through your actions, but at some point you must be willing to make your voice heard. Don't allow Satan to put a muzzle on your mouth because your focus is on your own shortcomings. The message you share is Christ. In Him we are made whole, and He is the One worthy to be praised.

I have found the two top reasons Christians do not share their faith are complacency and fear. All too often we are afraid of looking foolish and sticking out. The natural tendency is to casually camouflage ourselves and blend in with our surroundings. When we do this, however, we essentially lose our voice in the marketplace, and we place our message, our credibility, and ourselves at risk. Those who do not actively share the joy of their salvation slowly lose the joy of it. You must resist becoming so preoccupied with your own passions and pursuits that you lose sight of His.

I have learned that genuine and effective evangelism is simply the natural overflow of the heart. Jesus said, *"Out of the overflow of the heart the mouth speaks"* (Matt. 12:34). Witnessing need not be coerced or manufactured. It should be the natural expression of a life that seeks God. You may feel uncomfortable, inadequate, untrained, and unknowledgeable in the moment, but as God prompts you to step out He will give you the words to say and the wisdom to know when your presence alone does all the speaking needed for that person.

It is said that Saint Francis of Assisi said, "Preach the gospel at all times. Use words when necessary." The point of this famous quote is to let your life represent the gospel at all times. It's not our job to convert people. Our job is to be a witness, and witnessing is nothing more than loving people. James 1:19 states: *"Everyone should be quick to listen, slow to speak and slow to become angry."* Develop a genuine concern and interest in everyone you meet. Be an active listener. And as you do, you'll be amazed at the opportunities God opens up for you to share your faith.

The Davison Effect

There have been several men who have been instrumental to my spiritual growth, and one of them is my former Raider teammate, Napoleon Kaufman. Napoleon has inspired my family and me a great deal over the years through his friendship, encouragement, and teachings. He was at the peak of his six-year NFL career when he retired to go into full-time ministry. At that time, he was averaging a phenomenal 4.8 yards per carry as a running back for the Raiders, which was second only to Bo Jackson in team history.

People told him he was crazy to walk away from the money and the platform of the NFL, but to him there was no mistaking what God had called him to do. He understood that God didn't need his money or him to play football in order to use him. He just needed Napoleon's obedience.

Napoleon came to know Christ when free agent running back Jerone Davison shared the gospel with him in his rookie season. Observing Napoleon's demeanor and lifestyle, Jerone called him out and said to him one day, "You don't even look like someone who should be talking the way you do and acting a fool. Don't you know that God can use your life!" Like a firm slap of reality across his face, this conversation stopped Napoleon in his tracks and made him reconsider his priorities.

As Jerone shared Christ with him, Napoleon transformed into a mighty man of God, and it was remarkable to see. He came to the team a streetwise kid, having never known his dad and raised by a single mother who battled drug addiction. He ran the streets as a boy, loved his loud rap music, and stuck out his chest with his brash talk and vivacious confidence.

I watched as God molded him into a new creation before our very eyes. I remember the day he dumped thousands of dollars of his old music CDs into the dumpster. Then he poured out the alcohol bottles he had in his home, as God spoke to him about the areas of his life He wanted to refine. By the time Napoleon retired, he was a man after God's own heart. He was full of wisdom, both humble and willing to boldly stand up when his teammates were acting godless, which was quite frequent. The only music coming out of his locker was Christian, where he could often be found reading his Bible. He was always patient and kind in conversations with others, quick to bless and encourage his teammates.

Over the years I must have pestered the life out of Napoleon, as I would follow him around the Raider facility on a daily basis asking him numerous questions about his faith and about Scripture.

We shared countless Bible studies on planes and in hotel rooms as the team traveled, and he graciously and patiently poured spiritual life into me. Although persecution came from outside sources, he was well respected by his teammates because they saw the genuine transformation that consumed his life.

After his retirement, Napoleon founded the Well Christian Community Church in the East Bay area, and we had the honor of being one of a dozen families who initially helped launch it. I was a minister and my wife served in the children's ministry. I taught a couple adult education classes and an occasional message to the men of the church, but most of the time I served in children's ministry with my wife and kids.

I found that I enjoyed teaching the second through fifth graders the most. Learning to develop a message simple enough to hold the kids' attention was a great exercise in preaching. Serving snacks, leading worship, and prepping and cleaning the room also kept me humble and in a servant's posture. I absolutely cannot sing or key or stay on beat, so seeing this hulking giant standing in front of those kids doing hand motions and leading in worship was quite a sight. When others walked by the room, they would often stop, look in, and openly laugh.

It was a family affair as my wife and three young kids were by my side in the ministry. We colabored together as a family. It got to the point where my three young kids could lead the worship, manage the classroom, and teach the lesson better than I could. Years have gone by, and now, as young adults, my kids still fondly recall the hand motions we used in worship and some of the exercises we did to illustrate simple Bible lessons. Most importantly, it left an enduring memory of what servanthood and ministry were all about—humbling oneself to meet the needs of others.

Evangelism is the ultimate act of humility and servanthood. It may seem juvenile, but if you are willing to do the ridiculous more often than not, God will do the miraculous. Don't be afraid to step outside your comfort zone, because in so doing you will affect the lives of other people around you. If you love children, there is a child who needs your love. If you have compassion for sick people, there is someone in the hospital who needs your prayers. If you've had a particularly painful life experience, there is a broken person who could benefit from hearing you tell it. Don't discount yourself because of your past. There is a ministry, a need, and a way for you to reach your world and fulfill the Great Commission.

Jesus said, *"For this reason I was born, and for this reason I came into the world, to testify to the truth"* (John 18:37). Like Jesus, our lives are testifying to something. Whether righteousness, selfishness, or foolishness, each one of us are preaching a message to others. Why do you think you were born, and why did God place you in this world? There is a reason, and the reason is that you would testify to the truth of God's grace in your life.

The Extra Point

Gary was a football fanatic who abandoned his family for weekend sports until I spoke up and shared the gospel with him. God changed his reputation, and he became a light in his home, his church, and his place of employment—so much so that he didn't have time or interest in his weekend sports anymore. Ananias risked everything when he stepped out in obedience to meet with Paul (see Acts 9:10-19). Paul went on to testify and write thirteen of the twenty-six books of the New Testament.

Napoleon Kaufman was a streetwise, star-struck young man until Jerone Davison spoke up. God changed his reputation, and it has impacted thousands through his decades-long pastoral, preaching, and media ministry. I was named the dirtiest player in the NFL, and now I am sharing the good news of Jesus Christ.

Now it's your turn. If ever there was a time the world needed someone to speak up and step out, that time is now. Christ is the answer, and you are the messenger. Jerone, Napoleon, Gary, me—someone is waiting for you on the other side of your obedience. Someone had the guts to tell you. Now who will you tell?

Chalk Talk

1. Do you have a conversion story to share? Are you currently involved in a fellowship of believers that builds your faith, such as a Bible study, home group, or a local church?

2. List some ways you could possibly be a positive influence for Christ and more involved in your community? Do you see any voids you can fill? Do you know anyone who would fit the description of a community pastor?

3. What hobbies or activities do you naturally enjoy? Who is God putting on your heart to invite to join you in these activities?

4. Are you uncomfortable with sharing your faith in Christ? Why is it difficult to evangelize? What are you personally willing to risk in order to share Christ with the lost?

5. What are the central aspects of the gospel message that you could share with a nonbeliever? What Scripture verses can you put to memory that would help you?

6. What does baptism symbolize? How do we know this act pleases God? Explain why it's a God-idea to seek to be water baptized?

7. What should you do if someone wants to receive Christ? What do you pray, how do you follow-up, and where should you send them?

RESISTANCE

CHAPTER 8

BEATING THE BLITZ

When lives are at stake, leave nothing to chance.
—HECKLER & KOCH FIREARMS

The blitz is arguably the most exciting play in football. NFL defenses live and die by it. Named after *blitzkrieg*, a German war tactic involving speed and surprise, the blitz is a defensive attack that attempts to confuse, outwit, and disrupt an opponent by rushing predetermined defenders to the quarterback. Like a strategic game of cat-and-mouse, the blitz is bold and risky, but when successful it can wreak havoc on an opposing team's offense.

Blitzes come in a myriad of schemes, but they are universally timed-up to coincide with the snap of the football. The zone blitz, which sends safeties and cornerbacks to the football and drops lineman back into quadrants to cover downfield, has been popular since the early 1990s. Teams will often use a zone blitz to rush three, four, even five defenders to one side of the offensive formation in an attempt to completely overwhelm and shutdown their opponent.

The blitz is so effective that coaches spend extensive hours diagramming opponent blitzes and playing out various coverage scenarios as a unit. I have learned that there is one sure way to beat the blitz—to be prepared for it at all times. Defending the blitz and launching a counter-attack against it is much easier to do when you've eliminated the element of surprise.

As a man pursuing the call of God on his life, there is a blitz you must beat and be ready for at all times. Many great men have become casualties of this spiritual blitz. You don't have to be one of them. Life is a rush in more ways than one, and you cannot afford to rest on your heels and be caught off guard.

This chapter is a survival guide, a scouting report, and a war manual. It is designed to open your eyes to the unseen battle raging around you, reveal tactical operations behind enemy lines, equip you to fight through any ambush, and keep you armed and ready to rumble.

Prepare for War

Football is a game of preparation—physically, mentally, and strategically. In order to stay competitive, preparation for the next game begins with the final whistle of the previous one. For players this means hitting the weight room early Monday morning, reviewing game film, and making adjustments. After an off day Tuesday, the rest of the week consists of team workouts, long practice days, and reviewing scouting reports.

For coaches the schedule is more unrelenting. Most coaches rarely get a day off during the season, let alone an hour off. With little to no sleep, they put in long hours from Sunday to Wednesday researching and compiling a scouting report the size of an encyclopedia. These reports are typically presented during

Wednesday team meetings. When passing out these weighty one hundred-page scouting binders, our players would sometimes joke, "The trees! Save the trees!" due to the amount of paper it took to produce them. When I was a coach, the long hours and all-nighters spent producing these volumes nearly killed me. Even for players, it can be a burden to sift through the exhaustive material by game day.

When it comes to the opponent, simply no stone is left unturned. Coordinators factor in the biography of the opposing coach, defensive fronts, offensive philosophies, play-calling history, game-calling tendencies, and player propensities. All aspects of the opposing team are analyzed, diagrammed, and illustrated. Throughout the week each player watches many hours of film, practices against a scout team that mimics the opposition, and is given daily, up-to-the minute detailed notes on each and every player they are likely to square off against.

Football is a tough game. It's grueling, merciless, and unpredictable. But without preparation it is deadly. Whether it's beating the blitz or neutralizing a high-powered offense, there is no victory in football without a lot of preparation. It cannot be left undone. If found unprepared, you don't stand a chance at coming away victorious, let alone uninjured. Teams plan, train, scout, practice, and strategize for every aspect of every game before the ball is ever kicked off. Proper preparation is paramount to success. The moment a team stops preparing is the moment the opposition gains the upper hand.

Like football, the Christian walk is tough. It's grueling, unpredictable, and, at times, merciless. Without preparation, however, it can be downright deadly. You don't stand a chance at being victorious without it. Proper preparation is paramount to your spiritual success. For better or for worse, what you are doing today is preparing you for tomorrow, and the moment you stop reloading is the moment the opposition gains the upper hand.

In a spiritual sense, we are under attack from the enemy. We have been drafted into a war we did not enlist in. We have an enemy, and he has a long scouting report on us. He knows our weaknesses, our tendencies, and where we are the most vulnerable. He stands between us and the call of God on our life. His goal is to confuse, outwit, and prevent us from making forward progress. He has likely blitzed your marriage, your children, your health, and your identity. He's taken aim at your purity, your courage, and your thought life. Unless you put up a good fight, he will ultimately overwhelm you, wreaking havoc on every relationship in your life, especially your relationship with God.

When we take on Christ, we take on the mentality of a warrior. Paul exhorts Timothy to *"wage a good warfare"* (1 Tim. 1:18), *"fight the good fight of faith"* (1 Tim. 6:12), and *"endure hardships like a good soldier of Jesus Christ"* (2 Tim. 2:3). Why such aggressive language? This is because your life is on a collision course with hell, and you must decide if you will conquer it or if hell will conquer you. Only you can determine the outcome. God has given you a call that is destined to confront the forces of darkness. This is by design. He has fashioned you to be a premeditated weapon against the advancement of hell on earth. Simply put, you are heaven's answer to evil in this world.

In the first century, hell engineered a full attack against Jesus at His birth in an attempt to abort the purposes of God. Panic-stricken and threatened by the news of another king's birth, King Herod slaughtered every male child two years or younger in Bethlehem and its surrounding districts. But through a series of dreams, God forewarned Joseph and Mary and preserved the life of His promised child (see Matt. 2:13).

Abortion. Bombings. Ethnic cleansing. Famine. Genocide. Slavery. The enemy has always been about slaughtering the innocent because it's in his nature and in his best interests to do so. If he can abort something in its infancy, then he can stop it from growing stronger and becoming a genuine threat. To be ignorant of the fact that we have an enemy is to have already surrendered to defeat. Do not be deceived. Satan is present. Evil is real, and it stands in opposition to all that is pure, holy, and represents God.

RESISTANCE

Necessary Roughness

As an offensive lineman I bumped heads with other players every single time the ball was snapped. I would go through two helmets a year and still have a few spares with deep scratches and gouges lying around the house. On game day the skin of my forehead was often rubbed raw and would drip blood from helmet-to-helmet collisions and from constantly driving my face into defenders.

In your walk with Christ you will likely bump heads with the enemy on a regular basis. Spiritual confrontation just goes with the territory. You were born to fight, so you can expect a few scrapes and bruises along the way. And don't be surprised when it takes courage and vigilance to become the man God designed you to become. The will of God for your life is not automatic. It must be contended for. And so must your faith.

Sun Tzu wrote in *The Art of War*: "If you know the enemy and know yourself, you need not fear the result of a hundred battles. If you know yourself but not the enemy, for every victory gained you will also suffer a defeat. If you know neither the enemy nor yourself, you will succumb in every battle."[1] This quote rings true for soldiers, football players, *and* Christian men. Let's consider these thoughts in a little more detail.

You Have to Know Yourself

In the story of creation, God says something noteworthy, as He's breathing life into Adam's soul. He says, *"Let Us make man in Our image, in Our likeness"* (Gen. 1:26). From the very beginning we learn that mankind is the crown of all creation, the pinnacle of God's handiwork, formed in the likeness of God. In stark contrast to the theory of evolution, the Bible presents the human race as unique, special, and distinct from the rest of creation. Fashioned to look and act like our Creator, we reflect the very image of the Almighty and are to be His representatives on the earth.

What intrigues me most is the use of the word "Us" in this passage. Who is God talking to as He's spinning the potter's wheel and sculpting man from the dust of the ground? Scholars debate, but God may be speaking to Himself. Scripture presents God as three in one—what has been called the Trinity. He is God the Father, God the Son, and God the Holy Spirit. The "Us" could very well be the Father, Jesus, and the Spirit actively working as one to conceive the universe. If our Inventor is a tripartite being, and we are patterned after Him, it would seem logical that we are made to be three in one as well. Perhaps this is why we each possess a body, a soul, and a spirit.

Your *spirit* is the very core of your being; it is what is meant when we refer to our heart. Intertwined with your spirit is your *soul,* which encompasses your emotions, thoughts, feelings, and intellect. Your *body,* unlike your spirit and soul, is not eternal. It is vulnerable to sickness, disease, fatigue, injury, stress, and environmental influences. In the middle of all this, it is important to keep in mind that humans are first and foremost spiritual beings, not physical beings having a spiritual experience. Our spirit is the essence of who we are. For a short time we are put in a mortal body, but not for eternity. Our origins are of the spirit, and we will one day possess a spiritual body.

When a person is born of the Spirit (or born again), the Holy Spirit joins with their spirit and dwells in their heart. In this way the work of salvation starts from the inside out. God inhabits a person's spirit and changes their mind and sanctifies their body. Destruction, however, works in the opposite way. It starts from the outside in. Through sinful acts of the flesh, the devil attempts to ruin a person's mind to control their body and quench their spirit.

Salvation is holistic, meaning Christ came to save our whole being—body, soul, and spirit. It's important to your spiritual health that you exercise discipline and balance in all three aspects of your being. You need proper rest, exercise, and nutrition for your body; discipleship, godly fellowship, and laughter for your soul; prayer, worship, and a steady diet of God's Word for your spirit.

Of the three areas of your being, your soul is the most vulnerable to negative influences. If the enemy can gain access to your mind, like a rudder he can control your thinking, your words, your choices, and ultimately steer your ship. Holding me in a headlock, the words of my brother Leo come back to me: "If you control the head, you control the body."

Lust, pride, fear, greed, rejection, and resentment can all be entry points for confusion, anger, and unbelief. Once he has you swallowing his lies, the enemy becomes like a burglar picking a lock, methodically and tirelessly working his way closer to the valuables while simultaneously pickpocketing your soul. Our well-being hinges on being able to discern the areas of our soul that are most vulnerable and susceptible to Satan's vices.

Isaiah wrote, *"No weapon forged against you will prevail"* (Isa. 54:17). This means you have weapons forged against you that are specific and calculated. Ignorance is not bliss when it comes to a *blitzkrieg*. You must know your battlegrounds and be intentional about conquering them.

The Three Battlegrounds

Battleground #1: The Flesh

Flesh is not merely skin and bones. Rather, it denotes the disease of sin imbedded in our nature and inherited from the fall of man. There is a propensity toward pride and selfishness that resides in all of us. It is called our flesh, and it is this part in us that gravitates toward sin, rebels against God, and justifies unrighteous behavior. T. D. Jakes calls it "the enemy in-a-me."

Scripture has one graphic solution on how to deal with your flesh: murder it. Paul writes, *"Those who belong to Christ Jesus have crucified the flesh with its passions and desires"* (Gal. 5:24). Just as Jesus was crucified in the flesh, so must our sinful nature die with Him. God and Satan have this in common—they're both trying to kill you. While the devil may want to physically take you out, God wants to kill off your sin nature so that your spirit can rise above and prevail.

Are you truly living or are you just alive? If you're allowing your flesh to rule you, you are not living to your fullest potential and you are not tapping into the benefits of what walking in the Spirit has to offer you. Paul continues, *"For he who sows to his flesh will of the flesh reap corruption, but he who sows to the Spirit will of the Spirit reap everlasting life"* (Gal. 6:8 NKJV).

There's a story told about a man who owned a pack of wolves. Every week he invited over friends and neighbors to place bets as two wolves squared off in a ring. The results were seemingly random, with no one wolf remaining the champ for long. The owner made a handsome profit wagering on his wolves, as he seemingly knew beforehand which wolf would win. His puzzled friends finally asked how he knew which wolf would win from week to week. His reply was, "Simple. It just matters which one I feed more."

Within each believer live two wolves. One desires the things of God, and the other despises the things of God. One is our born-again heart, and the other is our fleshly nature. They are at odds with each other, and the one that comes out victorious is simply the one we feed more.

Paul writes to the Romans, *"We are more than conquerors through Him who loved us"* (Rom. 8:37) and, *"Do not be overcome by evil, but overcome evil with good"* (Rom. 12:21). The word *conqueror* and *overcome* is the same word stemming from the root word *nike*. We know them as shoes, but *nike* (nee-kay) in Greek means victory or conquest. Paul is saying that we are not just victorious in Christ but more than victorious through Him. When we stand with Christ, the enemy is indeed under our feet.

What army can boast that when it storms the battlefield it has already won the war? We can. Our General has defeated the enemy and secured our victory through His death, burial, and resurrection. Our battle is not *for* victory but *from* it. And you never have to enter this war zone alone. He fights for you, fights with you, and is your blindside help.

That is not to say you will never struggle to be triumphant in the area of your flesh. Actually, the opposite is quite true. You cannot be an overcomer without experiencing a struggle, and being an overcomer implies that we will have something to overcome. Your flesh is perhaps the biggest enemy you will encounter in your lifetime. Whether in football or in life, victory can only be gained through consistency and perseverance. To be an overcomer demands that you remain standing after everyone else has collapsed.

Surprisingly, the way to overcoming your flesh is through surrender. It has been said that the man who has surrendered to the Lord will never surrender to the enemy. That means that only those whose life is fully surrendered to Christ will take up the authority that is found in Christ.

Surrendering is not quitting, and there is a vast difference between quitting and surrendering. To quit is to *yield* to your fleshly desires, while to surrender is to *die* to your fleshly desires. Quitting involves submitting to your flesh, and surrender involves submitting to God. Quitters are merely those too proud or too weak to surrender to the King of heaven.

Sin is subtle, and the enemy will take what we do not defend. If we do not overcome, we will be overcome by what we refuse to overcome. In other words, what we refuse to overcome will overcome us. Give an inch to sin in your life and it can become a ruler.

I have noticed that men often do not fight for their family, their health, or their friends because they are too beat down and consumed by their own internal struggles. They never engage an external enemy because they are losing the war within. For this reason you cannot allow that sinful wolf within you to be gratified.

RESISTANCE

Be aggressive with your flesh and exercise your authority over it. We need your contribution on the field.

Most men are either aware of all their strengths or all their flaws, but usually not both. Part of knowing yourself means having a healthy knowledge of your own weaknesses. Take a step back, and make a list of your strengths and weaknesses. What's the scouting report on you? If you were your opponent, how would you go about shutting down your forward progress?

Battleground #2: The World

The Greek word *kosmos* is translated the world and has three definitions: (1) the earth or the material universe (see Acts 17:24; Matt. 13:35; John 1:10; Mark 16:15), (2) the inhabitants of the earth (see John 1:10; 3:16; 12:19; 17:21), and (3) the things of the earth (see 1 John 2:15; 3:17; Matt. 16:26; 1 Cor. 7:31). Much like the term *flesh*, the biblical idea of world is spiritual as well as physical. John is not alone in depicting the world as an unseen force. Scripture defines it as a spiritual institution and a corrupt system that has a mind and agenda of its own.

John writes, *"The whole world is under the control of the evil one"* (1 John 5:19). There is a spiritual entity behind the world that is controlled by evil forces and is hostile toward God. The evil one is pimping society to populate his kingdom and popularize his message. He will use technology, music, art, politicians, entertainers, and the media to his advantage. These mediums are not evil in and of themselves, but when not dedicated to God and when used outside their proper function, they can become conduits to push the enemy's agenda. We are not fighting against people; rather, we are fighting *for* them. And one of the ways we fight for them is to war against the perverse culture that is controlling them.

Originally, the physical earth had no connection with the satanic system of the world. Before the fall there was the earth, but after the fall there was the world. It is out of this world that we are called to depart. James encourages believers to keep themselves from *"being polluted by the world"* (James 1:27).

To come out of the world does not mean we all move to the mountains and become monks. Nor can we run away from the world's sinful desires or problems. We leave the world by dying to it, defecting to the other side, and living under another reality. Our challenge is to live in the world without living like it. Though we live in this world, we are not of this world. While we may utilize the things of the world, we hold no hope or future in them.

John writes:

> *Do not love the world or anything in the world. If anyone loves the world, the love of the Father is not in him. For everything in the world—the cravings of sinful man, the lust of the eyes, and the boastings of what he has and does—comes not from the Father but from the world. The world and its desires pass away, but the man who does the will of God lives forever* (1 John 2:15-17).

Sin leading to bondage often begins with a love for the things of this world. Instead of asking, "Is this thing right or wrong?" a better question might be, "Is this thing of God or of the world?" Often, its origins will reveal its destination and where it eventually will take you.

Everything belonging to the world is under a death sentence (see John 12:31). Strive to become a world-class Christian without becoming a worldly Christian. And do not be afraid to associate with the people of this world. Satan's hope is that he can either frighten us out of maintaining a presence in the world or get us so personally involved in the system of the world that we never stand up to it and influence it. We are called to love the people of the world, but not to love the world or the things of this world.

Battleground #3: The Devil

The existence of Satan is well documented throughout the Scriptures. Disguising himself as a serpent, Satan conned Eve into eating the forbidden fruit in the garden of Eden. In similar fashion, he tried to tempt Jesus to fall down and worship him in the wilderness. Satan's presence throughout biblical history is notorious: he is Job's afflicter (see Job 1-2), David's provoker (see 1 Chron. 21:1), Joshua's resister (see Zech. 3:1), Judas's influencer (see John 13:2), Haman's puppeteer (see Esther 7:6; 9:24), and the deceiver of the whole world (see Rev. 12:9).

Jesus Himself was not shy in speaking about the devil, referring to Satan dozens of times throughout the Gospels. He calls him a thief (see John 10:10), a murderer (see John 8:44), the enemy (see Luke 10:19), the evil one (see John 17:15; Luke 11:4), the father of lies (see John 8:44), and the ruler of this world (see John 14:30). A quick pass through the Gospels shows that Jesus seemed to take extra pleasure in freeing those bound by Satan. In fact, one of the stated purposes of the Messiah was to *"destroy the works of the devil"* (1 John 3:8).

The name *Satan* comes from the Hebrew word *HaSatan*, which means the Accuser. There are over twenty titles attributed to Satan in the Bible. Here are just a few of them: wicked one (see 1 John 3:12), adversary (see 1 Pet. 5:8), prince of the air (see Eph. 2:2), prince of this world (see John 12:31; 16:11), an angel of light (see 2 Cor. 11:14), the god of this age (see 2 Cor. 4:4), the prince of darkness (see Eph. 6:12), the accuser of the brethren (see Rev. 12:10), tempter (see Matt. 4:3), a murderer (see John 8:44), dragon (see Rev. 12:9), a roaring lion (see 1 Pet. 5:8), prince of devils (see Matt. 12:24), and the beast of the bottomless pit (see Rev. 11:7).

The name *Lucifer* appears to be Satan's original name. It is a name that means *shining one, morning star,* or *the brightest object in the sky before dawn.* While this king spoken of by Ezekiel was likely an actual king of Babylon, most believe it also metaphorically describes Lucifer.

> *Son of man, take up a lament concerning the king of Tyre and say to him: "This is what the Sovereign Lord says: 'You were the seal of perfection, full of wisdom and perfect in beauty. You were in Eden, the garden of God; every precious stone adorned you.... You were anointed as a guardian cherub, for so I ordained you. You were on the holy mount of God; you walked among the fiery stones. You were blameless in your ways from the day you were created till wickedness was found in you'"* (Ezekiel 28:12-15).

In conjunction with Isaiah 14 and Revelation 12, Ezekiel seems to depict Lucifer as a worshiping angel who at one time stood before the throne of God. Skilled in music he was one of the most beautiful and talented angels in all of heaven. At some point pride entered his heart as he craved a greater place of prominence and power. Desiring to be worshiped as God, he initiated war in the heavens by rallying a third of the angels in an attempt to overthrow the kingdom of heaven. His coup attempt was terribly unsuccessful. God and His angels cast the fallen one and his rebellious followers out of their places in heaven. Apparently, even angels have a free will to choose either good or evil.

Scripture makes it clear who your enemy is, and it's not your wife, your boss, your political opponent, or your mother-in-law. Many believers never engage the true enemy of their souls, so they wind up fighting each other. Meanwhile, the devil works in stealth, planting terror cells in our soul, laying mines in our spirit, and launching surprise attacks on our bodies. There is no neutrality or demilitarized zone in this war. Conscientious objectors and Christian escapists cannot escape the fact that they have an adversary who is fiercely at war with them.

The Devil Is in the Details

When it comes to the devil, there are three dangerous positions people tend to take:

Position #1: Everything Is Caused by the Devil

Let me be clear: I do not see a demon or an angel under every bush. The devil did not make me stub my toe this morning, and it's not likely that he possesses your truck either. Some people want to blame everything on the devil, and they happily use Satan as their excuse and their scapegoat for not taking responsibility for their actions.

There's an old joke told about the devil sitting on a curb sobbing his eyes out. Beelzebub, the head demon, comes over to console him, saying, "Oh, what's wrong, Lucifer?" Satan sticks out his bottom lip and whimpers, "It's those Christians. They're always blaming me for everything!"

"Blame it on the devil," "Satan made me do it," and "Could it be Lucifer?" We've all heard those lines before. Each of us are responsible for the choices we make, and Satan is not behind every struggle we face in this world. Granted, there are times we must discern what we're up against. Not everything has a natural cause; however, not everything has a satanic origin either.

Position #2: Nothing Is Caused by the Devil

Just as dangerous is the erroneous presumption that Satan has no ability to influence or affect our lives in any way. One of the enemy's best attributes is his ability to go undetected. While we may not often see him directly, upon further review we can identify his illegal procedures. To take the position that the spiritual dimension has no ability to influence the natural world and that Satan is either nonexistent or a nonfactor is to be spiritually and scripturally irresponsible.

Some people wrongly believe, "If I don't bother the devil, he won't bother me," or "If I pretend demons and hell don't exist, then they don't." Nothing could be further from the truth. This doesn't work when facing an opponent on the football field, and it doesn't work in real life either. My mother used to warn me not to speak of the devil out loud, because it could somehow wake him up and put him on my trail. Believe me when I say this: he's awake and already on your trail.

Why would the devil want to mess with you? Because you belong to God, and the devil is at war with God. Satan has not signed a peace treaty with heaven. He resents God and who we represent. And it's his objective to undermine the work of God in and through us. Make no bones about it, when you invoke God you provoke the devil. But do not fear. No matter what the devil may attempt to do, he only speeds the cause he seeks to hinder.

Position #3: I Can Live My Life Any Way I Choose and Not Be Affected by the Devil

Of the three, this position is perhaps the most dangerous and ignorant. For example, it's highly unlikely that a man can continually view pornography without walking away struggling with lust and perverse thoughts. If a man consults with psychics and the occult, he will likely open a door to witchcraft. A man who harbors deep resentment and hatred will likely develop a root of bitterness. It's nearly impossible for a man to watch horror flick after horror flick and not fellowship with a spirit of fear. A man cannot compulsively lie without finding himself deceived and further away from the truth.

Sin empowers Satan's kingdom and gives him legal access to oppress. Satan lives and traffics in darkness. He has access to every place of darkness, even if that darkness is in us. Any area of our lives that is not under the lordship of Jesus Christ is fair game. Like placing a vacancy sign on the door of our soul, we give him an invitation and the right of entry when we allow that darkness to remain in us.

Taking Out the Trash

Late one night during Raider training camp, Kevin Gogan and I returned to our hotel room and were shocked to find a mouse sitting in the corner of our room. When we pulled back the drapes, close to thirty mice and rats scurried out from under the curtains and darted past our feet in all directions. We both screamed like young schoolgirls, stumbling and sprinting toward the door as if our skirts were on fire. It was comically embarrassing.

Once outside the room, we could here the roar of laughter coming from our teammates. Center Dan Turk and punter Jeff Gossett were responsible for the sinister prank. They had bored a hole through the common hotel wall we shared with them and fed a small plastic PVC pipe through the tunnel. Then they went to the pet store and bought a dozen rats and two-dozen mice. They forced the vermin through the pipe and covered their side of the opening with a sock. I have to admit, it was very clever, but we got the last laugh when the organization handed them the $2,000 bill to cover the costs of patching the wall and fumigating the entire suite.

Like rodents, demons don't bother to check in at the front desk. Neither do they knock on our front doors asking to come in. They are trespassers and trash-passers, infiltrating our space and inviting all their friends over like its some kind of party. They find a corner in our minds and hide behind the curtains of our hurts. They go on performing unlawful practices on our property, and they will not leave until we pull back the drapes and expose them. If they can get away with something they will, and unless confronted and challenged, they will make themselves right at home.

What attracts a demon in the first place? The same things that attract rodents—rotting cheese, scraps in the basement, and crumbs under the refrigerator. Demons have an appetite, and like rats they feed off the emotional leftovers we leave in our basements and the garbage we fill our minds with. They cling to the hidden sin swept under our rugs and befriend the skeletons in our closets.

Demons are rightly called unclean spirits, for they can dirty up a place quickly—urinating, defecating, spreading deadly viruses, and multiplying their offspring. They litter our homes with shame and look to inhabit those places in us that are neglected, rejected, wounded, and unloved. They are doubt-peddlers, fear-mongers, and carry with them a medical journal full of diseases. They have the uncanny ability to squeeze past our defenses and enter through small openings along our perimeter. Any crack in our armor is seen as an opportune time to *blitzkrieg.*

When you have a rat problem, simply turning on the lights and shooing them away from your trash can will not suffice. The rats come back because the trash is still present. We've got to take out the trash in order to keep them away. Trying to get rid of them without removing what they feed on will only prove to be a short-term and ineffective fix.

As men of God, we've got to take responsibility for our bodies, our souls, and our spirits. It's high time we put our foot down and declare, "Not in my house!" It would benefit us all to ask for the Holy Spirit to shine a light on every trace of garbage that remains in our hearts and fumigate our souls with truth.

You might think about taking inventory of your entertainment and performing an audit on your thought life, or maybe forgiving your father and releasing that friend who betrayed you. Kick out the fear that tries to dictate your decisions and eliminate the rejection that influences your relationships. If you struggle with pornography, renounce it and confess it as sin. Now erase, delete, and throw out everything associated with it. Take out the trash, clean out those skeletons, and patch up the walls of your heart.

What Are Demons?

Satan has at his disposal a horde of well-organized, wicked forces. Demons are disembodied spirits seeking a habitation through a fleshly host. They serve as Satan's foot soldiers to deceive, defile, distract, dissuade, and carry out the desires of the evil one. According to Scripture, they have the ability to think, speak, hear, feel, and act (see Matt. 8:31; 17:18; Mark 1:34; 5:12; Luke 8:32; 10:17). They also will take on the characteristics of the sin that empowers them. For example, a demon of fear not only causes fear, but is itself afraid. In order to express itself it must find a host to express that fear. Likewise, a spirit of depression is depressed and is looking for a home to bring depression to.

The demons of the Bible are openly hostile to human beings. They oppress people, oppose the gospel, cause disease (see Matt. 4.24; 12:22; 15:22; Luke 4:35) and mental illness (see Mark 5:2-20; Luke 8:27-39). Whenever Jesus found a demonized person, He drove the demons out and delivered the person from their suffering. In fact, He often healed and delivered everyone He encountered who was demonized.

For those who think this all sounds far-fetched, think again. The popularity of demonic movies, ghost-chasing television shows, and mediums who claim to talk to the dead has never been higher. People have a true craving for the spiritual dimension and inwardly know there is something more to life than the physical realm. I remember sneaking in to see parts of *The Exorcist* movie when I was young, and it flat-out terrified me. I knew nothing about the Bible, but you couldn't convince me that that the demonic realm was not real.

We often think of demons as dark, hideous creatures, and indeed they are. But they are also con artists who have the ability to appear as angels of light. Seldom do they jump out of a bush and scream, "Boo!" They are smarter than that. Instead, they disguise themselves as spirit guides, dead relatives, benign apparitions, ancestral spirits, and imaginary friends intent on deceiving and nudging us in the direction they want us to go, which is ultimately always away from God.

How Demons Gain Entry

There are many different ways in which demons can gain entry into our lives, but I want to focus on a few that are specific to men in general. I've mentioned a few common entry points already—unforgiveness, fear, bitterness, and rejection—but here are a few more to consider:[2]

Greed

Money is not evil in and of itself, but the *love* of money is. It was Paul who first penned, *"The love of money is a root to all kinds of evil"* (1 Tim. 6:10). Money can be a source of great blessing or a cause for great temptation. It just all depends on who possesses it. While it's one thing to have material possessions, it's quite another to be gluttonous for it. Jesus said, *"No one can serve two masters. Either he will hate the one and love the other, or he will be devoted to the one and despise the other. You cannot serve both God and Money"* (Matt. 6:24). Jesus personifies money and likens it to a master who will either be loved or despised. Like any sin, the love of money will take you further than you wanted to go, cost you more than you wanted to pay, and keep you longer than you wanted to stay. The bumper sticker that reads "He who dies with the most toys wins" is a sham. He who dies with the most toys still dies and takes none of his toys with him.

Paul continues, *"People who want to get rich fall into temptation and a trap and into many foolish and harmful desires that plunge men into ruin and destruction"* (1 Tim. 6:9). Those who seek after riches are investing in the wrong kingdom and are placing their financial future in the enemy's hands. Only on their death-beds do many realize that money could neither prolong their lives nor buy them happiness. The more a person wraps their identity around their bank account, the closer they inch toward the allure and trap of materialism, jealousy, poverty, and lack. Greed must be resisted with all of our might.

Sexual Immorality

Sex is more than just a physical act. It is a spiritual transaction. When a man and woman come together, the two *"become one flesh"* (Gen. 2:24). There is an emotional tie and a spiritual union that takes place during sexual intercourse. It's a bond designed to protect the unity of a husband and a wife and should only be reserved for marriage. This is why sex outside the context of marriage is so harmful and hurtful to all involved. When a man sleeps with a woman who is not his wife, his soul becomes tied to hers and hers to his. It's called a soul tie, and like a sexually transmitted disease, any spirits she may be infected with can now be shared and passed on to him.

Fornication, adultery, homosexuality, pornography, and orgies are all perversions of God's original design for sex. Being immoral, however, doesn't just stop with illicit sex. Jesus said, *"Anyone who looks at a woman lustfully has already committed adultery with her in his heart"* (Matt. 5:28). Adultery starts in the mind before it ever gets to the bedroom. It is something that we should be vigilant in, taking every thought captive when it tries to enter our minds.

For this reason I do not watch movies, play video games, read magazines, or visit websites that have sexually-explicit content. I know myself too well and don't have the discipline not to be tempted. I refuse to willingly pay for something that only pollutes my mind and my marriage. Men are typically visually driven, and the enemy knows this. If he can access your spirit through your eye-gate, he can open you up to a world of fantasy, pornography, and masturbation.

Men who habitually fall for this trap are inviting sexual demons to come in and bring confusion, bondage, and shame. Don't let the enemy steal your purity and rob you of all the pleasures intended for you and your wife (or future wife). You should fight to stay pure with everything that is within you.

Traumatic Events

Traumatic events such as rape, abuse, murder, molestation, divorce, bankruptcy, career failure, accidents, and the death of a loved one can create opportunities for the adversary to sow seeds of fear and hopelessness in your soul. These spirits can further hold the door open for others, and if not properly dealt with they can profoundly affect the relationships and behavioral choices of that person their entire life.

Demons prey on the weak and vulnerable. Like archers, they shoot their arrows of doubt and rain down lies, hoping one of them pierces your soul. Your spirit has a memory even when your brain forgets what took place, which explains how traumatic events that took place in your childhood can affect you later on in life. Frank Hammond writes, "Without question the majority of demons encountered through ministry have entered the persons during childhood. The quickest way to understand what doors were opened for demons to enter is to hear an account of a person's childhood."[3]

Music

Have you ever found yourself singing a song and then stopped to think, "Wait...what am I singing about?" I have sometimes caught myself singing something that completely contradicts my worldview. When we sing the lyrics of a song, we are making a verbal profession of the lyrics, declaring the words over our spirit, claiming them as our own. Don't underestimate the power of your words. It was Charles Spurgeon who said, "Christians don't tell lies. They sing them." The lies that most people believe today are spread through the avenue of music. Whether we listen to lies, tell lies, or sing them, they are still lies nonetheless.

Just as singing songs of praise to the Lord has a powerful and positive effect on us, so singing songs that dishonor Him can have a negative effect upon us as well. One invokes God's presence; the other, well, you can guess whose presence it invokes. Remember that Lucifer was an angel skilled in music and created to make music (see Ezek. 28:13-17). It is not a stretch to think that he would use catchy beats and cool music to spread his message.

From the writer to the producer to the artist, music carries with it a spirit. What is the song about? What is its core message? Does it contradict what I am fighting for? Be aware of the spirit and the message of the tunes you are listening to. I am not suggesting every artist and every song on the radio is of the devil. But some are and they are not worth listening to.

Word Curses

Word curses are words spoken over you that set something into motion. They can be words that we say in the heat of the moment but don't really mean. Phrases like "It's killing me" or "I must be getting sick" or "I will never be loved" can become self-fulfilling prophecies that bring about what we have inadvertently proclaimed. Similarly, oaths, covenants, and inner vows can be an invitation for demon interaction.

Word curses can also come from other people. For example, a parent who says, "I never wanted you," or "You're such a disappointment," can open the door for a spirit of rejection. When a curse is spoken over (or against) you by another person, it acts like a spell intent on hindering and misguiding you. When a father says to his son, "You're so stupid; you'll never amount to anything," they are speaking a word curse over their son. Satan pounces on that declaration and uses it like a weapon against the child.

For these reasons, don't believe anything and everything people tell you, even loved ones. Make it a point to squash every word curse you hear, and make it your practice to speak life and blessings over yourself and other people.

Generational Sin

Some spirits we wrestle with are familiar and are passed on to us generationally. We contend with them on account of our last names, not our first names. While we may not personally be responsible for their presence in our lives, somewhere along the line an ancestor invited them in. When certain sin enters a family, it opens the door for certain spirits to travel from generation to generation. The tragedy of sin is that it not only affects those who commit it, but it reverberates for generations to come.

This is why an alcoholic often raises children who struggle with some form of addictive behavior too. If a son harbors bitterness toward his alcoholic father and does not rise up to defeat that addiction, he will likely fall into the same ditch that his father did. Disease is another example that has the ability to pass through the bloodline. One side of a family is plagued by cancer while the other is not. I've seen diabetes pass from parent to child to grandchild as if it were a family heirloom. Diseases and disorders that are congenial and congenital often have a spiritual root to them. In these instances, an ancestral spirit of infirmity may be at work.

Additionally, generational sin patterns have the ability to produce generational curses. These curses are like dark clouds that follow a person through life. Possible signs of a generational curse include, but are not limited to, premature deaths (including suicide), chronic marital problems, chronic financial problems, chronic family sickness and disease, accident proneness, female problems (including barrenness and multiple miscarriages), and a family history of mental illness and confusion. The good news is that curses of any kind can be broken through the four steps listed next.

How to Get Rid of Evil Influences in Your life

There are four words to freedom, and I would encourage you not to forget them.

The first word is to *repent,* which is a military term that means to turn around and march in the opposite direction. It is not an angry word, but a liberating word, and an act of defiance against the tyranny of sin. Repentance is both the decision and practice of fully turning away from all destructive and ungodly behavior. The person who repents takes personal responsibility for their conduct and chooses to proceed in a new direction. Instead of just changing the channel, repentance might mean unplugging the television set or unsubscribing from cable when it becomes too great of a temptation. It is a full and purposeful turn away from our sin.

Repentance is identifying the trash that the rats are feasting on and refusing to contribute to the pile any longer. If you need to get rid of evil influences in your life, taking ownership for your own actions is the first step. Determine what measures you took to open that door in the first place. Confess those measures as sin before God. Man up to a friend or an accountability partner and receive God's forgiveness. Now that you've turned your back on the behavior, you can now turn your face toward God and contend for your freedom.

The second word we are to remember when it comes to getting free is *renounce.* The second step to freedom is to renounce ungodly practices. To renounce is to publicly disown someone or something by making a formal statement against it. It is a verbal declaration that the influence or activity is no longer welcome in your life. Renouncing is like breaking up with the devil. When we repent, we are admitting we once had a relationship with him;

when we renounce, however, we are declaring that the relationship is over and that we can no longer be friends.

When I renounce sin and the strongholds that are associated with them, I like to be as specific as possible. Demons have names, and their names relate to their function. Some demons take on the names of emotions like depression, loneliness, rejection, grief, despair, anxiety, and fear. Others are in the family of addiction like lust, greed, perversion, masturbation, pornography, alcoholism, gluttony, and compulsion. Still others are strongholds of sickness like disease, cancer, pain, fever, infection, infirmity, virus, and affliction. That is not to say that all sickness and every emotion is demonic, but some are spiritually rooted, and these can only be healed through a spiritual remedy.

This is also a good time to forgive anyone whom you are angry with or you have a soul tie with. If you need to break a soul tie, verbally renounce any and all bonds that may exist between you and that person. It may benefit you to list by name those you need to forgive, those you have an unhealthy emotional tie to, and those you have had sexual interaction with. After repenting of resentment and the behavior that created the soul tie, in prayer let go of your bitterness and sever any remaining spiritual connection you may have with them. Declare they are forgiven, released, and have no power to influence or control you.

Once the sin is renounced, destroy those things associated with it. Unplug the computer, burn the magazines, delete the files, throw away the gifts from your exgirlfriend, and cancel the credit cards if need be. Don't flirt with it anymore. Be proactive and remove all traces of that stronghold from your life. Like cutting cancer from your body, you must move swiftly before it tries to creep back into your life.

Thirdly, to *revoke* means to remove any license or permission given to the enemy. Demons trespass legally and illegally.

They will claim any legal right they have to remain, and when they have no legal ground they will remain illegally until challenged and confronted. They are like squatters who occupy the uninhabited and abandoned places of our hearts. Revoking them forces them to pick up their seeds, pack up their bags, and sweep the place clean on their way out. This step also ensures that demons have nothing left to hold over our heads. Their access has been denied and their tracks are being erased.

The fourth word we need to remember when it comes to getting free is *remove,* which is the last step to freedom, removing the demonic presence from your life. This can only be achieved once you've fully repented, renounced, and revoked the sin that empowers it. I like to verbally call out demons as if I'm picking a fight with them. When you command a demon to exit, be specific and address one spirit at a time. Saying, "Hey you, spirits, come out of my life" will not do. The demons may just laugh at you. Say something like, "In Jesus's name, I command the spirit of suicide to leave my soul and my body and never return. You have been renounced and revoked, so leave me now."

Verbally state your commands and war against it as if you're assaulting an intruder who's breaking into your home. It can be helpful but not necessary to know the name of the spirit you're dealing with. Usually its name will reveal its nature and tactics. Francis Frangipane writes, "In the spirit realm the name of an entity always corresponds to its nature. To defeat the rulers of darkness, we must know their nature, their tactics and how they apply those tactics against our weakness."[4]

You will discover that Satan's army functions within a hierarchy and operates in groups of associated spirits. As you continue to press them, you will eventually uncover the head demon who is generally the first to enter. Jesus refers to it as the *strongman* (see Matt. 12:22-30), and this strongman often holds the door open for others to follow.

Keep praying and commanding these evil forces to leave until you feel a release. All power in this universe is subject to the authority of Jesus Christ. Be forceful and persistent until it vacates you, your family, and your home for good. It may be helpful to create an atmosphere where the presence of God is welcomed. Invite other believers to help you pray or to pray for you and ask the Holy Spirit to lead you. Read some appropriate Scripture like those listed in this chapter. Playing worship music in the background and anointing yourself and the room with oil can also be helpful.

Keep in mind that if you haven't dealt with all the access points of entry, your efforts to expel a demon will prove to be frustrating. It has the right to stay and will not budge. Go through the steps again and again until you have removed all legal ground. Don't be discouraged. Deliverance can be instantaneous, but many times it is a process. Every time you pray you are getting freer and closer to Christ. Like breaking a boulder with a sledgehammer, surrender fully to Jesus, and then use the Word of God and the name of Jesus to break that stronghold into pebbles one blow at a time.

When you are finished praying, ask the Holy Spirit to fill every void in you. Pray for a fresh infilling of the opposite virtue of your struggle. For example, pray for peace when there has been a stronghold of anxiety or anger, or joy where there has been depression.

These four steps can also be used to help someone else find freedom. If you know someone who is battling demonic oppression, walk them through these steps. Jesus spent nearly one third of His ministry directly opposing the work of demons, and I find it interesting that driving out demons is the first sign He said would accompany a believer (see Mark 16:17). He engaged the enemy, which means He expected His followers would have to do the same.

Hand-to-Hand Combat

Athletes know that the way to get faster and stronger is through struggle and discipline. Muscles grow when they are forced to work against resistance. In the same way, resistance stretches our faith and makes us grow. What we call spiritual warfare is often spiritual development. The goal should not be to get out of warfare but to get stronger through it. Through resistance, your persecution becomes your promotion and spiritual warfare becomes the training ground for your greatness.

The fact that you experience spiritual warfare shouldn't surprise you or threaten you. Rather, it should complement you. Spiritual conflict is an indication that you are doing something right, that you are fighting the good fight of faith, and fighting on the right side. It should concern us when we never experience opposition for our faith. Don't run from resistance. Instead, make it work to your advantage.

Football players wear helmets and shoulder pads for protection, but it's their hands that are their weapons. Punching can be an effective way for an offensive lineman to dominate at the scrimmage line. When I was playing I would try to get my hands on the opponent before they could even stand up out of their stance. My strategy was to hit the defender so hard that it would knock him off balance long enough for me to get my proper fit for the block. Like a gun fighter of the Wild West, the line of scrimmage usually comes down to who can draw their revolver out of their holster first. I was in it to win it, and I did not like losing. I hoped to punish my opponent and put such a legal beating on him that it would cause him to dread the day he had to play against me again.

In offensive line play, punching the fists has almost become a lost art. I have observed many NFL and college line coaches who fail to teach young players today how to properly use their hands and punch effectively. There is no shortage of talented athletes who gain in size and strength due to the advances in nutrition and weight training. But without proper training in hand-to-hand combat, they will continually get bullied and thrown around like a ragdoll at the line of scrimmage.

I included this chapter in this book because when you put your hand on the line for God, it is an act of defiance against the tyranny of the enemy and strikes a blow to the enemy. It is my prayer that your hands become a little better trained for war and more prepared for combat. Don't let the enemy intimidate you or push you back on your heels. Spiritual warfare is designed to keep the devil on his heels. Make him dread messing with you by responding to every one of his attacks with repentance and praise.

You are a dangerous warrior for God, but only if you realize it. Christ has armed you and has given you all authority for this fight. Use it wisely. A police officer who never arrests a criminal is still a police officer, but he doesn't yet fully value the weightiness of the badge he wears. Authority that is not exercised is meaningless. In similar fashion, a Christian man who never fights in prayer or lays hands on the sick or casts out demons will not fully appreciate the power they possess in Christ.

You want to be a hero? Here is your arena. You want to be a champion? Here is your fight. Satan only opposes that which he is threatened by. And you are Satan's greatest fear.

The Extra Point

Whether it's the red zone, the end zone, or the war zone, there is no victory in life unless you are pushed outside your comfort zone. I suspect this chapter did just that. It is my hope that this material did not make you afraid of the devil, as we should never fear an enemy that is already defeated. The best way to keep yourself free of Satan and his forces is to live your life wholeheartedly surrendered to Christ. Lives are at stake, and the way to keep the ground you have already taken is to keep taking more ground. I believe your life can be a living testimony of how God can break any bondage of captivity and turn your scars into stars.

RESISTANCE

Chalk Talk

1. Did this chapter freak you out a little bit? What characteristics of the devil were new revelations to you? What are the consequences if we don't teach Christian believers about their enemy?

2. Do demons really exist? If so, what is their role in serving or hindering the work of the Lord? Are they responsible for all the bad things that happen in the world?

3. Why does the devil hate you as a follower of Jesus? How do you threaten him and his kingdom? If you don't oppose him, what makes you think he'll give you a pass?

4. How does a person feed their flesh? How do they nourish their spirit? Do you have any emotional or physical trash in your life that the enemy could possibly use against you?

5. If you were your own enemy, what plan would you create to cause you to falter in your faith? What lies would you tell yourself?

6. Have you ever prayed in the name of Jesus Christ to rebuke a sickness, spiritual attack, bad thought, or some form of suspected demonic activity? Who has the authority to do so?

7. How do demons enter a host, and what must believers do to be set free from demonic influences? How do you keep evil spirits from returning?

Endnotes

1. Sun Tzu, *The Art of War*, chapter 3

2. Much of this material was gathered from various works from ministers Derek Prince, Doris Wagner, and John Eckhardt.

3. Frank Hammond, *Pigs in the Parlor: A Practical Guide to Deliverance* (Kirkwood, MO: Impact Books, Inc. 1973), 24–25.

4. Francis Frangipane, *Discerning Of Spirits* (Cedar Rapids, IA: Arrow Publications, 1991), 18–19.

PURITY

CHAPTER 9

BLINDSIDE HELP

No people can become great who
have ceased to be virtuous.

—SAMUEL JOHNSON

In the springtime when kings went out to war, the Bible records that Joab and the armies of Israel fought against the Ammonites. Israelite forces were deployed to quell an Ammonite uprising and besiege the city of Rabbah. King David, however, remained in Jerusalem while his military fought to preserve and advance his kingdom. It would prove to be a decision that David would forever regret.

One evening David observed from the roof of his palace a beautiful woman who was bathing. He inquired about her and was told that she was Bathsheba, the wife of one of his mighty men, Uriah. He promptly sent for her, took her into his chambers, and slept with her.

After learning that Bathsheba was pregnant, David devised a plan to cover up his indiscretion. He summoned Uriah from the battlefield, inquired about the war, and sent him home for a good night's rest. He followed it up by sending a royal gift to Uriah's house. But Uriah was an honorable man. Instead of going home, he slept that night at the palace entrance along with the king's servants. When David asked him why he didn't return to his house, Uriah responded, "The ark and my fellow countrymen are dwelling in tents and sleeping out in the open field. How could I go to my house to eat, drink, and be with my wife?" (see 2 Sam. 11:11).

So David came up with an alternative solution. He invited Uriah to dine with him and made him drunk. When evening had come, he sent Uriah home to Bathsheba, but Uriah didn't return to his house as David had hoped. He slept instead in the servants' quarters as before. At this point, David took things further than he ever thought they would go. In a devious act of treachery, he ordered Uriah to return to the battlefield with written instructions for Israel's commander in chief. The note directed Joab to position Uriah at the forefront of the battle and retreat from him so that he would be struck down and killed. The events happened just as David had conspired, and unknowingly Uriah had delivered his own death sentence to his commander.

When news came back to David that Uriah had been a casualty of war, Bathsheba mourned for him. When her time of mourning was complete, David took her as his wife, and she bore him a son.

If this story weren't found in the pages of Scriptures, we might think it was another Hollywood script. King David, a national hero and a married man, commits adultery with a married woman and impregnates her. After several failed cover-up attempts, the famous giant-killer betrays an honest man and murders him so he can steal his wife.

It is the nature of sin to multiply itself, to draw a person into greater enormities and harsher complexities. Sin is like anthrax in that it spreads quickly, is extremely deadly, and refuses to die easily. Once contaminated, anthrax spores rapidly multiply and can kill within two days. What starts out as cold-like symptoms quickly escalates into trouble breathing, shock, and eventual death. Somewhere along the line David took in a lethal spore of lust, and it rapidly multiplied into adultery, deception, ingratitude, injustice, betrayal, and homicide.

The story doesn't end there, however. David seemed perfectly content living with a guilty conscience for almost a year until Nathan rode into town. The prophet came with a tale of injustice.

The Traveler

Nathan said to David:

> *"There were two men in a certain town, one rich and the other poor. The rich man had a very large number of sheep and cattle, but the poor man had nothing except one little ewe lamb he had bought. He raised it, and it grew up with him and his children. It shared his food, drank from his cup and even slept in his arms. It was like a daughter to him.*

> *"Now a traveler came to the rich man, but the rich man refrained from taking one of his own sheep or cattle to prepare a meal for the traveler who had come to him. Instead, he took the ewe lamb that belonged to the poor man and prepared it for the one who had come to him."*

> *David burned with anger against the man and said to Nathan, "As surely as the Lord lives, the man who did this must die! He must pay for that lamb four times over, because he did such a thing and had no pity."*

> *Then Nathan said to David, "You are the man!"*
> (2 Samuel 12:1-7)

What is most shocking about this story is that the villain is not Cain, Haman, or Judas Iscariot—it is King David, the celebrated warrior, God's anointed king, and the writer of many psalms. David is generally considered one of the good guys in Scripture. A shepherd, a poet, and a prophet, he was a man after God's own heart. What could cause a great man like David to fall into such great sin? *A traveler.*

In Nathan's parable, a traveler came to the rich man's house and needed to be accommodated. Instead of taking from his own flock to feed his guest, the rich man steals the poor man's ewe to appease his hungry vagabond. If it weren't for the traveler, perhaps the man would have never thought to steal from his brother.

The traveler came to David, and David accommodated him. Who is this traveler? The traveler is a spirit of covetousness, and it personifies the inner urgings of sin and self-gratification within us. It is the desire to have something that doesn't belong to you. It is a man-stalking, lust-driven, self-seeking, lie-dispensing, equal opportunity destroyer.

To every man comes the traveler at some point and time in his life. He comes knocking on both your door and mine. He requires to be fed and will not be satisfied until we oblige him. His appetite is insatiable. His need is urgent, and he places upon us an obligation to appease him. We are delusional if we think that feeding him will make him go away. Pacifying him only encourages him to stay for a while and return for another visit. The more he is fed, the more his appetite grows, and the more his need becomes demanding.

I have a feeling you have entertained the traveler before. In fact, if we are honest, we all have. Through pornography, indiscriminate behavior, sexual fantasy, and masturbation, some men have polluted their minds and made themselves an attractive tourist destination for the traveler. It is my hope that by now you realize feeding your wanton sexual appetites will not gratify your urges but rather awaken a monster within.

Our sex-drives should never define us or control us, and unlike sleep or water, our bodies *can* survive without sex. A man who cannot control his sexual appetites has a spiritual problem, not a physical one. Blaming immoral behavior on hormones or testosterone levels is like blaming a crime on the murder weapon. You are under no obligation to feed the traveler indiscriminately, and when he comes knocking (and I guarantee that he will), David would highly recommend not answering the door.

David rightly assessed that the thief of the parable should be punished and pay back fourfold for his act of injustice. And for the rest of David's life, he did just that. The son born of David and Bathsheba's infidelity died in infancy. Amnon, David's firstborn son by Ahinoam, violated his half sister Tamar and was killed by her brother to avenge her rape. Ahithophel, a trusted counselor and friend, turned his back on David and joined a plot organized by David's son Absalom to overthrow the kingdom. David's relationship with Ahithophel, who happened to be Bathsheba's grandfather, was no doubt damaged by the king's scandalous and reckless behavior.

The consequences of David's actions had a lasting and devastating effect upon him and his family for generations that were to come—heartache, trouble, betrayal, incest, rebellion, dysfunction, and premature death. He paid a high price for his actions, a price that included the public airing of his dirty laundry. And here we are today, millenniums later, still talking about his transgressions. That is the ripple effect of sin. Fortunately, true repentance and faithfulness can create a heavenly ripple effect as well.

To his credit, however, David took ownership of his actions after being confronted by Nathan. David kept short accounts with God, and this is partly why he is so revered for many people today. In Psalm 51, we read of his heartfelt and genuine repentance.

Have mercy on me, O God, according to Your unfailing love; according to Your great compassion blot out my transgressions. Wash away all my iniquity and cleanse me from my sin. For I know my transgressions, and my sin is always before me. Against You, You only, have I sinned and done what is evil in Your sight; so You are right in Your verdict and justified when You judge....

Cleanse me with hyssop, and I will be clean; wash me, and I will be whiter than snow.... Create in me a pure heart, O God, and renew a steadfast spirit within me. Do not cast me from Your presence or take Your Holy Spirit from me. Restore to me the joy of Your salvation and grant me a willing spirit, to sustain me (Psalm 51:1-4,7,10-12).

David's heart of repentance and worship is exemplary, and this psalm always brings encouragement to me, considering my own failures and shortcomings. We can learn a lot from David's life, and one is that the traveler does not discriminate. If left to our devices, we would all self-destruct. I have no doubts that you are a great man, but that does not disqualify you from *"the lust of the flesh, the lust of the eyes and the pride of life"* (1 John 2:16). When it comes to sexual temptation, you have a blindside, just as I do. We all need help, and we need to stay sober and alert.

I like to fish, and I'm always amazed at the craziest things that can be used to catch a fish. From propeller lures to tandem-bladed spinner baits, I have caught fish using bread, cheese, lunchmeat, raisins, hot dogs, chicken livers, dog food, crickets, and even a bare hook with a few feathers attached. Bass in particular will snap at just about anything that flashes because they are easily provoked, very territorial, selfish, and, in general, have a bad attitude.

Once my kids needed to catch and observe some crayfish for a science project. So I took them down to a nearby creek along with a bucket, a fishing pole, and some bacon. They looked at me like I was crazy and asked, "Dad, where's the net?"

"Trust me," I replied, "we won't need one."

I attached the greasy bacon to the line and dipped it into the tiny trickle of the creek, which was so small you could easily jump across it. The kids were amazed that within a few seconds the line started to move, and we hoisted up three crayfish clinging to one diminutive piece of bacon. I swung the pole out over the water, slowly walked over to the bucket, and shook off the crayfish. The kids squealed with excitement, and we had a blast catching countless crayfish. I think we caught enough crayfish that day for their entire fourth-grade class.

The irony is that the crayfish should have known they do not naturally eat bacon. It's not in their daily diet, and it's not likely that they were accustomed to seeing a piece of uncooked bacon come floating down the creek. When we pulled them up out of the water, they could have easily let go at any point and scurried away. Instead, it wasn't until they were violently shaken and fell into the bucket that they realized they had become trapped without escape.

Men are not too unlike those crayfish. We tend to chase things that we have no business lusting after, and hold onto things longer than we should. We've been known to swallow the bait of Satan while pursuing unconventional and obvious lures. It's like the devil's playing chess while we're still playing checkers, and at times it seems like he's two or three moves ahead of us. His lies are his lures, and he knows just how to dangle the bacon. All along we could have let go, but we don't often realize we're being duped until we've been violently shaken and entrapped by our unholy desires. Temptations look inviting or they wouldn't be tempting.

Satan knows the vices that we find appealing, and he's more than willing to open our eyes to the bathing Bathshebas around us. Men who become casualties of this war either don't consider the consequences of their actions or are duped into believing they are the exception and will escape unscathed. All lies, however, have this in common: they come with a hook. Without exception, there is always a hook hidden within sexual sin. The only way to break free of it is to admit we made a mistake, open our claws, let go of the bacon, and learn from it. If you are currently entrapped in sexual misconduct, let go and run away from it before your stubbornness violently shakes you, imprisons you, and leads you down a path you never intended to go.

Encroachment

Proverbs 7 tracks a young man falling prey to the snare of a seductress. The woman's charm is deceptive and her honeyed words are bewitching. She leads him like a stag into an ambush or as a calf to the slaughterhouse. He is reduced to a fool in stocks, and like a bird caught in a net, she finishes him off with an arrow through the liver. Solomon writes, *"Do not let your heart turn to her ways or stray into her paths. Many are the victims she has brought down; her slain are a mighty throng. Her house is a highway to the grave, leading down to the chambers of death"* (Prov. 7:25-27).

This passage always reminds me of the sirens of Greek mythology. In Homer's *Odyssey*, sirens were female sea nymphs who inhabited an island at sea. Part woman, part bird, these seducing creatures captivated unsuspecting sailors through their enchanting songs and lured them to their deaths on the jagged shores of their island. Sirens were the *femme fatales* of ancient Greek mythology.

Covetousness is like a siren calling out to unsuspecting men seeking their destruction. She tries to captivate our attention and demands that we take notice of her. Even in our modern world, sirens warn us of danger. When we hear the sound of an ambulance, fire engine, police car, or car alarm, it tells us that something is amiss and that we should take caution. The sound of a siren should alarm us, not allure us.

In the same way, the voice of lust and the pull of seduction should raise red flags and send off warning signals in our spirit that the enemy is encroaching. Undoubtedly, David heard these warnings but chose to ignore them. Like a smitten sailor, we too sail into dangerous waters when we ignore the voice of the Holy Spirit and allow our desires to go unchecked.

Uriah's character and humility certainly did not make it easy for David to conceal his scandalous behavior. This should have been David's first clue. Still, David ignored the stop signs and continued to spin a web of lies that ultimately led to murder. Instead of manning up to his sin, David chose to plunge deeper into it.

Splitting the Heart of the Upright

It is obvious that the U.S. is fast becoming a sexually-drunken, sensually-perverse society. We revel in immodest expression, celebrate destructive lifestyles, and flaunt our sexual exploits. America is the number one exporter of pornography in the world, as the porn industry generates $13 billion each year in the U.S. alone.[1] Nine out of ten of our sons are exposed to pornography before the age of 18.[2] According to *60 Minutes*, Americans spend as much on pornography as they do on sporting events, eating out, and going to the movies.

In a culture where sex sells, men are the buyers. Placed before us every day is an unrelenting barrage of media stimulations and soft porn images designed to titillate our masculinity. Like *VISA*, it's everywhere you want to be—at the movies, via websites, in magazines, ollmusic videos, video games, sporting events, and beer commercials. Advertisers know that men are visual, and you better believe they use it to manipulate us. Is it any wonder that three of every five college males engage in Internet sex once a week?[3]

Godless forces want to split the heart of the upright by causing our affections to be attached to the things of the world while they watch us go down with the ship. Peter urges us: *"Save yourself from this perverse generation"* (Acts 2:40). This exhortation is as relevant today as it was 2,000 years ago.

God's desire for sexual purity is laid out in simple terms throughout Scripture (see Exod. 20:14; Eph. 5:3). Paul encouraged the Thessalonians toward this end:

> *It is God's will that you should be sanctified: that you should avoid sexual immorality, that each of you should learn to control his body in a way that is holy and honorable, not in passionate lust like the heathen* (1 Thessalonians 4:3-5).

And Paul reminds us in 1 Corinthians:

> *Do not be deceived. Neither fornicators, not idolaters, nor adulterers, nor homosexuals, nor sodomites, nor thieves, nor covetous, nor drunkards, nor revilers, nor extortioners will inherit the kingdom of God* (1 Corinthians 6:9-10 NKJV).

And Jesus added, *"Anyone who looks at a woman lustfully has already committed adultery with her in his heart"* (Matt. 5:28). Jesus is not introducing a new law here but interpreting an old one. He identifies lust as a central access point for sexual lawlessness. This is why pornography is so destructive in the lives of men. A man who looks lustfully at a woman steals from her what is reserved for her husband or future husband, and he steals from his own eyes the look of purity his wife deserves from him. Pornography of any type is a deadly trap that can be as explosive as a hand grenade blast to the heart and that of your spouse. The images you see will defile your marriage and cause a ripple effect of pain , rejection and betrayal in your closest relationships.

You and I can ill afford to tolerate any degree of sexual compromise in our lives. Why? Because sexual activity outside of God's design will not appease your flesh but rather arouse it. While an act of indiscretion may not initially appear to have adverse affects, unsatisfied and out-of-control sexual appetites will ultimately lead to your demise.

God created sex to be enjoyed and celebrated. He doesn't want to steal your joy; rather, He wants to protect you from pain. And we know it's only through following godly guidelines that your sex life can be guilt-free and fulfilling. Solomon writes, *"Drink water from your own cistern"* so that *"your fountain may be blessed"* (Prov. 5:15,18). Solomon is talking about being faithful to your own wife. I'm more than interested in my marriage, my sex life, and my fountain being blessed of God.

You can delete the history on your Internet browser, erase the call log on your cell phone, and have friends cover for you, but make no mistake about it: your sins will leave an indelible spiritual trace in your life. Too often men think that by using birth control or disease control methods they can avoid the consequences of fornication and adultery, but the issue is much greater than an unwanted pregnancy or a sexually-transmitted disease. You can't put a condom around your heart, and it is your heart that is at stake here (see Prov. 4:23). Sexual sin of any kind will create an unseen barrier in your relationship with God and that of your spouse that will block intimacy until it's acknowledged and confronted.

Sex creates a bond between two people that can, without the cord of marriage securely fastened around the relationship, never produce the intimacy, trust, and security it is designed to produce. Only in a monogamous marriage can a man and woman be protected from the vices and consequences of sexual promiscuity.

We fool ourselves if we think we are immune from falling into sexual sin. All men are susceptible, which means all men need to stay vigilant, especially in our sexually charged world. I guarantee you that a one-time sexual encounter will not satisfy your urges. It will only serve to awaken your desires, amplify your loneliness, and leave you drowning in shame. In a culture where sex is overrated and intimacy is undersold, what you crave is not an ejaculatory release but intimacy in a committed, God-honoring relationship.

The incident with Bathsheba was not an isolated event for David. Hints of compromise can be detected throughout his life, and when it came to sexual gratification, David was no saint. He practiced polygamy, he had concubines, and he had accumulated a large harem of women. By the time he was 30, David had six wives, which was in direct violation to God's instruction for the king of Israel (see Deut. 17:14-17). In total, he entertained ten concubines and had anywhere from eight to twelve wives. F. B. Meyer writes that David's multiple wives and concubines fostered "in him a habit of sensual indulgence, which predisposed him to the evil invitation of that evening hour."[4]

Clean Machine

Most men take pride in their vehicle, and if you're anything like me you like to keep your ride looking and smelling clean. People tell me I should own a carwash business, because it puts a smile on my face to see a freshly detailed car or truck on the road. My first car was a used 1980 root beer brown Toyota Corona hatchback I purchased used for $4,000. That baby had a ninety-five horsepower, four-cylinder engine, three-speed automatic transmission, hand-operated roll-up windows and two-tone tan-and-brown fabric seats. It went from zero to sixty in like thirty seconds.

I was only a sophomore in high school at the time, but I loved that car and treated it like it was a baby named Ferrari. To me it symbolized my freedom. I hand washed it, detailed the engine, and waxed it so often my mother used to say I could eat off the hood. She was always perplexed as to how I could keep my car so spotless yet fail to pick up my room. To this day I like to wash my own vehicles and keep them waxed and well maintained. My old Chevy pickup with 120,000 miles still gets some weekly love and a healthy dose of Armor All.

The truth is that we are God's possession, and He has paid a steep price to redeem our lives. He is lovingly concerned about our condition and is continually working to cleanse and protect us. It is my prayer that I use the same energy to keep my heart pure and spotless as I do with my possessions. I want to communicate my appreciation to God by making His priorities my priorities and choosing His moral standards as my own.

What if we took such painstaking measures to keep ourselves pure in the eyes of God? Staying spiritually, physically, and mentally clean in today's society is not easy, yet it is not impossible. It takes a full commitment to it. It requires proactive, creative measures and a good dose of the Holy Spirit. We would do well to examine our lives daily so that we can pass inspections and present ourselves spotless before God. The Lord does indeed examine our lives, and it's through these examinations that He prepares us for the ultimate examination—the day we all must stand before His throne and give an account of our life.

Pick Six for Purity

How can a man shut out the traveler, avoid the pitfalls of sexual temptation, and successfully navigate through siren-infested waters? Here is your pick six for sexual purity.

Bump and Run

When you walk through a crowd, inevitably you are going to bump into people. The polite thing to do is say "excuse me" and keep walking. In the same way, you cannot walk through the digital age without bumping into an image, a commercial, or an advertisement containing explicit content. The right thing to do is bump and run. Bump away from the Victoria Secret store and run to the other side of the mall. Bounce your eyes off that billboard and look the other way. Grab the remote and change the channel.[5]

What do you do when a woman bends over in front of you? Do you stare at her figure like a pitcher staring at his catcher? It is not the first moment that we have control over, but the second and third moments. We may notice with our first glance, but God notices our second glance. It was Job who said, *"I have made a covenant with my eyes, not to look lustfully at a girl"* (Job 31:1). When David saw Bathsheba from his balcony, he should have been averting his eyes instead of reaching for his binoculars.

Paul exhorts men to run from "youthful lusts" and to "flee sexual immortality" (see 1 Cor. 6:18; 2 Tim. 2:22). When Potiphar's wife grabbed Joseph by his garment and threw herself at him, Joseph had to run out of his coat in order to escape her clutches. Joseph modeled for us the ultimate bump and run strategy. And we would do well to follow his lead.

Stay Inbounds

In football, in order to keep yourself in the game, you've got to stay on the playing field. Similarly in life, we've got to stay within our boundaries as well. We must not go wandering into places and websites we have no business visiting. Create boundaries for yourself, and when you cross them, throw yourself a penalty flag. Billy Graham, for example, resolved to never dine with a woman other than his wife or be alone in an elevator with another woman. If a lady were to step in, he'd kindly step out.

If you travel for work and are tempted by the in-room movies, then simply unplug the television or your computer. Read a book, call a friend, do some exercise, or take a nap. Problem solved. We all need to police ourselves in some way. Treat sexual sin like it's a high voltage electric tower and build a fence around it, both for yourself and for others. Don't even flirt with it. It's not worth the heartache, pain and isolation that is certain to accompany the sin.

Defend Your Home Turf

Men who fall into immoral behavior have faltered in their thought life many times over before the actual encounter ever occurred. Paul says we are to *"bring every thought into captivity and make it obedient to Christ"* (2 Cor. 10:5). Not every thought that floats into our brain is worth dwelling upon. Guard your thought life like you would defend your home. You wouldn't let disgusting, ungodly, and vile people walk through your home unannounced. Protect your mind as it if it's a prized piece of real estate. Paul reminds you to *"set your minds on things above,"* (Col. 3:2), and *"whatever is true, whatever is noble, whatever is right, whatever is pure, whatever is lovely, whatever is admirable—if anything is excellent or praiseworthy—think about such things"* (Phil. 4:8).

Have a Strong Safety

Every man needs another man to be strong for him when he is weak. There is strength in numbers and there is safety in accountability. It is a known fact that when bad behavior is observed, the behavior changes. We all need man-to-man coverage—someone who loves us enough to blow the whistle on our behavior, get in our face, and call us out. Accountability is fundamental to any good defense. Do you have a brother in Christ whom you can be painfully honest with and who asks you the hard questions? Very few men are willing to allow their lives to be examined by another, but those who do are better for it and are often leaders among us. Silence feeds our shame, but vulnerability and sharing our true self builds liberating intimacy with those we love.

Avoid One-on-One Isolation

Isolation is a setup for disaster and the result of overconfidence. We err when we think we are strong enough to make it on our own. Solomon warns that *"a man who isolates himself seeks his own desire; he rages against all wise judgment"* (Prov. 18:1 NKJV). Winning this war is not an individual accomplishment. It will require a team effort. Avoid enemy isolation, and pursue fellowship with other believers.

When we traveled as a team, I usually requested a roommate. I enjoyed the company, the clowning around, and the fellowship. Also, in doing this, any temptations I could possibly have in being away from my family were greatly reduced. In ministry, most pastors and evangelists I know also travel in pairs for much the same reasons. They value the fellowship and prayer support of another brother, and it helps them stay focused and free from any possible spiritual distractions.

Throw a Decisive Block

Temptation is not a sin in and of itself. Eve was tempted, and so was Jesus. The fact that you get tempted is just evidence that you've got something beautiful that the devil wants to pervert. Sin is born when we give into that temptation and disobey God. Scripture doesn't just tell us to resist temptation; it instructs us to avoid it altogether. We are called to take proactive steps to remove or reduce the temptations in our life. Take some things to the chopping block, and throw a chop block on the devil.

I always felt at home in the huddle.
We all need other men around us to stay encouraged

Purification in Process

When it comes to the battle for our purity, many young men get frustrated and don't have the fortitude and strength to resist unholy desires. But if you have opened your heart to the working of God's Spirit, the process has begun. Your progress may seem slower than you would like, but over time the heaviness of sin will dissipate. No matter how dark or filthy the nature of your sin, God forgives, washes, and transforms you. Your mind can be filled with clean and pure thoughts. If you diligently seek God's presence, you will one day be a vessel of honor ready to be poured out as a drink offering to God and useful to others.

I love television shows about car collecting and car enthusiasts who perform amazing restorations on old automobiles. I have attended my fair share of car shows and heard owners describe the hundreds of hours they put into rebuilding and restoring their cars. They did it with a clear purpose, passion, and at a significant expense. Often, however, the only thing they get out of the project is satisfaction. They simply loved the process of restoration. The sight of seeing an old junker transformed into a showstopper is worth all the time and effort.

God is no different. He loves to roll up His sleeves and get to work on us: *"He who began a good work in you will carry it on to completion until the day of Christ Jesus"* (Phil. 1:6). To see you transformed into what you were created for brings Him great satisfaction and joy, and for this reason it is a labor of love. He starts by stripping us down bolt by bolt. Hardheaded people like myself tend to resist Him like a rusted bolt, but His Spirit slowly loosens us until the decay of rust and lust are removed. At times it may feel like He's hammering on, because He is. It's all just part of the process of restoration. Because He is our Maker and our Model, He knows how to rebuild us again piece by piece, straightening out our steering and tuning up our alignment.

Restoration can be a grueling and time-consuming process, but God is unbelievably patient and up for the task. You can trust that He knows what He is doing because He loves you, and He's the One who engineered you in the first place. When complete, He's delighted to get us back on the road, fulfilling the purpose for which we were created. Only He can redeem us and spiritually restore our inner being. Only He can make us whole again and function properly, and it is then that we can serve the purpose of our call. We are all works under construction at differing points in this transformation process. God isn't done with any one of us entirely until we are made perfect in the presence of our Lord. Until then, He still has some buffing to do.

The Extra Point

Sexual purity is a battle worth fighting and a war you must win. In order to achieve it, you've got to be like a salmon. Salmon are not afraid to go against the flow. There is nothing easy about what they are called to do. They must swim upstream if they want to fulfill their destiny and finish strong.

Since men are a lot like fish, you might as well be determined to swim upstream and fight against the currents of our culture. The journey may not be easy, but it is worth it. I can guarantee you that the rewards will far outweigh the cost.

Chalk Talk

1. Would the sight of Bathsheba have tempted David if he were on the battlefield with his troops? What are the dangers of idleness? Is there a welcome mat for the traveler in your mind? If so, what do you need to do to remove it?

2. What sexual lures are you prone to? What in your life do you have no business chasing that currently catches your eye? What proactive measures can you take to stay mentally and sexually pure?

3. Who can you trust for advice, accountability, and encouragement in the things of God? Do you have three such relationships with other men in your life?

PURITY

4. List three personal boundaries you can start putting into practice today to guard your purity.

5. Do you feel God's process of purification and restoration at work in your life? What evidence do you have of the changes that have taken place? Are you fighting Him like a seized-up bolt, or allowing Him to do His work?

6. What are the consequences of your life if you never allow God to purify your sinful heart? Will you be the man God intended you to be? Do you expect your children to do what you say when you are not willing to do it yourself?

Endnotes

1.   This information is taken from Covenant Eyes, http://www .covenanteyes.com/pornstats/, accessed February 17, 2015.

2.   Ibid.

3.   Ibid.

4.   F. B. Meyer, *Great Men Of The Bible, vol. 2* (Grand Rapids, MI: Zondervan, 1982), 58.

5.   This is a technique taught in the Everyman's Battle series of books written by Stephen Arterburn and Fred Stoeker.

FAMILY

CHAPTER 10

HOME TEAM ADVANTAGE

*If you want to know the character of a
man, look into the eyes of his wife.*

"They're not ready for us," I heard him shout above the deafening roar.

This was only the second home game since the Raiders moved back to Oakland, and the crowd was rowdy and boisterous. We were squaring off against a storied franchise with one of the most notorious fan bases in football—the Philadelphia Eagles. I was in uniform, lined up, and ready to take the field. Willie Brown, a former Raider Hall of Famer and director of squad development stood with his arms stretched out, blocking me from entering the field. "Wait until you hear the bells Wiz," he remarked with a big grin.

At the Oakland Coliseum, players have a long trek to get to the playing field. Upon leaving the locker room, there is a lengthy corridor that passes the Oakland A's clubhouse, followed by a steep flight of stairs leading down to the field level. My locker happened to be the closest to the exit. After the pregame speech, I hit the double doors fired-up, shuffled down the corridor, and bounded the stairs to the double doors that led out to the field under the bleachers.

I thought to myself, "Bells? What bells is he talking about?"

Just then a red light from a television camera appeared from under the bleachers and zoomed in on my face. I've never been comfortable on camera and have always shied away from media interviews, but I had no choice but to look sheepishly into the camera lens. Then I heard the bells. AC/DC's song *Hells Bells* blasted so loud through the stadium sound system that I could feel the reverberations of the bass rumble through the bleachers. This was a new pregame introduction that played as the team took the field. At that, we were released and stormed onto the field.

There are not many feelings in life that compare to the thrill of running onto the field in front of a stadium full of screaming fans in anticipation of a nationally televised game. You might think that the big stage wouldn't faze professional athletes. But think again. Though football players may be tough, they are no different from anyone else. My heart was pounding during warm-ups that day. I had butterflies in my stomach and even a few goose bumps as the national anthem was being sung.

The game couldn't have started more poorly as we quickly found ourselves behind 17–0 in the first quarter. That was no way to win the affection of our rekindled fan base. However, we rallied together as a team and slowly and methodically battled back, scoring forty-eight unanswered points to win the game 48–17. Our head coach Mike White praised the jubilant team afterward for staying united in the face of adversity as we advanced to a record of 3–1 on the season. After the game my wife told me it was fun to see my face on the jumbo screen as I led the team out onto the field. Several friends and fans said likewise, but I didn't think much of it.

After our pregame ritual the following week, we lined up in the locker room, and this time I was toward the rear of the pack because I had gone to get a roll of tape from the training room. As the coach released us, a few veterans yelled, "Wait a minute. Wiz has to lead us out." As you know, athletes can be extremely superstitious, and apparently it was determined that because we won the previous week, somehow the order of us filing out of the locker room could have a bearing on the outcome of the game. I'm not superstitious at all, but I've learned to never disrupt the confidence of a player or coach on game day.

Willie Brown (right) and myself leading the team
onto the field at the Oakland Coliseum

From that day forward, it was somehow decided that I was the guy to lead the team onto the field before each and every game. There were other guys probably more deserving of that honor, but reluctantly and humbly I accepted the role. As a team captain, I never wanted to take for granted the gravity of my responsibility as a leader. I considered it an honor that my teammates saw something in me that they thought worthy of representing them.

Not many of us will get the opportunity to lead an NFL team out onto the field, but all of us will have the opportunity and responsibility to lead our wives and children into the things of God. While not many feelings compare to running out of the tunnel before an NFL game, there is one for sure that exceeds that feeling—the thrill of leading your family to heaven. I can't begin to fathom how raucous the atmosphere, the cheering, the praise, the music, and the celebrations will be on that glorious day. It will be a crazy reunion unlike any other.

Taking It to the House

It is no secret that the family unit is under assault and has been for quite a while. With the divorce rate in America hovering around 50 percent, we are told that six in every ten marriages eventually lead to separation. That means more children today are being raised without the benefit of their biological parents functioning together in the same home. It is also evidence that the foundation of the family is being dismantled before our very eyes.

The first institution that God established on the earth was not a government, a church, or a religion. It was marriage (see Gen. 2:21-25). It was through this bond of unity that the planet would be populated and the world would be strengthened. Safe, loving, unified, committed relationships are what we are designed to enjoy from the day we were conceived to the day after eternity.

Those who even dare to share what the Bible has to say about marriage are most often attacked publicly and ostracized by the media. Many people have lost their jobs or had their businesses boycotted simply because they agreed with the traditional definition of marriage—that it is between one man and one woman.

It should come as no surprise to us then that God desires strong families. They are the backbone of society.

The logic behind why we oppose abortion, homosexuality, adultery, the porn industry, and the teachings of evolution is not because we are old-fashioned and narrow-minded. It is because they stand in direct opposition to God's established truth and the biblical model of what the family is supposed to look like. The institutions of marriage and family are God-engineered initiatives worth protecting and preserving.

In the ancient Hebrew culture, the noblest profession was not a doctor, lawyer, or a scholar. In fact, neither was it to be a prophet, priest, or king. The highest call in life was the call to be a parent—to be the mother or father of a child that you could raise in the ways of God. What if our culture honored fathers and mothers in the same way we esteem athletes, musicians, and actors today? It would likely turn our world right side up and make heroes out of those most deserving. And, undoubtedly, it would cause us to grow in appreciation for our wives, our parents, and our roles as fathers.

It should be no surprise to us that marriage, family, and traditional values are under siege today. The enemy knows the commanding influence that a godly marriage can be to our communities and to the generations that follow. If he can break down a single marriage, he can tear apart a family. If he can break apart enough families, he can weaken a society, and thereby infiltrate a culture. Once he changes the definition and standards of a single generation, he can redefine it indefinitely however he sees fit.

As men we must boldly stand up to represent our family's best interests, no matter the subject or the circumstance. Whether it's in regard to the definition of marriage, our rights as parents, public education standards, or the politically-correct agenda enforced upon our kids, we need men who will love, lead, and defend the family unit.

FAMILY

The Bible offers plenty of wisdom on marriage and family. In his letter to the Ephesians, Paul gives two charges: one to husbands and the other to fathers. The first one is addressed to fathers: *"Husbands, love your wives, just as Christ loved the church"* (Eph. 5:25). And the other is addressed to fathers: *"And you, fathers, do not provoke your children to wrath"* (Eph. 6:4 NKJV). These two admonitions offer a unique perspective on developing strong families, so let's take a closer look at each of them.

To Husbands: Love Your Wife

The way that Jesus loves us is a model for how we are to love others, especially our wives (see Eph. 5:25). Paul uses the phrase *"loved the church"* as a sort of code language to convey the way Jesus lived and the manner in which He died. Paul writes elsewhere about this love, saying, *"God demonstrates His own love for us in this: While we were still sinners, Christ died for us"* (Rom. 5:8). How does Jesus love? He does so sacrificially. How far does His love go? All the way, ultimately leading Him to lay down His life for His bride, which is the church.

As husbands we should be willing to pay the ultimate price for our brides as well. If an intruder broke into your house, threatening to rape and kill your wife, what husband wouldn't risk his life to protect her? We must practically do for our wives what we are willing to physically do for them. Just as any husband would rise up and confront the intruder, so we should rise up and defend our marriage from all possible intruders that seek to threaten us. I would willingly die to protect my wife, but the question is, am I willing to die to my pride, selfishness, and stubbornness for her sake and for the sake of our marriage? Am I willing to make myself vulnerable and be emotionally intimate as well? To me, and maybe you, that is far scarier than fighting hand to hand with an intruder. This is what it means to love our wives as Christ loves the church.

How well do you love your wife? If you want to know how loved your wife feels, ask her. Also look for clues in her countenance. A husband has a direct influence on the emotional well being of his wife, and you can determine how well a woman is loved by the condition of her heart which is often reflected in her face. Her countenance will communicate how she's being treated and may reflect the kind of leader you are at home. I hate to see my wife in emotional pain, especially when I know my actions have been the culprit. It's one thing to unintentionally cause the pain, but love sees another in distress and reaches out in humility to address the source of the conflict.

There's a story told of a man and woman who had been married for more than sixty years. They had shared everything, talked about everything, and withheld nothing from each other. They kept no secrets except that the little old lady had a shoebox in the top of her closet that she requested her husband to never open or ask about. Over the years, the man had never thought about the shoebox, but one day his wife got sick and the doctor said she would not recover. In the process of sorting out their affairs, she asked her husband to take down the box and bring it to her bedside. When he opened it with her, he found two crocheted scarves, and a stack of money totaling $20,000.

He asked her about the contents. She explained, "When we were to be married, my grandmother told me that the secret to a happy marriage is to never argue. She told me that if I ever got angry with you, I should just keep quiet and crochet a scarf."

The old man was so moved that he had to fight back tears. Only two scarves were in the box. In all those years of living together, she had only been angry with him two times. He almost burst with happiness. He said to her, "Dear, that explains the scarves, but what about all of this money? Where did it come from?"

"Oh," she said, "that's the money I made from selling the scarves."

Paul adds to his admonition by quoting from Genesis 2: *"For this reason a man will leave his father and mother and be united to his wife, and the two will become one flesh"* (Eph. 5:31). In the Genesis story, no suitable counterpart could be found for Adam, so God put him into a deep sleep and created Eve from one of Adam's ribs. When he awoke, Adam said, *"This is now bone of my bones and flesh of my flesh; she shall be called 'woman,' for she was taken out of man"* (Gen. 2:23). Scripture records that upon their union, both Adam and Eve were naked and unashamed.

Unfortunately, for the first family it didn't remain this way forever. Satan sought to put a wedge between Adam and Eve by tempting Eve to eat the forbidden fruit. He knew that if he could get Eve to disobey God, it would force Adam to make a choice— Adam would have to choose between his wife and his Creator. Tragically, Adam chose the former and ate the fruit offered him. In so doing, he damaged his relationship with God, relinquished his authority over the earth, and was forced to leave paradise.

Adam sinned in that he gave in to Eve's lead. Husbands are to accommodate their wife's *need,* not their *lead.* God requires that our love for Him come before any other earthly relationship that we have. When we do this, it always makes us better husbands and fathers.

Paul employs the word *proskollao* when describing a man *uniting* or *cleaving* to his wife. This Greek word means to be completely inseparable, as if the two are glued or cemented together. In God's eyes, a husband and wife become one flesh. Though there is no marital status in heaven, the covenant of marriage is one that brings two people and two families together for eternity. Your marriage survives you. This means that even after you die, your DNA remains on this earth through your offspring and is perpetually passed down from generation to generation.

I took a position as an assistant coach with the Oakland Raiders in 2011. I really enjoyed working with the younger guys, and I found it rewarding helping them become better players and men. However, I'm not sure that I was prepared for the demands of the schedule. During the football season, the position called for seventeen-hour days with no time off other than a couple days during the bye week.

I discussed it with my wife, and on a good month we would have dinner together once or twice. Although she fully supported my work, I felt I should resign the position. I was grateful for the opportunity, but I felt that the rewards of the job were not worth the concessions I would have to make, namely, giving up time with my wife and kids. No amount of job security, money, or success was worth sacrificing my relationships.

I have learned that there is no substitute for quality time spent with my wife. Even if you have been married for many years, you cannot put your marriage on cruise control and expect it to survive. You may be the kindest husband on the planet and the best communicator in the world, but if you do not spend quality time with your wife and have consistent heart-to-heart conversations with her, you will end up losing her. I am still learning and growing in the area of vulnerability and sharing emotional intimacy. I now see it as essential to any dynamic and healthy relationship, and I strive to push through until it Is second nature to me. We all have areas we can improve in our relationships, but are you willing to identify those areas and work on them with all your heart?

Your marriage is like an oak tree growing in the middle of your living room. It is the center of your household, and its roots hold your entire family together. When it is thriving, it brings life to everything around it, especially your children. However, when it is dying, not even money, success, or your children can revive it. As your marriage goes, so goes the rest of your family. It has the ability to steer your kids in the right direction or drive them off the edge of a emotional cliff.

The single greatest thing you can do for your kids (other than lead them to Christ) is to love your wife, and let them see you demonstrate that love to her. Children understand love in two different ways: in how their parents love them, and in how their parents love each other. Your children need to see you being affectionate with your spouse and praising her in front of them. When children grow up in a home with a strong marriage, they are given the best foundation for a successful family of their own.

My high-school-aged daughter blessed me when she came downstairs the other night from doing her homework and asked us what all the raucous was about. My wife and I were laughing loudly and chasing each other around the center island of our kitchen. My daughter said her friends' parents were always fighting, but in our home her biggest problem was that we were too loud laughing and clowning around. I guess that's not the worse thing in the world.

Success in marriage is not so much about finding the right person but in being the right person. If you are unhappy in your marriage, it is not your wife's fault. No one can steal your happiness or choose to make you miserable. Happiness is yours to keep or to squander—the choice is yours. Happy marriages come from happy people, and the key to a happy marriage is by choosing to be happy being married.

A few years ago I bought a good book in the Christian bookstore that caught my eye called *The Power of a Praying Husband* by Stormie Omartian. I thought this was great and would tell me how to pray for my wife so that she would be molded into the woman God wants her to be. I was deeply convicted when I started reading and highlighting the book. The gist of the author's opening remarks said that if I bought this book hoping to make my spouse more of a woman of God, and if I wanted to see my kids and my home blessed of God, then I first needed to drop down on my knees and pray for myself. "What? Me, pray for myself?" I felt like returning the book.

I was convicted enough to keep reading, however, and as I did the truth became clear. If I wanted my wife to be more like Christ, my kids to walk with integrity, and my home to be blessed of God, then it all had to begin with me. I have to be the man, the husband, the father, and the child of God He wants for me before I can ever hope to see a Christ-natured change in my household—God has ordained that the husband be the spiritual leader in the home. If I want a strong marriage relationship with my wife, I need a strong and prayerful relationship with my heavenly Father.

Without exception I have found that when my relationship with God is at its strongest, my marriage is never stronger. It thrives, it is healthy, and it is vibrant. Perhaps this is because Christ loves the church so much. When a man is close to God's heart, Jesus empowers him to love and be the best husband, father, and son imaginable. Conversely, when my relationship with God is weak, my marriage always suffers as a result. Even though my wife is amazing, the times when I have been spiritually neutral and have run from God have sadly taken a toll on our marriage. My heart was deeply saddened when I recently asked my wife her thoughts about an edit for this book. She made a comment, and I quickly snapped at her in an ugly tone. She confessed that she didn't like talking about this book project with me, because when she does I get mean. Once again I allowed my frustration with this task to damage the best supporter I have in this life outside of God. Praise God that He and my wife still forgive idiots like me. If I were to die today, I would regret that I have not been the best husband God would intend me to be. After twenty-five years of marriage I am still learning from my mistakes and growing into being a better husband and spiritual leader in my home.

It is your responsibility to make your love for your bride a sacrificial priority, just as Jesus did for His bride. Don't allow your career, your hobbies, or even your kids' activities to take priority over your relationship with your spouse. When money or raising kids becomes a higher priority than our marriage, we run the risk of losing both our money and our children to divorce. Take time out of your busy schedule to spend time with your wife. Do something that she would enjoy. Work less. Be around more. Invest yourself emotionally. The reward will far outweigh the investment.

To Fathers: Do Not Provoke Your Children to Wrath

Fathers, do not provoke your children to anger by the way you treat them. Rather, bring them up with the discipline and instruction that comes from the Lord (Ephesians 6:4 NLT).

There is no role in modern society that suffers a greater attack or a pitiful neglect than that of a father. It was Billy Graham who said, "A good father is the one of the most unsung, unpraised, unnoticed, and yet one of the most valuable assets in our society."[1] Fathers are so instrumental and formative in our lives that God reveals Himself to us as a Father. Of all the needs of a child, none is greater than the need of a father, as George Herbert wrote, "One father is more than a hundred schoolmasters."[2]

From this verse in Ephesians, we learn that it is a father's responsibility to train and instruct the children, not the wife's. Too often we rely on the church, the school, or the university to educate and prepare our children for the future. However, they can't do our job for us, nor can they do it as well as we can. Any efforts from teachers or pastors should only supplement the discipleship that is already taking place in the home. It's when a man begins to impart wisdom to his children and teach them about life that he becomes keenly aware of what he *really* believes.

Paul cautions fathers to not be so harsh with their children that it provokes them to wrath and rouses them to rebellion. Children are not an aggravation; they are an adventure. We should be their advocates, not their adversaries. They deserve to be celebrated by finding the treasures hidden within their hearts. And it is on us to create a positive and healthy learning environment for them, a secure place for them to grow, learn, succeed, and fail. Our home should be like a high-wire walker's safety net. One day they will be an adult and move out on their own. When they fall (and they *will* fall), they won't have the benefit of our net to catch them, but if we have done our job well they will have the experience and the maturity to make the right choices with their lives.

Notice that Paul's antidote to heavy-handed fathering is a godly discipline and guidance. Parents exasperate their children by overdisciplining them or by a lack of discipline altogether. In a culture that preaches hands-off parenting, the call to properly discipline our sons and daughters is a refreshing reminder of our role as a father. If a parent's role in the life of their child is to merely be a placeholder for society, and that passing on to them our moral values hinders their individuality, then why did God make it so that every child must have a biological mother and father? This idea that a parents' role should be reduced to caregiver or advisory status is absurd and flies in the face of science.

Albeit not easy, disciplining your child is a worthy investment. It takes time, effort, and a stronger will than your child. Godly discipline looks more like love than anger, however. Its purpose is to teach a child how to have self-control, not to berate or belittle them. Well defined, loving, and fair boundaries give kids the sense of security and structure that they need early in life. Proverbs 22:6 says, *"Train up a child in the way he should go, and when he is old he will not depart from it"* (NKJV). Proper discipline is an important ingredient to the discipleship of your children. Determine to always be firm, fair, and consistent with them. Though a child may get sideways or even take a step backward for a few years, they can't outrun the Holy Spirit or escape the voice of your instruction.

Furthermore, Paul adds to this by instructing the children:

> *Children, obey your parents because you belong to the Lord, for this is the right thing to do. "Honor your father and mother." This is the first commandment with a promise: If you honor your father and mother, "things will go well for you, and you will have a long life on the earth"* (Ephesians 6:1-3 NLT).

Often the key to a man's relationship with God is in his relationship with his natural father. Men who have a healthy relationship with their father can more easily come to understand God as a Father. That goes for you and your sons as well. A wise father takes time to know his son, but an even wiser son takes the time to know his dad.

Do not demand that your children honor you. Rather, demand of yourself that you honor your parents, thereby teaching your kids to honor you by the example you set. We cannot expect our children to respect us if we do not respect our own father and mother. Kids follow our lead. When we honor our own fathers and mothers, and when we honor our wives, we are giving our children a demonstration on how we believe fathers and women should be treated. If you are concerned with the lack of honor shown to you or your wife, perhaps your children are not the problem. Be the kind of father the Bible describes, and in so doing you will set in motion the proper standards of living that bless your children for years to come.

Children are products of their environment. They are like mirrors that reflect our actions and our attitudes. They are no different than anyone else, just younger and more easily influenced. Like sponges, they soak up our words and yield what we sow into them. They learn integrity by witnessing it in us, they learn honesty from hearing it spoken from our lips, they learn humility by the way we carry ourselves, and they learn respect by seeing it demonstrated. Our sons will likely respect a woman in the same way we treat their mother, and our daughters often find their self-worth in our opinion of them. Your kids are watching you closer than you may think, and they will glean far more from *what* you do than from *what you tell* them to do. The best inheritance you can leave them is a good example.

Four Ways to Love Your Family

Lead

Men are leaders by nature. For better or for worse, voluntarily or involuntarily, you will influence others by the leadership you take and the way you live your life. The sooner you come to grips with this truth, the sooner you will become the man you are meant to be and the sooner you will change the world for the better.

We have the opportunity to lead our families down the road of righteousness. We are anointed to disciple them and lead them to the water of God's Word. We care for them when they are sick, carry them when they are injured, and lay down our preferences for theirs. We are the protector of their innocence and the provider of their confidence. We are husbands and we are fathers—this is what we do and this is who we are. We are not afraid to ward off the wolves that threaten the flock, and we won't desert them when the weather gets sketchy. The work of a shepherd is no joke. Neither is it for the faint of heart.

Too often men leave the spiritual leadership of the home to their wives. They let the woman take the lead in prayer, worship, church attendance, and family devotions. While women are certainly more than capable to lead the family in these ways, shirking our God-given role as spiritual leaders takes a devastating toll on our families and ultimately shoves them into a vulnerable corner. Our passivity forces our wives to make an unfair choice—to carry a spiritual load they are not designed to bear or to sit back and watch their family grow spiritually anemic. Our children also suffer in this process. It teaches them that dad is too weak to lead and leaves them left to decide if our words are even worth listening to.

My wife has been involved in leading women's Bible studies for many years. She reports to me that the top prayer request from the wives she ministers to is that their husbands would be the spiritual leader of the home. God is waiting for you to rise up and take your rightful place of leadership, and likely so is your family. If you would only just lead them to the cross, your wife and kids would willingly follow. It is not likely that your children will grow up to know and love God unless you teach them how. This teaching starts with developing a loving and thriving relationship with God on our own, and then it spills out onto them. We can't give someone directions to a destination we haven't been to ourselves.

Determine to lead your children spiritually and to lead them by example. It is not enough to follow your family to heaven. You must escort them there. Don't be the kind of man who drops his family off at church and then drives away. Light a torch, hold it high, and blaze the trail. A father who runs from his responsibility runs from his legacy, and we can't expect God to change our wives, our marriage, or our families until that change first comes to our own hearts.

When I speak of being a spiritual leader, I don't want to paint a picture of a man who is out of touch with reality. Too often we overspiritualize things. Ministry in your home might involve cleaning the kitchen, sharing your emotions honestly, or washing your wife's car. Men should be willing and able to change diapers, fold laundry, cook dinner, do the dishes, and sweep the floor when necessary. Being actively involved in sharing the responsibilities and workload of the home is a spiritual activity. I see no difference between serving your wife, serving your children, and serving in the local church. All can be legitimate acts of worship.

We tend to divide our lives into two areas: the sacred and the secular. We treat things like prayer and church attendance as sacred, while work and mowing the lawn are considered secular. But the Bible does not draw such a bold line. First Corinthians 10:31 teaches, *"Whatever you do, do it all for the glory of God."* When we offer worship to God, the areas of our lives that seem unspiritual undergo a spiritual transformation and are raised to the level of the sacred. By doing this, every activity of our life can be an act of worship.

A. W. Tozer calls this the sacrament of living. He writes:

> Let us practice the fine art of making every work a priestly ministration. To say this is not to bring all acts down to one dead level; it is rather to lift every act up into a living kingdom and turn the whole life into a sacrament. It does not mean that everything we do is of equal importance with everything else we do or may do. It is not what a man does that determines whether his work is sacred or secular; it is *why* he does it.[3]

Helping your wife clean up around the house truly can be an act of worship. Disciplining your children is a spiritual exercise. Getting up early to earn a living and put food on the table is a godly and righteous pursuit. This is what it means to lead.

Serve

Servant leadership is touted by some as the latest and greatest leadership style among business executives, but it is actually a concept that comes straight out of the Bible:

> *Jesus called them together and said, "You know that the rulers of the Gentiles lord it over them, and their high officials exercise authority over them. Not so*

with you. Instead, whoever wants to become great among you must be your servant, and whoever wants to be first must be your slave—just as the Son of Man did not come to be served, but to serve, and to give His life a ransom for many (Matthew 20:25-28).

Jesus's life modeled what it means to be a servant leader. He came to serve, not to be served; He came to give, not to receive. In this passage Jesus contrasts two opposing leadership styles: *rulers* and *servants*. Rulers are here-I-am leaders who lord it over people by exercising their authority and demand that their needs be met by those they govern. For rulers, the arrow always points in. When they walk into a room, it's, "Here I am!" Servants, however, are there-you-are leaders. They feel an obligation to serve the needs of the people they lead. For servants, the arrow always points out. When they walk into a room, it's, "There you are!"

Being a leader is not the same thing as being controlling, for there is a fundamental difference between taking charge and taking control. The controlling man is not really a leader at all. He is a dictator. His word is law, and he rules his kingdom with an iron fist. No one dares spend money, make a decision, or challenge him without his knowledge or permission. He commands obedience, bullies his wife, intimidates his children, keeps a death grip on the checkbook, stacks the cards in his favor, and is a master manipulator.

Some men think that by controlling their wives they can keep them in check, or that they can gain leverage with their children by barking out threats and commands at them. The truth of the matter is that you are not leading your family when you control them. Rather, you are suppressing them. Servant leaders, on the contrary, lead with unselfish motives, not self-seeking ambition. They serve the ones they lead instead of demanding their servitude. Though humble, they are far from passive. They are not afraid to take charge and lead the way. They roll up their sleeves and get to work, and they don't ask people to do something that they themselves are not willing to do.

A servant leader can embrace correction because they are confident and secure in who they are. When another person is more gifted then they are, they are not threatened by it. Instead, they seek to encourage them and empower them even if it means losing status or being replaced. Servant leaders quite simply are willing to serve a cause greater than themselves and, in so doing, they serve the ones they lead.

Over the course of my athletic career, I was exposed to a number of good leaders, but none greater than the example set by University of Michigan Head Coach Jim Harbaugh. Before coaching at Michigan, and the San Francisco 49ers, Jim Harbaugh was the head coach at Stanford University, and I was privileged to be apart of his coaching staff. He hired me to be an offensive assistant prior to the 2010 season, and I watched him courageously mentor and inspire young men in an amazing fashion. Prior to Jim's arrival, Stanford was the doormat of the Pac-10 with only one win and an average margin of defeat of twenty-eight points. After four seasons he transformed that team into being a national powerhouse with a record of 12–1 and a mindset that they could defeat any challenger, anytime and anywhere. He did what many people thought was impossible all while maintaining a high code of conduct and academic standards.

I learned far more from him and his staff than I contributed. In fact, I learned a great deal just by witnessing his style of servant leadership. Without a doubt, he is a take-charge, what-you-see-is-what-you-get kind of leader. There is no hypocrisy or pretense with Coach Harbaugh. He is as genuine as they come. He is not one to pander to the media or cave in to popular opinion. Whether addressing the team, the staff, the media, or a parent, he was the same man in every situation. Anyone who knows him knows that he's a true competitor who doesn't accept defeat easily, and his players tend to take on the same discipline and toughness that he possesses.

Once I was doing the monotonous task of emptying scouting binders and refilling them with new weekly reports. Seeing that I was buried in the conference room in offensive binders, he jumped in to lend a helping hand. I told him, "You don't have to help me, Coach." He responded, "Hey, we're all in this together," then he proceeded to fill them faster than me until the job was completed. And this happened on more than one occasion.

I watched him frequently jump in and run the scout team, which is usually a position for the youngest and lowest tenured coaches. Holding up cards and setting the huddle, he instructed the freshman in what they needed to do to give a good look to the defense. When the team traveled, we would leave from a private terminal so the team buses could pull up on the tarmac and get close to the airplane. The support staff, of which I was apart of, was given the task of carrying all the luggage and equipment to and from the cargo loading area by hand. It was a sweaty and sometimes smelly job as we lugged several bags at a time past the hot jet blast of the engines. With the players and coaches comfortably seated on the plane, it was not uncommon for Jim to be one of the first to help organize the equipment on the ground. No job was beneath him, and seeing him jump in to serve further inspired me and the rest of the team to do our part even better.

I was impressed with the way he took time to help others, even though head coaches rarely have any free time during the season. Once he had heard about a young man who was paralyzed from an off-road vehicle accident. He was a high school quarterback and had been brought to Stanford Medical Center. When Jim heard the story, he said instantly, "We have to go see him. Let's go, Wiz. I'll get the golf cart."

I balked, "Coach, I have to get cards ready for practice today."

He replied, "That can wait. This is more important."

He made a number of visits across campus to visit that young man, and he had players stop in just to say hello. Jim is just like that—never too busy to help someone in need and never looking for personal attention or praise.

Whether it's the life of Jim Harbaugh or Jesus, an effective servant leader is courageous, decisive, and compassionate, willing to make the right decisions even when they are unpopular. These kinds of leaders set an example that others willingly follow. In the primary language of Ghana, the only way to ask, "What is your religion?" is by saying "Whom do you serve?" The assumption is that everyone must serve someone. We tend to elevate people based on their gifts, but God elevates people based on servanthood. I encourage you to dig down deep and ask yourself, "Who am I serving? God? My family? Or myself?"

Bless

Men are environmentalists in this way: we create the climate and the atmosphere of our homes. We are thermostats, not thermometers. We don't just read the temperature, but we actually set it. Through our attitudes, behavior, and our words, we set the tone for our households. This means that your words are more powerful than you give them credit. Through them you can shape the world around you. Your tongue actually has the ability to build your wife up or tear her down, to bless or curse your children. Every situation you face together with your family is an opportunity to speak life and destiny over them. I'm convinced our home life would be much more peaceful if men could display as much patience with their kids as they do when they are fishing. Jesus said:

> *The good man brings good things out of the good stored up in him, and the evil man brings evil things out of the evil stored up in him. But I tell you that men will have to give account on the day of judgment for every careless word they have spoken. For by your*

*words you will be acquitted, and by your words you
will be condemned* (Matthew 12:35-37).

Great coaches know when to praise, when to critique, and
when to simply give a pat on the back. I've seen it played out dozens of times. A player gets cut or traded and leaves a team dejected
and doubting his ability to even play the game. Next thing you
know he has a breakout season with a new team. What happened?
Often it's a coach that takes the time to develop a connection and
a relationship with that player. He speaks words of affirmation
and shows that he believes in him. With a few slight modifications
to his game and a boost in confidence, the player's performance
greatly improves.

Players will tell you that success in professional sports is largely
mental. Everyone has talent or they wouldn't be there in the first
place. But it is those with the mental perseverance to push through
the pain and pressures of the game who become the great ones.

You are the coach of your home, and it is your job to redeem
your wife and instill confidence in your children. Your goal is to
maximize their gifts to their fullest potential and to help them
fulfill their destiny in Christ. For better or for worse, your wife
and your kids will become what you envisioned they could and
would become.

I recently spoke to an auditorium full of teenagers at a school
assembly. Illustrating the power of our words, I asked for two vol-
unteers from the audience. Both were given a tube of toothpaste
and instructed that this would be a race to see who could completely empty the tube the fastest. The young audience cheered
in anticipation as we counted down the start of the race. In the
frenzy, the toothpaste came squirting out all over the tarp I had
laid down, and we all cheered the victorious sixth grader.

After the cheering had stopped and I restored order, I told
them that the toothpaste represents the words we speak. Sometimes we don't think carefully, and we just spit things out that

could be hurtful to others. Cleaning up the mess is usually a sticky, humbling, and a laborious job. I then informed them the race was not yet over: they were to see who could put the toothpaste back in the tube the fastest. The kids looked at me with bewilderment as I said, "Go!" They quickly discovered that it was next to impossible to get the toothpaste back in the tube, and after a few minutes they gave up trying.

The words we speak are like a fountain of spewed toothpaste. Once we speak them, it is nearly impossible to take them back. We must be especially careful and intentional about what we say to our wives and children. You and I can have a supernatural influence on those around us if we simply purpose to speak blessings to them on a daily basis. Prayers and words of kindness are two of the most effective weapons we can use to squash contention and squelch anger in our homes.

You can practice speaking blessings to your spouse and your children on a daily basis. Pray for your family, pray *over* your family, and pray *with* your family. It may sound cheesy but it's true: the family who prays together stays together. And never let a day go by without giving them a hug and telling them that you love them.

Defend

There once was a thief who masterminded a unique way to rob a local department store. The robber entered the store as a customer and, unbeknownst to the management, secretly rearranged the price tags on some of the items. The most expensive items were swapped with the lesser expensive items. What was of high value was now grossly discounted and what was cheap was overpriced. The thief was able to walk out the front door having looted the store for just pennies on the dollar.

The enemy uses this strategy with our priorities. If he can get away with it, he will leave us confused as to what is really important in life. The precious becomes underappreciated and what

FAMILY

is of little importance is overinflated in our minds. Soon we are concerned with trivial pursuits like image and bravado and the pursuit of material possessions. When these take precedence over our family, it leaves them vulnerable and susceptible to attack. The enemy easily steals our valuables without a fight because we were too busy guarding the petty (see John 10:10).

Don't let the thief steal what is valuable to you by getting you distracted with the trivial, the urgent, or the convenient. Guarding your home and defending your family is not just a physical exercise—it is a spiritual one as well. Guard your time and your heart connection with your family. Walk through your home and remove anything that could defile you, your wife, or your children. Walk around your property line and pray for God's blessing on your family members and possessions. Play Christian music throughout your house, and contend for the spiritual atmosphere over your household.

Primary Receivers

Your family should not be treated like they are third string. They are the starters you are molding to get the job done. Jesus taught us to love God and to love one another, and who is one another? First and foremost, they are those who are closest to you. Your family should be the primary receivers of your love. You are the coach, and your home is your practice field. It is the place where you put into motion all that you have acquired from your previous instructors and pastors. If I can't love those I see on a daily basis, how can I love God whom I can't see? If I can't even take care of my own family, how could I ever think I can take care of God's family?

The famous missionary C.T. Studd once said, "The light that shines the farthest shines brightest at nearest home."[4] This means that your influence in the world must begin with your influence with your family. You cannot push back against the darkness and export a love to the lost that you are not putting into practice within the confines of your own home. In fact, one of the biblical qualifications for ministry is that a man must be able to manage his own household well (see 1 Tim. 3:2-5).

A young man recently approached me and asked for a letter of recommendation to attend seminary. Knowing his marriage and home life were in shambles, and knowing how he had miserably shirked his responsibility as a spiritual leader, I replied, "Not a chance." I love good preaching, and I have no doubt that he could preach well. Being a pastor or missionary is an admirable aspiration, but I don't want to hear someone teach me the truths of God's Word if they aren't following the very basics of shepherding their family in the home.

Do you desire to be in ministry? Do you want to be a missionary? If prayer and instruction are not taking place under your roof at home, then you are not qualified to take it elsewhere. You will merely be teaching an impersonal and inexperienced theory, and your message will have zero impact. If you consider yourself a Christian minister and cannot take loving care of your own household, you, my friend, are a fraud.

The Extra Point

Men, it's time to restore our home field advantage. If you don't lead your family, who will? That honor may fall to those on social media, the Internet, the public school system, the video game industry, a drug dealer, gang member, Hollywood or some other ungodly influence. In our quest to win the world, let it not be said of us that we lost our family in the process. You can achieve and attain this high call of God. When our time is up and we stand before the Lord, may it be said of us that while we may not have done it all perfectly, we did it sacrificially and gave our best to those we were called to love.

FAMILY

Chalk Talk

1. Are you comfortable spiritually leading your family? What proactive measures are you taking or can take to meet and serve their spiritual needs?

2. What does it mean to love your spouse like Christ loved the church? How did Christ love the church? To the married or those in a relationship, are you following this biblical model?

3. As a spouse, father, or employer, would you willingly follow someone who exhibits your characteristics and style of leadership? What does it mean to be a true servant leader? How can you improve on being a servant leader in your home, work, or school?

4. How does God define marriage, and why it so important to Him? What proactive steps can you take to improve your marriage? In terms of your marriage relationship, what is one of the most powerful things you can do to bless your children?

5. Discuss your role in the lead–serve–bless–defend model for Christian leadership in the home. Where do you feel challenged and in what areas are you doing well? What things have you learned from this chapter?

6. Are you regularly and purposefully speaking blessings into the life of your loved ones? Do you need to ask forgiveness for harsh or misplaced words spoken out of anger or frustration?

7. Do you see the importance of making your family the primary recipients of your love and spiritual shepherding? They are your primary mission field. Ask the Lord

FAMILY

to empower you to lead courageously and with a compassionate and tender heart. No matter the fatherly example you had, lean into Him, who is your heavenly Father, for guidance and grace. Perhaps doing the dishes tonight is of greater benefit than preparing a sermon.

Endnote

1.   Christian Quotes, http://christianquotes.taberstruths.com/christian-quotes-about-fathers/, accessed February 19, 2015.

2.   Ibid.

3.   A. W. Tozer, *The Pursuit Of God*, (Christian Publications, Inc. Camp Hill, PA 1993) 117–128.

4.   Goodreads, https://www.goodreads.com/quotes/805699-the-light-that-shines-farthest-shines-brightest-nearest-home, accessed 3/10/2015

SUCCESS

CHAPTER 11

THE APPLAUSE OF HEAVEN

*Today I will do what others won't, so tomorrow
I can accomplish what others can't.*

—JERRY RICE

"If I don't finish this race, I'm not coming home!" I snapped at my wife on the other end of the line. "I will crawl across that finish line if I have to!" Abruptly I said good-bye and hung up the phone. It was not the most shining moment in my career as a husband. My wife had simply called to wish me well on the eve of my race and to lovingly remind me "not to overdo it, as I had nothing to prove." In retrospect I should have been much more appreciative and kind. I was admittedly on edge and my unscripted response was short, but I had everything to prove. Regardless of my time or the risk of injury, I was determined to somehow find a way to finish this race. I *had* to finish it. And I knew I would finish it—failure was not an option.

It was May of 1997, and I was in Olympia, Washington, for the Capital City Marathon. I had just turned 30 and was coming off my eighth season in the NFL. Several months prior to that, I got inspired to challenge myself beyond anything I thought I was capable of. Defying my coaches, teammates, and agent's best advice, I decided to train for and run a full marathon during the off-season. It would be my first attempt ever at running 26.2 miles. I didn't know of any other active NFL offensive lineman who had ever attempted that feat, so it was the perfect challenge. For an offensive lineman, distance is usually measured in yards, not miles.

It was probably not the wisest way to prolong an NFL career or to let my body heal in preparation for another grueling football season. My strength coach Garrett Giemont tried to talk me out of it, but when it became obvious there was no dissuading me, he decided to join me. He was turning 40 that year and had run a few marathons himself, so he decided to train me how to run without injuring myself. He was true to his word and ran the marathon with me, but so as not to interfere with my personal experience he ran at his own (and much faster) pace.

The day of the race came, and I experienced more butter-flies than during a big playoff game. I could barely speak or even keep down my breakfast of a bagel, oatmeal, and half a banana. Thousands of runners moved to the starting line. At 277 pounds, I felt like an elephant in a rat race. Even though I had lost over forty pounds in four months of training and was quite lean for an NFL lineman, I was still enormous compared to the other run-ners. Around the Raider facility I tried to hide my weight loss by wearing two thick sweatshirts, but it was becoming obvious to everyone. My teammates teased me by saying that I looked like I was suffering from rickets.

I was amazed at the diversity of runners gathered that day. All body types, ages, and demographics were represented—young, old, men, women, children, fit, fat, and everything in between. I inched forward as the shot was fired, and we were off like a slow moving sea of polyester. Steps became yards, and yards became miles. Mile after mile, hour after hour, I kept my pace. I started with a smile. I laughed. I sang. I prayed along the way and even cried as I approached the twenty-one-mile mark, which was my previous longest distance.

The pain really started to settle in at this point. I forced myself to walk when I got to the aid stations to drink water, but quickly returned to a slow trot. I witnessed people around me fall to the ground from cramps, exhaustion, and dehydration. I felt my calves tighten and pain run up my shins, but I was determined to stay the course. Five miles to go, then four, three, two, and then one. Triumph was only a few football fields away. As I came down the stretch, Garrett appeared. He had doubled back to run the last several hundred yards with me. I pushed through each pounding step and accelerated through the finish line with my hands in the air and a smile on my face.

When I reached the finish line, my body was numb. My clothes were permanently stained from dried sweat and snot. My eyes were blurred from salt and tears, but I had never felt more alive as I did in that moment. I felt as though I had accomplished something great. It took me over five hours to cross the finish line. I didn't break any records, and no one in particular took notice, but in my heart I felt like a champion. "Thank You, Jesus," I uttered, grateful that my foolishness hadn't killed me. It was the best sense of personal achievement I have ever felt in my athletic career.

Football is a team sport where a number of individual battles and strategic decisions determine the outcome of the game. But running is a different animal altogether. It is intensely personal. No one can run a race for you, and it's up to every runner to overcome his or her own personal challenges and limitations.

Finishing that marathon for me was symbolic for a couple rea-sons. First, it taught me to *tune into* the voice of God and *tune out* the voice of the naysayers. What was outlandish and outrageous to some became outstanding to me. Second, it showed me that anything was possible with God, and that I possessed the kind of persevering faith to see a project through to the end. I now thought of myself as an overcomer, not a quitter, and I learned that I had the fortitude within me to push through pain and dis-comfort to achieve any goal.

The Bible uses the analogy of a long-distance runner to paint a picture of our faith walk:

> *Do you know that in a race all the runners run, but only one gets the prize? Run in such a way to get the prize. Everyone who competes in the games goes into strict training. They do it to get a crown that will not last; but we do it to get a crown that will last forever. Therefore, I do not run like a man running aimlessly; I do not fight like a man beating the air. No, I beat my body and make it my slave so that after I have preached to others, I myself will not be disqualified for the prize* (1 Corinthians 9:24-27).

Racers run the race in order to win, and the exhortation here is that if we are going to claim Christ and take up the Christian life, then we should run it to win it. Entry does not guarantee victory. Many start out strong in their Christian journey, but not all put forth the necessary discipline, effort, and perseverance to win the prize. No one can run this race for you, and a halfhearted effort will not do. Success demands maximum effort.

If you feel like you have already failed God and dropped out of the race, the good news is that your marathon is not yet over. There is still time left to dust yourself off and get back in the race. Not all of us start out so well in life, but it's not how you begin but how you finish that matters. If you run well, if you are consistent in your walk with Christ, persistent in your pursuit of God, and exercise mastery over yourself, you will not fail. You will finish strong. And your prize will not be an earthly or temporal wreath, but an eternal and victorious crown. Your prize will be the high call of God in Christ Jesus.

Defining Success

Success can be defined in so many different ways. When we think of a great leader, teacher, entertainer, artist, athlete, or entrepreneur, what makes them accomplished? We could come up with a list of qualities found in successful men and start trying to emulate them and incorporate those qualities into our lives, but we would be wasting our time. We'd be asking the wrong questions. Before we can ask what makes a person great or successful, we must first answer, what is success? If we fail to answer this question first, we will tragically find ourselves chasing after something we think is success only to be terribly disillusioned once we achieve it.

Success is often found in the eye of the beholder. To some it is starting their own business, running a Fortune 500 company, or achieving their career and financial goals. Success for an athlete might be winning a gold medal, being inducted into the Hall of Fame, or becoming a household name. To a musician it could be signing their first record deal or seeing their name in lights. To some success is buying a vacation home or retiring young. To others it's simply survival—just getting by and making enough money to pay the bills each month.

Success to me on that day was crossing the finish line. The fact that I was able to finish the race with a smile on my face and still walk upright was a legitimate accomplishment for me. I was so happy that I wore the cheap finishers medal I received around my neck the next day and on the flight home. Walking through the airport, I must have looked like a 277-pound fifth grader who just won his first spelling bee.

How do you define success? Do you judge your success in light of the pace and body weight of the other runners around you? Is success all about being first—first class, first rate, first string, or first place? Do you define success in terms of the amount of possessions you own, the kind of car you drive, the size of your portfolio, the position you hold, or the clout you have among your friends? Those might all be notable personal achievements, but do you ever wonder if there is more to success than this?

Not everyone can have their own Hollywood star or live the lifestyle of the rich and famous. Raising a child to be a respectful and honorable member of society is truly a success. Celebrating a golden anniversary and leaving behind an inheritance for your children is a success. The vast majority of the people in the world will never be rich, famous, or celebrated by the masses. Are they unsuccessful?

Life has a way of coming into better focus as we age. Sitting in a Roman prison cell and approaching death, Paul reflects:

> *I have fought the good fight, I have finished the race, I have kept the faith. Now there is in store for me the crown of righteousness, which the Lord, the righteous Judge, will award to me on that day—and not only to me, but also to all who have longed for His appearing* (2 Timothy 4:7-8).

Paul's notion of success was not fame, fortune, or prestige. It was fighting the good fight, finishing the race, keeping the faith. It is liberating and a little terrifying to learn that earthly success is no guarantee of heavenly success. Eternal success is not based on comparative peer status or what society thinks of us. It is solely found in the eyes of God. Roger Staubach said, "Winning isn't getting ahead of others. It's getting ahead of yourself." For Paul, success wasn't luxurious living or being better than the next guy. It was living life faithfully and finishing strong, hearing the applause of heaven.

Be encouraged to know that heaven's definition of success is vastly different than society's definition. We think in terms of prosperity while God thinks in terms of humility. We focus on the destination, but He focuses on the journey. We look at material wealth while He looks at spiritual capital. For us it's about what we accomplish, but to Him it is about who we become and how we live.

In the framework of my Christian faith, my personal definition of success is to know God and be known by Him; to be fully submitted to Him and to live in the center of His will. With all my abilities, talents, and treasures, I want to give God glory for my entire life. If I can accomplish this, I will be a successful man.

Public Success, Private Failure

In my second season with the Los Angeles Raiders, we reached the 1990 AFC championship and were matched up against the high-octane Buffalo Bills. We went 12–4 that year and locked horns with a tough Bills team that secured home field advantage by going 13–3. A record-breaking 80,324 fans filled Buffalo's Rich Stadium to watch one team be crowned AFC champion and advance to Super Bowl XXV in Tampa.

It was a game I remember all too well, though it was not a game to remember. We experienced one bad bounce after another, and before you knew it we were down 21–3 in the first quarter. Bills quarterback Jim Kelly and his talented band of merry men in Thurman Thomas and James Lofton couldn't be slowed. At one point Kelly dropped back to pass and slipped on the icy turf for what appeared to be a certain sack. Before any defenders could reach him, however, he bounced back on his feet, scrambled a few steps, and threw a beautiful touchdown pass to James Lofton. By halftime we were down 41–3.

During the game I was running around like a madman hitting anything that moved. On the sidelines, I found myself playing the role of motivator and pumping up my teammates. As we went into the locker room at halftime, I told the guys, "Hey, they scored forty-one in the first half. We can score forty-one in the second. Let's start with getting one and go from there." It would not happen. I'm glad I'm not a gambler, because going into it I was absolutely certain we were going to win that game. Win we did not, and it wasn't even close. It was brutal. We went on to lose by a humiliating score of 51–3.

Success is not always how we envision it to be. Yet neither is defeat. Perhaps you feel beat up by life. Circumstances have dealt you a devastating blow, bulldozing your dreams and fracturing your vision. Maybe you can't find a job you're qualified for. Your boss is unreasonable or your retirement account is nonexistent. Perhaps you've been ridiculed, passed over, and unappreciated by your colleagues. Your friendships are strained, and you're just trying to hold your family together. You've invested your time and hard-earned money but with little return. You question if your ship will ever come in. None of this for a single moment should ever make you feel unsuccessful. Setbacks are not the measure of your success. Rather, it is how you respond to life's setbacks that determine your success. Vince Lombardi said, "It's not whether you get knocked down, it's whether you get up."

To the Corinthians, Paul outlines the not-so-glamorous life of an apostle. He speaks of hardships, troubles, tribulations, distresses, beatings, imprisonments, riots, sleepless nights, and empty stomachs:

> *Through glory and dishonor, bad report and good report; genuine, yet regarded as impostors; known, yet regarded as unknown; dying, and yet we live on;*

beaten, and yet not killed; sorrowful, yet always rejoic-
ing; poor, yet making many rich; having nothing, and
yet possessing everything (2 Corinthians 6:8-10).

By all accounts Paul's life at the time seemed like a miserable failure. He forfeited his path to position when he chose to follow Christ. He left his countrymen to minister to the Gentiles, suffered much for the gospel, and died an early death at the hands of Nero. But why are we are still quoting him today? It's because he *had nothing yet possessed everything.* This might be our best definition of success yet.

In my over twenty-five years of playing and coaching, I've gotten to know some famous people and have been privileged to meet men from every corner of the country and from every walk of life. What I've come to realize is that whether a man is venerated or vilified, social status does not make a man what he is. A panhandler on the street is no less of a man than one walking around in a three-piece suit. Men have different lots in life, and we all have to face similar struggles, trials, victories, and defeats.

For this reason I'm not star struck by celebrities. I've never been one to seek out an autograph or look to take my picture with a well-known personality. I've observed those whom people idolize. Some are truly wonderful people while others are scumbags. Some are committed to their teammates and their families, while others merely to their image. It is a little disappointing when you meet a celebrity whose values are the polar-opposite of Paul's brand of success. Instead of having nothing yet possessing everything, it seems they *have everything yet possess nothing.*

Beware of becoming a public success and a private failure. Just because you are successful before others doesn't mean you are successful before God. Our goal is to succeed both in our public and private lives, but there can be no lasting public success without consistent private victories. For this reason I would advise you to focus less on public success and give more attention to private victory. When we do, two positive things will happen: first, our public setbacks will not affect our private success, and second, public success will eventually find us.

Though it stung in the moment, I can look back now and laugh at the playoff loss to the Buffalo Bills. Though a public setback, it was not a private failure. The loss would not define me or the careers of any of my teammates.

You've Got Talent

The Bible has much to say about achieving lasting success. In the parable of the talents, Jesus tells the story of three servants who were entrusted with a delegated sum of money while their master was away (see Matt. 25:14-30). This large sum of money, called a talent, was equivalent to about fifteen years of wages for a day laborer.[1] The implication was that the three servants were to conduct business with the money while the master was gone. To one was given five talents, to another two talents, and to a third was given one talent.

After a long absence, the master returned from his journey and settled accounts with his servants. The one who had been entrusted with five talents presented to the master ten, reporting that he had doubled his master's money. The master was pleased and said, "Well done, good and faithful servant! You have been faithful with a few things; I will put you in charge of many things. Come and share in your master's happiness!" Likewise, the second doubled his sum and the master rewarded him similarly.

The third servant came to the master and said, "I knew you were a hard man, harvesting where you have not sown and gathering where you have not scattered seed. So I was afraid and went out and hid your talent in the ground. See, here is what belongs to you."

The upset master replied, "You wicked, lazy servant! So you knew that I harvested where I have not sown and gather where I have not scattered seed? Well then, you should have put my money on deposit with the bankers, so that when I returned I would have received it back with interest." He then ordered this man's portion be given to the one who was most profitable and that he be kicked off his property and cast out into the darkness. This story helps bring God's definition of success into better focus. Let's define success from this parable.

1. Success Makes Good Investments

The master encouraged his servants to make wise investments and expected them to be profitable. The most important investments a man can make are not financial but spiritual. The goal of your life is not to *live* it and *spend* it. Rather, the goal is to *invest* it. This parable teaches that success is defined by how well we invest the life we have been entrusted with.

We exist to glorify God, and we demonstrate our love for Him by depositing love into others. Godly success is not evidenced by experiences, accomplishments, or possessions. It is better evidenced in what we give and leave behind. The notion that life is merely a roller-coaster ride of reckless living and that we should go to our graves used up, screaming, "What a ride!" is an irresponsible way to live. It is the duty of every man to make himself profitable and useful to those around him.

There is a saying that says, "Money is like manure—good for nothing when heaped up but useful when spread around." The same could be said of our God-given gifts and talents. What we withhold we lose, and what we give away we keep for eternity. The man who goes through life having left no contribution of love and having not made the world a better place has wasted his potential.

2. Success Is Faithfulness

Jesus's story paints a stark contrast between the faithful and the unfaithful. The difference between the profitable and unprofitable servants was fidelity. The unfaithful servant devalued what the master had delegated to him. He was untrustworthy with what he was entrusted with and treated it like refuse. The faithful servants, however, were good stewards of what had been assigned to them. Even though the talents belonged to their master, they cared for them as if they were their own. The reward for their faithfulness was promotion and exaltation.

What you have been given, whether great or insignificant, is God-given. Do not devalue it. God has plans to promote and exalt you, and He is observing the degree of faithfulness you display with what He has already entrusted to you. Make it your aim to show Him that you are a good investment. Take personal responsibility for the duties you have been given. Don't think of faithfulness as a quality that will make you more successful. Think of faithfulness as success.

3. Success Wears a Hard Hat

The context of this parable is linked to the previous parable about being prepared for the return of Christ. How can one ready themselves for that day? I can assure you that spiritual readiness is not sitting around waiting for God to show up and do something on your behalf. Readiness is being responsibly active and producing the kind of results that God can see and approve of. In a similar parable, the instruction to the servants was to *"occupy until I come"* (Luke 19:13 KJV). Spiritual work is what keeps you occupied and prepared for the coming of the Master.

Contrary to what you might have been told, work is not a consequence of the fall of man. Before sin entered the world, Adam had a job assignment: *"The Lord God took the man and put him in the Garden of Eden to work it and take care of it"* (Gen. 2:15). Among other things, Adam was to manage the garden and name the animals. When you think of the size of the animal kingdom, Adam must have put in some long days completing that job.

Successful men understand that work is neither a chore nor a curse. It is a blessing and is good for the soul. The dictionary is the only place where success comes before work. Think of a garden for a moment. If success is the harvest, work is the seed. The success of your tomorrows depends on the work of your today. The more you can see life through this lens, the more purposeful and enjoyable work of any kind will be for you.

The bumper sticker that reads, "I owe, I owe, so off to work I go," misses the original design of men and work. Men work to provide for their loved ones, but also because it pleases God. Scripture says, *"Whatever you do, work at it with all your heart, as working for the Lord, not for men, since you know that you will receive an inheritance from the Lord as a reward. It is the Lord Christ you are serving"* (Col. 3:23-24). And the book of Exodus says, *"Six days you shall labor and do all your work, but the seventh day is a Sabbath to the Lord your God"* (Exod. 20:9-10). Just as we take pleasure in rest, we can take pleasure in our work too.

Remember that *what* you do for a living is not as important as *how* you do it. And it is the attitude with which you go about your work that is most noteworthy to God. The famous college football coach Lou Holtz once remarked, "Your talent determines what you can do. Your motivation determines how much you are willing to do. Your attitude determines how well you do it."

If you drive a truck, care for your load and your rig as if they belong to God. If you are a soldier, recognize that God is your highest commanding officer, and you are in His army and represent Him. If you are an athlete, compete as if God is your coach and take that winning attitude to the field. I had the ultimate respect for opposing players who modeled Christ and pulverized their opponents. Their competitiveness demanded my respect and their work ethic testified of their faith. If done before God, your workplace can be a place of worship and your work ethic a positive witness to those around you. The original disciples were men who held various jobs in the marketplace. They were tradesmen, shepherds, tent makers, tax collectors, fisherman, and doctors. They were not the professional clergymen of their time, yet Jesus chose men who held everyday occupations to change the world.

The master accused the unprofitable servant of being wicked and lazy. At times men can be lazy, but I have found most men to be hard-working. The question this parable raises is not, will we labor? but, are we willing to labor for someone else's gain? The faithful servants worked hard for their master's benefit regardless of the rewards.

You are probably diligent when it comes to personal gain, but how about when there is seemingly nothing in it for you? The great news is that God promises to reward our labors. We have much at stake and much to gain, but that should not be our strongest motivating factor. Successful people are industrious regardless of who gets the spoils or the credit.

Jesus said, *"Seek first the kingdom of God and His righteousness, and all these things shall be added to you"* (Matt. 6:33 NKJV). The *"all these things"* is a reference to the very things that men work for—food, clothing, shelter, tools, and the basic necessities of life. Jesus's encouragement is that when we seek God's kingdom above our own interests, He is faithful to give us all that we need in this life and in the life to come. By being about His business, we are communicating that we trust Him to be about ours. It also gives Him permission to work on our behalf. If you will consciously make God's business your priority, He will see to it that your interests are His priority.

No servant in this parable started out empty-handed. The fact that each man was given something means that you and I have a God-ordained assignment to fulfill on this planet, and each of us has something to give and to invest into the lives of others.

4. *Success Never Stops Growing*

When God gifted you, He did not give you a fully mature gift. He gave you a gift in seed form. Within that gift is the potential for

SUCCESS

exponential growth, but that growth is up to you. Maturity is your responsibility, not God's. Gifts do not grow in a vacuum. They bloom *when* they are planted and they mature with use. The more you step out in your God-given gifts, the more you will step into them. Neither football nor public speaking came naturally to me. Both of those skill sets had to be cultivated and put into practice for many years before I flowed in that gifting.

The wicked servant buried his talent, but the profitable servants *planted* theirs, and they yielded a return on their master's investments. Burying and planting may appear similar, but there is a completely different motive behind each. Burying is a ritual of death; planting an activity of life. Burying brings about decomposition, but planting spawns reproduction.

When a person buries something, they leave it in the ground and forget about it. They neither water it nor care for it. Burying may, in fact, preserve something, but it also prevents it from developing. Planting, on the other hand, involves risk and maintenance. The purpose of planting is not for safekeeping but growth. While it requires care and upkeep, the potential for increase is endless. A farmer knows that one way to protect his seed is to sow it and allow it to yield a harvest.

We are all compelled to do something with what we have been given, and it's through application that we achieve multiplication. Rewards are given to us not based on what we have but what is made of what we have. Whether it's teaching, giving, singing, writing, encouraging, fixing, healing, leading, or praying, a gift that is sown will always increase. It's when we don't use it that we tend to lose it.

This analogy of bearing fruit is found elsewhere in Scripture. Jesus said, *"I chose you and appointed you to go and bear fruit— fruit that will last"* (John 15:16). And He said in another place:

> *Do people pick grapes from thorn bushes, or figs from thistles? Likewise every good tree bears good fruit,*

but a bad tree bears bad fruit. A good tree cannot bear bad fruit, and a bad tree cannot bear good fruit. Every tree that does not bear good fruit is cut down and thrown into the fire. Thus, by their fruit you will recognize them (Matthew 7:16-20).

And in the Book of Galatians Paul speaks of the fruit of the Spirit, saying there is no law against *"love, joy, peace, patience, kindness, goodness, faithfulness, gentleness and self-control"* (Gal. 5:22-23).

Success in God's kingdom comes by bearing good fruit. When we receive Christ, the Word of truth is planted like a seed deep in our spirit. The Holy Spirit tills the soil of our heart and prepares us for growth. His presence photosynthesizes our faith, and His Word waters our roots. Through prayer, worship, and obedience we bear fruit.

Who of us couldn't use more fruit of the Spirit in our lives? An opinion poll once asked what Americans really wanted out of life, and the top three answers boiled down to love, joy, and peace. Good fruit is a product of God's Spirit within us. It will not come naturally to our flesh, and we cannot fake these qualities for long. Consistent fruit will require consistency in Christ. When your family and your coworkers see the fruit of the Spirit displayed in and through your life, they will take notice and be drawn to you like I was drawn to Clyde.

Clyde was a ticket man who greeted players and coaches on game day at the VIP gate of the Oakland Coliseum. The player parking lot at the Coliseum is located on the north side of the stadium. All Raider personnel and employees park in parking lot F and proceed through a turnstile ticket gate just as fans do. Clyde was always there to greet us with an infectious smile. He was a middle-aged, African American man who was small in stature but always had a big smile, a positive word, and a warm embrace.

Clyde was in a perpetually great mood, and there wasn't a single player or coach that didn't enjoy being greeted by Clyde when they arrived at the stadium. Only once in my career was Clyde absent. On that day, as I approached the gate, I was shocked to see some other guy standing there. It felt like I just received a punch to my gut. I stopped in bewilderment and asked, "Who are you? Where is Clyde?" Others asked, "What's wrong with Clyde? Is he okay?" We were told he was at a wedding and couldn't make it back in time for the game. Several suggested that we call off the game because Clyde was not there to greet us. The pregame chatter in the locker room was, "Can you believe Clyde's not here today?"

It comes as no surprise that Clyde was a Christian. He never forced his faith on anyone. He never preached a message that I know of, but the testimony of his good fruit spoke volumes. He was just a humble guy doing a menial task, yet we couldn't help but notice him and be drawn to him. This demonstrates how the fruit of the Spirit can shine through a person.

Does your life make a lasting impression upon others? Does it deliver consistent, fresh fruit for others to enjoy? One of my coaches used to say, "Beauty is only skin deep, but ugly is to the bone." It is too easy to sacrifice long-term success for short-term gain. Good looks and charm can only get you so far. Power plays and smooth words may garner votes, gain followers, and grow congregations, but they can never earn us the applause of heaven. We may fool others for a while, but we cannot fool God, and sooner or later the truth about us will be made known.

Bad fruit indicates the absence of Christ and is merely a product of not abiding in Him. When our fruit is not pleasing to the eye, to the smell, or to the taste, people will be repelled. No one is drawn to diseased, spoiled, or moldy fruit. Leaders who aren't bearing good fruit have to resort to manipulation or control to make others follow them. But the man who bears good fruit will find success in all areas of his life. His wife, his children, and his employees will want to be around him to *"taste and see that the Lord is good"* (Ps. 34:8).

Keep growing in Christ. Anything that is not growing is by definition dying, and we die a slow death when we stop learning and maturing in our faith. Physical therapists will tell you that the hardest people to work with are the elderly who are the most set in their ways. Their bodies become like their mindsets—rigid. Christians must be flexible and resist the tendency to become rigid. As you age, be intentional about staying limber, both physically and spiritually.

5. Success Is Knowing God

Your concept of God determines what kind of life you will lead and what kind of person you will be. Famous author and pastor A. W. Tozer writes, "What comes to our minds when we think about God is the most important thing about us."[2] In this parable, all three of the servants can be commended for having a desire to please their master, but one man's misguided opinion of his master hampered his ability to please him. In an attempt to justify his behavior, the unprofitable servant said, *"I knew you were a hard man, harvesting where you have not sown and gathering where you have not scattered seed. So I was afraid and went out and hid your talent in the ground. See, here is what belongs to you"* (Matt. 25:24-25).

The servant thought the master was hardhearted, miserly, and tough to please. Because he was mistaken about his master's character, his good intentions fell regrettably short. Instead of trusting his master's benevolence, he was critical of him. Instead of having confidence in his abilities, he was afraid to fail, and consequently failed miserably. This erroneous perception paralyzed his decisions and led him to bury his talent.

How we view God and who we believe Him to be will greatly dictate what kind of servant we will be. If we see Him as an unjust judge, we will despise Him. If we regard Him as a hypocritical bully, we will oppose Him. If we think of Him as an ambivalent parent, we will ignore Him. If we deem Him a nonexistent force, we will reject Him. If we consider Him to be a giant Santa Clause in the sky, we will approach Him like a slot machine. But if we see Him as the loving, strong, just, and faithful Father that He is, we will respect Him and trust His wisdom to guide our behavior.

Reducing the Almighty to mere mortal status distorts our view of ourselves and devalues what is designed to be precious. Presuming Him to be other than He really is or substituting our likeness for His likeness is a form of idolatry. Man was fashioned in the image of God, not the other way around. When we make God in the image of man, we warp our God-image as well as our self-image.

We can extract a lot about God's character from this parable. He is not an exacting master or unjustifiably harsh. He is fair, generous, trusting, encouraging, honest, consistent, and wise. His mercy warms our hearts, His holiness demands our reverence, and His might commands our respect. Having a clear and accurate view of God helps us to confidently step out on the waters of faith to achieve a maximum return on His investment in us.

Most wrong conduct has at its roots in a wrong view of God. A. W. Tozer once again writes, "There is scarcely an error in doctrine or a failure in applying Christian ethics that cannot be traced finally to imperfect and ignoble thoughts about God."[3] Many people have a desire to please God, but not all possess the necessary knowledge of Him to help them accomplish it. Some believers fall by the wayside due to a misunderstanding of His nature. If a person sees God as hardhearted, demanding, and impossible to please, it will have a negative influence on their faith and will make it difficult to trust Him.

The unprofitable servant feared God, but in an unhealthy way. Instead of taking responsibility for his actions, he made false excuses and actually tried to shift the blame for his behavior on a perceived stinginess in his master. It was a backhanded complement, but the master called his bluff: *"If you knew I was after the best, why did you do less than the least?"* (Matt. 25:26 MSG).

The servant's actions were not only irresponsible but inconsistent with his stated beliefs. If he thought the master was unreasonable and unjust, the last thing he should be doing is burying his talent in the ground. He should have at least put forth some degree of effort. Something is always better than nothing. It just proved he had no love or respect for the master or for himself. When all was said and done, his rationalization was merely a ruse to cover up his own fear and laziness.

The foolish servant failed to recognize his master's good intentions and substituted security for service. By failing to grasp the magnificent character of God, he failed to grasp the magnitude of his responsibility. Instead of investing his faith in a heavenly kingdom, he invested it in an earthly pit and effectively grounded his talent. In so doing he sent his potential to an early grave and prevented it from ever reaping a heavenly return that could reach supernatural proportions.

As a Christian, focusing on knowing God as revealed through His Word is a worthwhile endeavor. Christ keeps our vision on the desired target and helps align us to the will of God. When our priorities are in proper alignment, He is faithful to make our impact hit the mark and count for His glory. The more we set our sights upon Him and learn through His Word how He acts, the clearer we see the true nature of God. Let's not hesitate to firmly grab hold of God's Word and hone in on the very nature of God. Take up any slack in your life, strive for self-control and a prayerful lifestyle. And don't be afraid to act as God prompts you. Speak up in the face of godlessness, witness to the lost, lay hands on the sick, feed the hungry, and cast out demons. In short, fulfill your ministry and be the man God intends you to be. Be an example of the kind of Christian the Bible prescribes.

6. Success Hangs on God's Every Word

When God was looking for a successor to Moses, he found one in Joshua. Joshua and Caleb, two of the twelve spies selected to survey the Promised Land, returned with a good report, coming back full of faith in God's ability to give them the land. The other ten spies spoke of fortified cities and intimidating giants, frightening the people and discouraging them from entering Canaan. Sadly, the people believed the ten spies and refused to conquer the Promised Land. Because of their fear and unbelief, that generation was denied access to God's promises. God would need to raise up the next generation to take the land.

After Moses had passed and Joshua was anointed the new leader, God spoke to Joshua, saying: *"Do not let this Book of the Law depart from your mouth; meditate on the day and night, so that you may be careful to do everything written in it. Then you will be prosperous and successful"* (Josh. 1:8). For Joshua there would be no success apart from God's Word. With it he would prosper, and without it he would fail. The Book of the Law was pivotal to his future and his prosperity. And it is no different for you and me. God's Word gives direction, protection, provision, inspiration, and wisdom for every circumstance. It is truly the greatest personal game plan in the world.

As you dive into the Bible, you will discover that Jesus Christ is the spotlight of both the Old and the New Testament. He is the central figure of Scripture, the fulfillment of prophecy, and the living Word of God. For this reason, applying biblical principles to your lives without acknowledging or submitting to Christ misses the whole goal of God's Word, which is to lead us to faith in the Messiah. I have known some wonderful people who possess a high moral system of personal conduct. They recognize that the

Bible has some great teachings and even want their children introduced to it, but they don't know Jesus, the living Word of God, for themselves.

The Bible was never intended to just be just a good coffee table read or a self-help book. While it is good to be a moral person and apply biblical concepts to your life, that is not enough. Starting with Jesus, we need to give God ownership and mastery over every compartment of our life. Only then can we access the true power of success found in the Bible.

Reading God's written Word helps attune our hearts to hearing God's spoken word. This is the beautiful wonder of Scripture. As you read it, it reads you. Jesus said, *"My sheep listen to my voice; I know them, and they follow Me"* (John 10:27). The goal of Scripture is to direct us to the Good Shepherd and teach us how to follow His voice, which requires the same attentiveness and patience that an offensive line must possess when hearing an audible at the line of scrimmage. Just like a player must know the playbook by heart in order to know what to do with the play call, we must know the Bible inside and out to properly respond to the play calls of our quarterback.

Success is not just in hearing God's voice. Success is spending enough time with God to recognize His voice when He does speak and trusting Him enough to follow through with it. As men we can't walk away from God's directives and expect to be successful. We are delusional if we think we can do things our own way and count on God's anointing, presence, and power to remain with us.

7. *Success Stays Connected*

The unprofitable servant forged out ahead on his own and effectively veered off the road and into a ditch. If he felt he was in over his head, why did he not ask for advice or help? He could have easily consulted the other servants and gained wisdom from their business strategy. Instead, he isolated himself and tried to navigate it alone. The truth is that there are no successful lone rangers in the kingdom of God. You need others, and others need you. There is always strength in numbers, and surrounding yourself with other committed believers is a wise strategy for success.

When I ran the marathon, Garrett was there to encourage me and push me on. He developed a personalized training regiment that helped me accomplish my required team workouts in addition to sticking to a long-distance running schedule. By his own volition he ran the last half-mile by my side and would have carried me across the finish line if need be. I couldn't have done it without him.

When God gives you a task, He supplies the grace, resources, and supporting cast to see it to completion. Where He guides He provides, and with His vision He gives the provision. He won't ask you to swim just to watch you drown. Despite our wishes, His provision is hardly ever money falling from the sky, but almost always people who support and believe in us.

Success advises that we choose our companions wisely (see 1 Cor. 15:33). Whom you allow to speak into your life can influence the direction of your life. Just as it's imperative to have voices of encouragement in your ear, it is equally important to block out those who try to dissuade you from following the call of God. They are nothing but vision vandals. Because your vision conflicts with their opinion and their way of doing things, they shoot down your God-inspired ideas. They aren't realists; they are opinioned pundits who don't have a lifestyle of prayer and don't have your best interests in mind. They may mean well, but in the end they are just mean. Don't allow their words to sway or manipulate you.

Those you allow closest to you should be doers of the Word and serious about following the call of God for their lives. That does not mean that you surround yourself with yes men and people who never challenge your opinion or hold you accountable for your decisions. It means you should gravitate toward those who share your same values and love you enough to support you, pray for you, and lovingly get in your face if need be.

I am cautious whom I allow to speak into my life and whom I seek spiritual counsel from. I'm not interested in emotions, opinions, or good ideas. I want God-ideas, and I need to know that my counselor has an ear tuned toward heaven. Likewise, choose your business partners and those you invest your money with wisely. Lay any decision out before the Lord and seek His wisdom and direction. I have lost valuable time and a great sum of money investing with people and businesses that ended in dead ends, only because I did not first seek God's directives.

8. *Success Follows Discipline*

You will scarcely find a successful man who is not self-disciplined. Success warrants gaining victory over thoughts, appetite, and will. A body that is undisciplined is more prone to sickness, weakness, and poor health. A mind that is undisciplined is more susceptible to fear, depression, and poor attitudes, and it can be more easily led astray by false teachings. You will have a far better chance of succeeding in this life and in the life to come if you can learn to live a disciplined lifestyle.

Discipline isn't devoid of weakness. Neither is it being rigid or unwilling to deviate from routine. Discipline is making a positive contribution to one's growth in righteousness. It instructs, guides, and develops us through correction and training. Don't think of discipline as punishment but rather an investment of love. In fact, it is through His discipline of us that we can see God's deep love and commitment to us.

I have several friends who have served in military special forces. They relate that all the applicants who wish to join elite teams are physically fit, motivated to serve, and mentally sharp. These qualities alone, however, will not cut it. The special forces are looking for those who have the grit and tenacity to see a task through to completion, even if it kills them. They are not only looking just for the fastest, strongest, and smartest. They want the guy who won't quit. The great Tom Landry once said, "A winner never stops." Quitting is habitual. Once you learn it, it becomes a habit.

Every man can benefit from discipline—athletes, students, ministers, and businessmen (see Ps. 94:12; Prov. 10:17; 13:18; 15:32). One of the wonderful benefits of discipline is that it is transferable. What I mean is that when you gain discipline in one area of your life, you can apply those same principles to another area of your life that is yet to be disciplined. For example, if you are undisciplined in your prayer life, you can transfer the discipline you have learned at your job to your prayer life. Or if you are disciplined in exercising your body but not disciplined in your thoughts, simply use the same measures you use with your mind as you do to stay physically fit.

9. *Success Masters the Art of Contentment*

As a young man, Solomon grew up privileged, comfortable, and financially secure. He was a royal prince, a son of the king, an heir to the throne. He was intelligent, articulate, educated, and gifted. After David's death, he assumed the throne and ruled for forty years. During his reign he undertook elaborate building projects and had many wives and concubines—900 to be exact—but who's counting? When it came to women, not only did the apple not fall far from the tree, but it sprouted and produced a densely populated forest.

Despite his faults, Solomon found favor in the eyes of God. He built the temple at Jerusalem and brought about unprecedented peace and prosperity to the land. In addition to possessing notorious wisdom, Solomon became one of the richest and most influential kings in the ancient world. In the midst of public success, however, Solomon grew excruciatingly barren on the inside.

Have you ever thought, "If I had money, women, and prestige like this star or that big shot, then I wouldn't have a care in the world"? We probably have all thought this at one time or another, and how foolish we were. If the high life was really that gratifying, then why do so many celebrities wind up in debt, rehab, or divorce court? Look at the elites. Do they look happy? I have had my taste of public recognition, and let me tell you with confidence that there is no lasting contentment in the applause of man. The accolades of others cannot cure the ache of the heart.

Blaise Pascal, the French philosopher, physicist, and mathematician, wrote, "There is a God shaped vacuum in the heart of every man which cannot be filled by any created thing, but only by God, the Creator, made known through Jesus."[4] Your contentment will never be achieved through trophies, tributes, milestones, or anything else that is temporal. Your contentment can only come from something eternal. The answer to the void in life is a God who is unavoidable.

I have friends who have won Pro Bowls, Super Bowls, and national championships only to wake up the next morning asking, "Is that it?" Many professional athletes suffer from career-hangovers. When age settles in and the stadium lights start to dim, the sporting community quickly moves on without them. I have observed that those who got too accustomed to the big stage tended to struggle the most in finding their place in the post-sporting world.

It should come as no surprise that many successful icons are desperately lonely and hopelessly depressed. This is because contentment does not come from an outside source but from an inward reality. It is a choice that springs up from a heart devoted to God. I can guarantee you that any Christian man who is not content in Christ will search for contentment from another source, only to fail and be left frustrated, vandalized, and hollow.

If you think that money can buy you happiness, remember that there are just as many miserable poor people as there are miserable rich people. The misery comes from thinking that money is the answer. Those who are poor are miserable when they presume that their unhappiness is on account of their poverty. They strive to get money and despise the rich, all the while secretly envying them. When they do come into wealth, they are disappointed with it because it isn't all it's cracked up to be because there never seems to be quite enough of it. The high life deals them a low blow, and when it becomes evident that money will not make them happy, that disillusionment leaves them even more miserable.

Contentment is not being slothful; neither is it striving. Contentment is enjoying what we have more than wanting what we don't have. You know you are content when you do not demand the things you do not possess. The wicked servant was anything but content. He was a lazy malcontent. He neither appreciated what he had nor was happy to receive more.

There are those who have more than they know what to do with but are still not content. May that never be said of us. Spiritual contentment does not mean we are satisfied with our current level of devotion to God; it only means that we can appreciate what we have been given while eagerly anticipating what God still has in store for us. We don't need more possessions to be successful. We need to be satisfied with our earthly stuff and strive to store up treasures in heaven.

When we contrast Solomon's experiences to that of Paul's, we can see that star-studded achievement does not necessarily make a person content. As we learned earlier, Paul had to overcome great hardships in his effort to fulfill the heavenly call upon His life. Even in the midst of those struggles, he was able to find the source of meaning and true contentment:

> *I know what it is to be in need, and I know what it*
> *is to have plenty. I have learned the secret of being*

SUCCESS

content in any and every situation, whether well fed or hungry, whether living in plenty or in want. I can do everything through Him who gives me strength (Philippians 4:12-13).

Paul identifies Christ as the source of his contentment and admits that only through Him and Him alone could he be strengthened to do all things required of him. My friend Napoleon Kaufman once told me, "The most content man in the world is the one who is in the center of God's will." Success is finding the very core of God's will and thriving in it. The man who can remain in the center of God's will has found a place of strength. Of course this is easier said than done. It will require a single-minded focus on your purpose and goals. Nothing in this life is easy, but God supplies us with the necessary grace to meet every challenge.

10. Success Is Hearing, "Well Done"

When the master said to the first servant, "Well done," he was paying him the ultimate complement. He was saying, "You passed the test. You graduated. I'm giving you a promotion beyond your wildest dreams." That is music to the ears of any employee.

My former offensive line coach Joe Bugal used to say, "Well done. You are a true professional." He didn't throw that compliment around lightly. To him, that statement and a hug was his highest form of praise. A professional to Joe was someone who took his craft seriously, who meticulously studied, trained, and executed when the game was on the line. When Joe told me that, I felt great, and it assured me that all my hard work and effort was not going unappreciated. His praise, love, and encouragement fueled in me the desire to work all that much harder.

Someday you and I will stand before the Master of the universe to give an account for our lives. Suddenly those things that the world propped up as so important will seem painfully frivolous.

SUCCESS

The measure of a man will not be his money, titles, or reputation. His reward will not be based on how much wealth, ability, or the intellect he amassed, but rather how responsible he was with what was at his disposal and how well he devoted his life to the service of the King. Success on that day will be hearing the words, *"Well done, good and faithful servant! You have been faithful with a few things; I will put you in charge of many things. Come and share in your master's happiness"* (Matt. 25:21).

The man who hears that has finished the race, kept the faith, and won the prize. He has succeeded at life. It is the well done of God that we are living for, and it is for the well done of God that I have written this book. I want nothing more than for you to hear these words on that day.

It is worth noting that the master's standard of judgment was not the same for the servant with five talents as it was for the man with one. On the day of reckoning *"everyone who has been given much, much will be demanded; and from the one who has been entrusted with much, much more will be asked"* (Luke 12:48). The master would have accepted simple interest on his one talent given to the unprofitable servant, implying that he would have been happy with small returns over no returns at all. This helps us to know that any real effort to serve Christ is better than spiritual sloth. God will not judge us for what we don't have. Rather, He will judge us for who we refused to become.

The Extra Point

Great athletes know that lasting success does not come from their strengths but by overcoming their weaknesses. To be the best, you must identify your weaknesses and work on them daily. When I was playing football, I would purposely wash and wax my car with my left hand in order to improve the coordination of my left-handed punch. I would jump rope and work on balance drills to improve my foot quickness and control.

SUCCESS

Most men succeed not because they're destined to but because they're determined to. Be determined to finish this race and finish it well. To be successful you must be relentless. Don't just settle for crawling across the finish line. Sprint for it and finish strong. It's not "go big or go home"; it's "go big and then go home."

Chalk Talk

1. How should your personal definition of success alter in light of God's definition of success? Discuss the ten reflections of success and share some new insights you can apply to your life from the chapter.

2. What amount of hardship or personal sacrifice are you willing to endure to achieve success in the eyes of God? What will have a greater impact on your children—your worldly success or your spiritual obedience?

3. Would others who spend time with you know you're a Christian without you telling them? What areas of your life are bearing good fruit? What areas need to be pruned, replanted, or plucked from the ground?

4. What areas of your life are disciplined? Undisciplined? Are there priorities in your life that need to be adjusted in order to spend more time abiding in Christ?

5. How effective have you been in putting your God-given talents to work for His glory? Have you buried some of your abilities, gifts, or resources in the ground? Pray that God would establish the work of your hands to be a builder for His kingdom.

6. Do possessions bring you lasting happiness, or have you learned the Christ-centered art of contentment?

7. At this point, how profitable has the spiritual investment of your life been? If the Master returned today, what would He say about the way you have used what was given to you?

Endnotes

1.   D. J. Harrington, *The Gospel of Matthew* (Collegeville, MN: Liturgical Press, 1991), 352.

2.   A. W. Tozer, *The Knowledge of the Holy* (New York: HarperCollins, 1961), 9.

3.   Ibid., 10.

4.   This quote was taken from http://www.famousquotesabout.com/quote/There-is-a-God/69316, accessed February 19, 2015.

LEGACY

CHAPTER 12

THE END ZONE

Every man dies. Not every man really lives.
—WILLIAM WALLACE, *Braveheart*

Every locker room has its fair share clowns and gregarious characters. During my career I played with dozens of jokers who left me a trove of colorful stories and comedic memories. Of all of the characters I came across, however, none had a greater imprint on my life than Dan Turk.

Dan came to the Raiders as a center in 1989 after playing two seasons with the Steelers and two with Tampa Bay. He earned the nickname "Psycho" from his previous teammates for his fearless play on special teams, reckless lifestyle, and willingness to confront coaches. As the story goes, Dan drank himself out of Pittsburgh and physically strangled his Buccaneer offensive line coach. Although he was talented, both teams weren't convinced he was stable enough to commit to. The Raiders seemed like the perfect landing spot for him.

Dan's locker was right next to mine, which meant I got a front row seat to his hilarious and copious shenanigans. In football, a player's locker is like their office. It's the place where they like to kick back and relax after a hard practice. When not in meetings or in the weight room, players tend to hang out at their locker and clown around. Dan and I were locker mates for eight years, and for eight years his antics kept it lively.

Danny, as I called him, loved to wrestle and was always talking smack. He was the kind of guy who would leg sweep you as you walked by just for the fun of it. On countless occasions, he tried to put me in a headlock when I bent over to tie my shoes. In some ways, Danny was like an older brother to me in that he knew how to push my buttons and get me riled up. He was constantly goading me to make a bet with him on some golf related event and was always boasting about his alma mater—the Wisconsin Badgers.

As a football player, Danny was a superb center and very quick for a guy of his size. His long snapping abilities rivaled anyone in the league. He was strong, explosive, and had the grip of a wrestler. His most dominant quality was his competitiveness. He played with a chip on his shoulder as if he had something to prove to the world. He openly heckled opposing players and teammates. In practice, he would jeer coaches and kickers, betting the kicker would miss the next practice field goal just to add pressure to the situation. He often ran the scout team and would openly mock the defensive coordinator if his fellow scout team members had success against the starting defense.

I remember once we were in a tight game against the Chiefs in Kansas City. We had a long drive down the field and were preparing for a critical field goal. All of us starting linemen were exhausted from the drive and competitiveness of a hard-fought game. Dan comes running off the bench like a puppy looking for some mischief. He was our feisty long snapper and had only seen limited action on special teams at that point. He began to openly

LEGACY

mock and call out the Chief defense during the television time out. He referred to them as a bunch of female body parts, calling them punks, and yelling at them to bring all they got. He told Pro Bowl defensive end Neil Smith that he is an embarrassment and should have retired years ago.

As both teams lined up in preparation for the field goal attempt, the Kansas City defense shifted seven men directly over Dan, me, and our other offensive guard, Kevin Gogan. Back then there weren't any rules prohibiting defenses from "teeing off" on the center or using players to physically ramrod other defenders in the back to create extra penetration. We interlocked our feet and hunkered down in our stance as Dan quickly snapped a perfect dart back to the holder Jeff Gossett. The defense charged forward like stampeding bulls released from the rodeo gate. I was a strong guy at that time, but all I remember was being hoisted in the air and getting knocked flat on my back as my helmet bounced off the turf. Miraculously the ball somehow sailed just above the outstretched flood of defenders and through the middle of the uprights.

A few punches and some pushing and shoving ensued before the referees separated us and left us retreating to our respective sidelines. I was seeing stars, which was an all too frequent occurrence and a possible side effect of a concussion. Dan seemed proud and invigorated from the whole experience. Kevin Gogan promptly grabbed him by the collar and threatened him, saying, "Dan, if you ever do something like that again, I will personally kick your butt." That was Danny, a loud and proud Raider, and always ready to mix it up.

A few years into Danny's stint with the Raiders, things started to change dramatically in his personal life. One off-season a random bus driver engaged Danny in a lengthy conversation about God en route to a charity basketball game. Later that night, Dan prayed to receive Christ into his life. He soon fell in love and married a wonderful woman, and they had a beautiful little girl together. Dan's wife and daughter were the apple of his eye. He clearly became more visibly joyful and at peace with his life and even with his role on the team.

His humor was still there, but less biting and more light-hearted. The coaches and even Al Davis noticed the changes too. Danny eventually became a starter for the 1995 season and started all sixteen games at center, as well as handling the long snapping duties. When he was released by the Raiders after the 1996 season, I was saddened to lose Danny as a teammate but happy when the Washington Redskins signed him. It was a good situation for him, as he had the opportunity to snap the football to his brother, Matt Turk, who was the punter for the Redskins.[1]

Danny played three seasons for Washington. In his final season in 1999, he developed a chest cold that didn't seem to respond to antibiotics. He thought it was just a case of the flu. His conditions worsened, but never one to complain he played through it and did his best to support his teammates. In the divisional playoff game against his old Buccaneer team, Danny made a rare high snap on a 51-yard field goal attempt that could have won the game for the Redskins. The kick was missed, and with it went their hopes for a Super Bowl birth.

Washington terminated his contract after the season, and Danny's condition worsened. When it got to the point that he was not able to climb a simple flight of stairs without gasping for air, he sought the advice of a doctor not affiliated with the team. He was quickly diagnosed with mediastinal germ cell tumors. Within a year, it would take his life.

In December of 2000 I had received word that Danny was not doing well. We happened to be playing in Pittsburgh that week, so Coach Gruden allowed me to fly to Virginia to visit him rather than travel back with the team. I spent the rest of Sunday and all day Monday with Danny at his home in Ashburn.

It took my breath away to see him in such a weakened state. On a good day he could make it downstairs from his upstairs bedroom by himself. That trek alone, however, depleted him of all his strength for much of the day. One of the most powerful guys I had ever known, a guy who had taught me how to punch and use my hands as a weapon, was incapable of caring for his own needs in what should have been the prime of his life.

When your body begins to fail you and your life is fading away, you don't waste your words. Dan was dying of cancer, and he knew it. Typically we would clown around with each other, but on this occasion we spent most of our time praying, singing, and talking about our families and about the Lord. It was something we had never done together before in such a meaningful way. We read Scriptures about death and about the promise of eternal life. We had the most amazing time, and I had never felt closer to Danny than during those two days at his house.

When he was with the Raiders, Danny lived only forty-five minutes away from the Raider facility in El Segundo. He must have invited me over to his home on dozens of occasions. To my regret, I never once took him up on the offer. I had a million excuses not to go see his house and the koi pond that he was so proud of. One day it was the Los Angeles traffic; the next time I was too tired or too busy. I said, "Dan, I love you, but I see you all day every day at work." I'm convinced now that God brought Dan into my life for a reason, and I only wish I would have developed a more meaningful friendship with him earlier on. We both could have benefited from it.

Before I left his home, he shared with me a story that only a dying man could articulate. The week before my visit, Dan determined to drag his body out of bed and force himself downstairs to eat breakfast with his daughter before she left for school. Like recounting a heavenly vision, Dan described in vivid detail even the smallest facet of their breakfast together. It was like time had stood still for him in that moment. His daughter was simply eating a bowl of oatmeal, but something about it gripped his soul. Without her being aware of it, he stared at her and marveled at her beauty as she smiled and giggled when talking about their upcoming day.

As he was narrating this story, he looked at me with his steely eyes and said in a low, serious tone, "Wiz, that was the most beautiful thing I have ever seen." He told me to never take my family for granted and to enjoy every moment I share with them. These were some of his very last words to me. Danny died three weeks later on December 23, 2000. He was only 38 years old. When he died, I was told he was sitting upright in his recliner with his eyes closed and a huge smile came over his face. He gasped and stopped breathing completely. I don't know exactly what Danny saw that made him smile, but I have a really good idea.

At his funeral, I was so delighted to hear the stories of how God was glorified through Danny's life. Here was a guy who was once called a psycho but now is a saint of God reigning with Jesus in His kingdom. The memorial honored Danny's request to celebrate his life and give all glory to Jesus. His beautiful daughter, recited Dan's favorite portion of Scripture—Psalm 23. That day we were all reminded that Danny was not lost. Things are only lost when we don't know where they are. Dan was not lost, because we knew exactly where he was.

Making Sense of Death

Death doesn't negotiate. Sooner or later every person must stand toe to toe with the grave and face his own mortality. Death is our final battle and man's greatest enemy. It is the king of terrors and the terror of kings. For thousands of years, people have pondered life after death and made preparations for it. Virtually every culture and religion adheres to a belief system regarding death and what happens after we die.

The Egyptians supplied their dead with basic needs that could be used in their passage through the afterlife. The Aztecs killed a dog to serve as a spirit guide to the dead. The Greeks buried a coin with the dead to pay the boatman Charon when crossing the River Styx. Buddhists pledge objects of value like jewelry, money, articles of clothing, and food. Hindus believe the dead are reincarnated. Hollywood has popularized the notion that a person's spirit wanders around their favorite locations for centuries until they find their way heavenward. Even atheists have faith in a self-created hypothesis, betting that there is nothing more to their existence than the material.

But the basic questions about life and death still remain and have not been solved by ancient religions, Eastern mysticism, or humanistic philosophies. Noted atheist and Nobel-prize winning author Albert Camus confessed, "Mankind is plagued with the two basic problems of sin and death."[2] He admitted that Christianity addresses these problems.

In order to make sense of life, we must be able to make sense of death. Until we do, life will hold no real meaning for us. What we believe happens after we die has a lot to do with how we live our life before we die. I once saw a billboard that read, "Live like there's no yesterday." These kinds of philosophies about life and how to live it are just fanciful thinking. Living like there's no yesterday and living like there's no tomorrow is no way to really live, since no one can ever escape the past or the future. Yesterday and tomorrow will always be—that is reality.

What if a person really did subscribe to one of these mantras? Their life would be one gigantic mess. Those who lived like there was no yesterday would never gain the benefit of learning from their past mistakes and would be destined to repeat them. Those who lived as if there's no tomorrow would make foolish and short-sighted decisions and be forced to live with the consequences of their actions for the rest of their lives.

In one sense we are all dying from the minute we are born. None of us are guaranteed another day, and it is only a matter of time before our days are complete. Paul writes that we should *"die daily"* (1 Cor. 15:31 KJV) and *"carry around in our body the death of Jesus so that the life of Jesus"* (2 Cor. 4:10) would be revealed. Our lifespan is short and our window to strike a mark in history is rapidly closing.

The fact that death is certain, however, does not give us license to throw off all restraint and live morally reckless lives. The fool says, "We only go around this crazy merry-go-round once. I might as well live it up while I'm alive." The error in this thinking is two-fold: the first is that giving into fleshly lusts equates living it up—I can assure you that compared to the high call of God, debauchery is definitely living it down. The second misconception is that there is no justice or reckoning or permanence beyond the grave. Scripture assures us that all men are *"destined to die once, and after that to face judgment, so Christ was sacrificed once to take away the sins of many people; and He will appear a second time, not to bear sin, but to bring salvation to those who are waiting for Him"* (Heb. 9:27-28).

All men must stand before God and give an account for their life. If we could save ourselves through lifetimes of good deeds, then Christ did not need to die. Likewise, if we could purify ourselves by living a series of reincarnations, then there would be no need for accountability or justice. The Bible clearly does not support reincarnation.

We are each given one life, and we are accountable to our Creator for what we do with it. We live, we die, and we will all stand before our Maker. This is it. We have only one shot at this. This is our moment in time, and we have the opportunity of a lifetime to change history and set our trajectory for eternity. Our actions, our words, and even our thoughts will one day be carefully examined, and how we lived will determine how we will spend eternity.

While it may be true that all will die, it is equally true that all will live forever. This is why living like there's no yesterday or living like there's no tomorrow is so foolish and so out of touch with reality. Living like we're dying is a good idea, but a better idea might be to live like we'll live forever.

It is not easy for a finite mind to comprehend an infinite continuum that dwells outside the realm of time and space. I once heard a pastor try to illustrate eternity by stretching a rope from one end of the sanctuary to the other. With a permanent marker he ticked a small mark roughly in the middle of the rope. He said the dash represented our earthly existence and the span outside the mark represented eternity. This life is just a drop in the bucket compared to our entire existence. Death then serves as a passageway into eternity.

When a man comes to faith in Jesus, eternity is altered and his relationship with death changes. Where death was once his demise, it is now his reward. Before Christ we fear it; after Christ we confront it. What once mastered us, we now possess mastery over. A Christian man is no longer subject to death, because death is now subject to him through Christ. Death for the believer is not the end. It is merely the blowing out of a candle because the dawn has arrived. From this perspective, our best days are not behind us as Christians, but in front of us.

The Second Death

There is a riddle that says, "Born once, die twice. Born twice, die once." It simply means that all born into this world are subject to die two deaths. The first death is natural; the second is spiritual. Because all men are born into sin, we all must face death on both accounts. But those who are born again (or born of the Spirit) are only subject to one death—they are saved from a second death. While the believer will die a natural death, he or she will not die a spiritual one. He is protected from what the Bible refers to as "the second death."

Of this second death, John writes: *"Blessed and holy are those who have part in the first resurrection. The second death has no power over them, but they will be priests of God and of Christ and will reign with Him for a thousand years"* (Rev. 20:6). After Satan is thrown into the lake of fire and dead are judged, he writes, *"Then death and Hades were thrown into the lake of fire. The lake of fire is the second death"* (Rev. 20:14). And Jesus promises, *"He who overcomes will not be hurt by the second death"* (Rev. 2:11).

Adam and Eve were introduced to the second death firsthand. They were created to never taste death of any kind, but they disobeyed and ate the forbidden fruit. Their consequence was death. God said to them, *"For dust you are and to dust you will return"* (Gen 3:19). They died that day—not a natural death but a spiritual one. They were banished from the garden and prevented from ever entering it again. They and all their offspring now possessed a sin nature and were in need of a Savior. As harsh as this judgment may seem, it was God's mercy to prevent them from eating of the tree of life. He did not want Adam and his descendants to have to live forever in their sinful condition.

Whereas death separates the soul from the body, the second death separates the soul from God. Those who don't believe in original sin or absolute truth have no explanation for death. To them, death is cold, harsh, and final. It is death, however, that proves that sin has entered the world. If there were no sin, there would be no death. This is why heaven will be so heavenly.

Adam and Eve did eventually physically die. Their bodies returned to the ground, as we all do, but there is One whose body never saw decay—He is called the Last Adam. Through Jesus we gain access to the garden of Eden and can partake of the tree of life. Only through Him can we avoid the second death. This is what Paul referred to when he wrote about death through Adam and life through Christ. Just as death entered through Adam, life entered through Jesus. He reversed the condemnation of Adam's fall. Whereas the first man's disobedience caused us all to be born into sin, the Son of Man's obedience allows us to be born again and made right in God's sight (see Rom. 5).

The Lord Is Waiting to Greet You

If you live long enough, you will most likely outlive your parents. It's the natural order of things. Children should survive their parents, not the other way around. And trust me when I say that parents would have it no other way. As painful as it is to lose a parent, there is no comparison to the agony of losing a child. If your parents are both still living, then you should be grateful for the days you have left with them. Now is the time to invest in your relationship with them and gain their wisdom before they pass.

When my father was dying, I was with him in the hospital and stood at his bedside, with my stepmother and two of my sisters. I remember wrapping both of my hands around his massive right hand as he lay motionless in the bustling intensive care unit. I spoke quietly in his ear for what I knew would be the last time. Even though he was in a coma and the warmth of his spirit was slowly departing his body, I had no doubts that he could hear me. I told him he had been a great father and that I loved him very much. I assured him that there was a reward awaiting him in heaven and that we would be together again soon. Tears steamed down my face and down the faces of all who were present. My last words to him were, "It's okay to let go, Dad. The Lord is waiting to greet you."

The words I spoke to him were not just comforting things to say in an awkwardly tender moment. I believe them to be the absolute truth. I have found God's Word to be irrefutably truthful, and I have staked my life on it. My father's conversion and commitment to Christ could not be denied.

When the medical staff came in and examined my father, they pronounced him dead and began to make preparations to move him. We took some time to collect ourselves and the few remaining personal belongings of my father. When his spirit left, we all felt a peaceful kiss good-bye, and what remained in that bed was only the worn-out shell of what had been my father.

Even though my father was gone, something still remained—hope. Jesus truly does take the sting out of death. Whether you are facing the death of a loved one or you are the one dying, there is hope for all who believe in Christ. Even peace can be found in an untimely death. There is no hope, however, for those who pass away without faith in Christ. They are often left alone, fearful, and do not know what to expect. They leave no certainty, no closure, and no peace for the loved ones who survive them.

My father was loud, proud, and patriotic. He enjoyed a good day's work in the sun, a nice meal, and a glass of wine with dinner. He lived much of his life on his own terms, but his repentance and his faith were genuine. He was indeed a sinner who had been saved by grace, and he left me with something significant the day he died, something worth far more than property or an inheritance. He left me with a legacy of faith.

Creating a Spiritual Legacy

There is a legacy that money can't buy, that carves our names onto people's hearts and leaves behind a lasting heritage. It is the legacy of a good name. Dying with a good name is far better than living with a bad one. Raider defensive coordinator Dave Adolph used to say, "Refuse to become what you despise." We do this by being intentional about dedicating ourselves to the people and things God loves. The measure of a man is not what he inherits from his ancestors but what he leaves behind to his descendants. More than money, your children need a legacy, and a spiritual legacy is worth far more than riches.

I was privileged to inherit a rich spiritual blessing from my ancestors, particularly from my mother's side. My grandfather, Vincenzo, came to this country from Italy when he was 13 years old. Along with his two brothers, he and his family settled in Massachusetts. From that day forward, he held down a job for the rest of his life. His first job was delivering water to the men working on the dam at the Clinton Reservoir. One day a foreman asked Vincenzo his name, and he told him his full name in Italian. The foreman replied, "Your name is too difficult to pronounce. Your new name is Jimmy." From that day on he was known as Jimmy.

Nonno, as I knew him, worked full time all the time. He worked in construction and later as a barber. He grew a large garden and bottled his own wine. He saved his money wisely and even purchased a few modest rental homes. Jimmy was well respected in the community. He was known for his Christian faith and charity, which included giving out free haircuts one day a week during the Depression. He believed it was important to give people their dignity, which is why he gave complementary haircuts to anyone who couldn't afford one.

I remember my grandfather as always being full of joy and gratitude. He believed that God was real and was with him, and he found the Bible to be 100 percent accurate. He had four daughters and one son who served as a monsignor in the Catholic Church, and he instilled his faith in all of them. This was the home my mother grew up in.

My mother, Valia, was an amazing woman of faith as well. She had an infectious love for God that spilled over onto all she did. She enjoyed the simple pleasures of life and never put her own needs first. She took pleasure in serving others and always saw the best in people, even when others didn't. She was the kind of person who would invite anyone and everyone over for a home-cooked meal or to sample her amazing baked goods. Being

LEGACY

full-blooded Italian, she took personal offense if she couldn't spoil you with her hospitality.

Life handed nothing to her, but she did an amazing job raising six children, volunteering in ministry, and working to make ends meet after the divorce. She was a hard worker and, somehow, in the midst of juggling a full-time job, cooking, cleaning, washing, shopping, sewing, and meeting all the demands of a mother, she found time to volunteer in the prison ministry. She believed her highest call was to be a Christian woman, a wife, mother, and grandmother, all in that order.

Anyone who knew my mother knew that she was a prayer warrior, and she prayed with me every night. Her prayers moved heaven and shook hell. Although fragile and meek, she prayed with conviction and an expectation that something would happen. I remember opening my eyes and looking around the room quite frequently after her prayers. I fully expected to see angels filling the house and God moving in a mighty way—for all I know they probably were.

Through my grandfather's faith, the ways of Jesus were instilled in my mother. And from my mother that faith was shared with my five siblings and me. We all have our own rocky stories to tell, but we have all received Christ as our Savior.

I had the privilege of sharing my faith with my high school girlfriend and now she is my wife. As they say in football, I outkicked my coverage. In other words, I married a great woman I probably don't deserve. My wife and I have shared our faith with our kids, and they have all earnestly made a commitment to follow Christ on their own. My prayer is that this legacy of faith will continue to expand through their lives and yours as you read this book.

Whether you come from a godly heritage or a godless one, you can start creating your own spiritual legacy right in your own home today. If you choose to follow and obey Christ, you can't help but make an impact on future generations and leave a spiritual footprint for others to follow.

Businessman and motivational speaker Jim Rohn once said, "All good men and women must take responsibility to create legacies that will take the next generation to a level we could only imagine." Let your ceiling become someone else's floor. Set up others to surpass that which you couldn't or didn't. By leaving a spiritual legacy you can actually outlive yourself. Eighteenth-century author John Allston penned, "The only thing you take with you when you're gone is what you leave behind."

The Extra Point

Whether in sports, business, or ministry, great leaders replicate themselves in the lives of others. They are not insecure micro-managers. They are team builders, enablers, and macro-managers. They freely give away trade secrets for the privilege of strengthening the team. They have the courage to tell others what they know to be true, lead them to the source of all knowledge, then step back and allow them to grow.

I am eternally grateful for the knowledge that has been passed onto me from those who have already passed through the end zone of life. Their wisdom still is with me. I learned from Danny to enjoy the small joys of life, the tender moments with my family, and the laughs around the dinner table. I learned from my father that God's grace can reach and transform anyone at any time in their lives, no matter what they have done—that God truly is *"gracious and compassionate, slow to anger and rich in love"* (Ps. 103:8).

I learned from my grandfather that taking time to invest in other people's lives is worth the cost. I learned to love work, to give others the dignity they deserve, and to leave the legacy of a good name. I learned from Coach Paterno the greatness of humility, the beauty of modesty, and the value of giving back to my community. And I learned from my mother to put the needs of others before my own, to find joy in serving those around me, and to change the world from my knees.

Each of these people left me with a legacy that I now strive to leave behind. And just as my father left me with a good name, so our heavenly Father has left us with a good name. Jesus Christ is our legacy. He poured His life out so that we could take on His name. Now it's your turn to put your hand on the line and leave a legacy that lasts for generations.

Chalk Talk

1. What concerns you the most about your own eventual death? Are you fearful, hopeful, or fully assured of your salvation? If you knew the day that you would die, how would that affect your behavior today?

2. What kind of legacy do you want to leave to your family and to the generations that follow?

3. Is there a "Danny" in your life that you would regret not developing a deeper and more meaningful Christian relationship with if they should pass? Who is it? What are you going to do about it?

4. At your funeral, what would people say about the man you are today? What would you like them to say about you as a father, brother, Christian, athlete, or a businessman? Would you want your son or daughter to emulate your current witness for Christ?

5. Who may be standing on the other side of your obedience to following God's call? Are you ready to put your hand and your life on the line? I encourage you to take the action steps listed in this chapter to receive Christ

and take hold of the new life you have in Him. If you made that decision, I want you to tell another believer.

Endnote

1.   I remember Matt working out at the Raider facility in the off-season. He boomed punt after punt, yet for some reason he never got a formal tryout. I heard that he was living with Danny in southern California as he tried numerous times to get NFL tryouts without much success. He was finally signed by the Green Bay Packers in 1993 and released. The Rams signed him in 1994 but was released again before catching on with the Redskins in 1995. He went on to have a seventeen-year NFL career. He played for nine different teams and was an All-Pro three times.

2.   Roy B. Zuck, *The Speakers Quote book,* (Grand Rapids, MI. Kregel Publications 2009), 128

NO REGRETS

I have held many things in my hands, and
I have lost them all; but whatever I have
placed in God's hands, that I still possess.
—MARTIN LUTHER[1]

One Last Message

If I only had one message to pass on to you it would be this: put everything you have, everything you lack, and everything you hope to be in God's hands. Invest yourself fully in following God's call, in building personal relationships, and in your God-given family and place of employment. Seek God's blessing on every area of your life and give Him glory and thanks for what He has already done and for what He will continue to do. In doing so you will likely live a life without regrets.

My experience has been that everything I have entrusted to God He has blessed, and everything I have tried to keep from Him has come to ruin. The success I experienced as an NFL player was largely due to the blessings of God, hard work, and the fact that I played with no regrets. Regrets suck. Many of us have them and know that haunting feeling deep in our soul of what we could have or should have done. Like trying to escape your own shadow, regrets follow your every movement. At times you don't see them, and those closest to you may not even be aware of them, but you seldom lose the sense that they are stalking you.

In my athletic career, I was determined not to have any regrets. I've known dozens of talented men at every level who for one reason or another just didn't put it all together. I've heard and seen story after story of guys who said, "If I had only tried harder, not got injured, listened to my coaches, or not messed around with drugs and alcohol..."

Not me. I sought to take advantage of every opportunity given to me, to learn, improve, train, and play until the whistle blew. I didn't walk in fear of injury, nor did I question my coach's direction. I was ready to play anytime, anywhere, and I exhausted myself fully in that pursuit. I'd play in the parking lot or on the dark side of the moon if needed. I played with a reckless abandon like each game could be my last, and I backed down from no one, as if to say, "Let's meet at the bus and get this fight started." I never wanted to be old and look back on my life and say, "If I had only... I wish I had... I should have known to trust God."

Proverbs 28:1 states, *"The wicked flee though no one pursues, but the righteous are bold as a lion."* As a one belonging fully to Christ, we have absolutely nothing and no one to fear. God has our back, and His angels go before us. The Lord gives us No Fear Gear through the blood of Jesus and the Word of God. His power and wisdom are unmatched, and He takes pleasure when we strive to follow His will.

We all have once-in-a-lifetime opportunities in our path on a daily basis. God doesn't want you living in fear or intimidation, for He is with you. What He's called you to do, He promises to provide the resources for. Where He's called you to go, He will provide the protection, grace, and anointing to complete the mission. You must realize that you have a mission to accomplish here on earth, and you only have a short unspecified time to get that mission done. Your personal game clock is winding down.

Tomorrow is not promised to any one of us. Christ may return in two years, twenty years, or 2,000 more years, but that's not the question at hand. He is coming back—that much is certain. The relevant question is, are you ready to meet Him if you don't survive the night? If you were to die today, do you have areas of unfinished business or areas of regret that you need to address?

Personal Regret

It's normal for great men to have personal regrets. However, it's what we do with these regrets that determines the outcome of the game. In the movie *Schindler's List*, the main character, Oskar Schindler, is a German businessman who saved the lives of over 1,000 Polish-Jewish refugees by hiring them to work in his factories during the Holocaust. He spent all of his personal net worth bribing German guards and officials to allow Jewish workers to work for him instead of sending them to their certain deaths in the concentration camp at Auschwitz.

Oskar Schindler took extreme chances time and again to put his fortunes and his personal well-being on the line to save these Jewish refugees. When Germany finally surrenders, he is completely out of money and must flee or risk being captured by the advancing Russian Army. As he bids farewell, his workers give him a ring engraved with a Talmudic quotation: "Whoever saves one life saves the entire world." He is deeply moved by their act of appreciation and weeps, as he feels ashamed as though he could have somehow done more.[2]

At the end of our lives, all that matters are the relationships we have formed and the work we have done in building the kingdom of God. The great evangelist Billy Graham said in his autobiography *Just As I Am* that he had three personal regrets: If he got to live his life over again, he would have spent more time in prayer, spent more time studying God's Word, and spent more time with his wife and kids, especially in their early years.

I left no regrets on the field, but I do have some off of it. I wish I had told my mother how much I loved her and how much I appreciated her sacrifices before she passed away. I wish I had a better husband, more emotionally vulnerable and transparent in my relationships. I wish I had listened more carefully to the voice of God in my investments instead of blindly following "good ideas" that often evaporated. I wish I had obeyed the call of God on my life sooner and written this book when God had instructed me. Who knows the lives it could have touched in that appointed season? I wish I had set a better example of work ethic for my kids by maintaining full-time employment after my playing career was over. I wish I had invested myself more fully in my community and the lives of other men.

Recently, we moved from our California home of many years. As we made preparations for the move, I was terribly convicted by all the truckloads of junk I came across. I had an attic, garage, and storage room full of old sporting goods, auto parts, furniture, artwork, and cancelled checks for items long since discarded. Things I once considered valuable, I had to now pay just for people to haul away. As I shredded boxes of old documents, I was confronted with so many poor investment decisions and regrettable purchases. Items I researched, craved, and paid dearly for were often quickly broken, discarded, and devalued; so many wasted dollars, wasted years, and countless distractions. Had I obeyed God when He told me to write this book, I seriously doubt I would have spent a decade in this manner of indecisive living.

I tried a number of different jobs, numerous hobbies, and seemingly worthy pursuits, and yet there was no peace. Looking back, the common denominator was that I was not doing what God had clearly called me to do. Therefore, I was walking in my own willful disobedience and not fully giving myself to any one pursuit. In the back of my mind, I could hear the Holy Spirit saying, "Steve, this is not what I've called you to do." My disobedience led to an undisciplined and discontented life. But praise God, that season is over and a new one has begun.

Do you have any personal regrets? If so, I encourage you to verbalize them, write them down, and give them to God. Romans 8:28 says, *"And we know that in all things God works for the good of those who love Him, who have been called according to His purpose."* God will not waste a personal scar, a bad memory, or even a disobedient action, if we truly release it to Him. Write your regrets down on paper and prayerfully offer them up to God. Then shred or burn the paper as a prophetic act and allow God to remove the pain from your soul. In doing so, it will bring healing to you and your experience may now be offered up to bless others and glorify God. No matter how bad you feel about yourself, or your poor decisions, God hasn't given up on you. We have to see ourselves as God sees us. Dearly loved children that want to spend time with and use for His glory. Like the Prodigal Son (Luke 15), when we return home to Him, God runs out to greet us and wrap us in His arms.

Where you have sinned, confess it. Where you have disobeyed God, renounce it. Where you were wrong, admit it. Come clean and move forward, asking the Holy Spirit to fill every void in your life and direct every step for His glory. God has great things in store for those who love Him and are called according to His purposes. He uses everyday people like you and me to do the extraordinary. He is an amazing Daddy who wants to know us intimately, blessing us and our descendants for generations to come.

I believe the time has come for us as men to make our way to the cross. The key to us being good stewards of our lives is not all the activity that we do in Jesus's name. It's that the activity we do and the pursuits of our life are in accordance with our heavenly Father's will. We must submit ourselves fully to God and allow Him to lead us and direct our steps. In so doing, we invite His presence into our relationships, homes, and places of business (see 2 Chron. 7:14).

I don't believe any of us will ever regret the time we spent reading God's Word or in prayer. I doubt we will ever regret following God's call on our life or investing ourselves fully in the lives of our family members. I doubt we will ever regret sharing our faith in God or building community with other believers.

It's Time for Action

At pivotal times in a man's life, he is forced to choose between two courses of action, each with their own certain outcome. Growing up in Texas, we studied Texas history, and in particular the state's fight to win independence from Mexico. The famous battle of the Alamo was a pivotal turning point in the war and became a battle cry for the rag-tag assortment of Texas freedom fighters. In late February of 1836, the Mexican general Santa Anna accompanied by over 1,500 well-armed soldiers surrounded a small mission near San Antonio, known as the Alamo. Inside were a little over a hundred poorly equipped rebels, including frontiersman Davy Crockett, and commanders James Bowie and William Travis.

A thirteen-day battle ensued and was the most intensely fought blood bath either army had ever been involved in. Miraculously, the resilient and hopelessly outnumbered rebels somehow held the mission against multiple and repeated assaults. With their ammunition, food, and water nearly exhausted, William Travis reportedly called his men together for what would be the last time. On March 5, 1836, he clearly explained their dire situation and explained that each man must now make the personal decision that will decide their future. With his sword drawn, he marked out a long line in the dusty dirt in front of his remaining men. Travis told the men that if they wanted to try to escape the mission under the cover of darkness, they would have his blessing. He promised no one would think badly of them or report them as deserters. But if they wished to stay and fight to the bitter end, he asked them to mark their decision by stepping over the line.[3]

Reportedly, every man stepped over the line but one, including a severely injured Jim Bowie who reportedly asked to be carried across. Inaction was not accepted. It's fascinating to me that Travis required these exhausted men to signify their decision by action. He didn't say, "I know you're tired, thirsty, and injured, so I will make this easy for you. If you wish to stay, just stand where you are." No, he said if you wish to stay, put your faith in action, and step up and over this line.

The next morning, on March 6, the Mexican Army again assaulted the fort in a brutal attack. With the Texans ammunition completely exhausted, they resorted to hand-to-hand combat. The Mexican Army reportedly killed Travis with a gunshot and breached the northern quadrant of the fort. Within two hours they had captured the fort and killed every man accept for a few men who were left critically wounded.[4] No mention was ever made of the man who tried to escape. I can't help but think he was most likely shot in his attempt to flee. I wonder if his dying thoughts were of regret for leaving his fellow soldiers, or, if he did escape, did he regret his decision and see himself as a coward until the day that he died?

Now that you have been presented with the information in this book and God has had some time to speak to your soul, it's time for you to decide. Either way, action is demanded on your part. Step across the line, and fight for what you know to be true, although it will cost you your life. Or flee in the night and attempt to run away from God and those whom you love. Either way, you will face death. One death leads to freedom, the other to regret, remorse, and continued separation from God and the plans He has for your life.

Some of you are ready to commit your life to following Jesus. Maybe others of you are still scared. Maybe you're fearful that you will just slide back into your old habits. Maybe you've quit on yourself before: you quit on loved ones over the years, your education, diet, finances, exercise program, or your employer. No one has to tell you that you've blown it in an area or two of your life. You know it because you've let yourself down. That's okay if you feel that way, because it just means you're seriously counting the cost of following God. Many of the most faithful men in the Lord throughout history were once the staunchest skeptics.

We need to push through our emotional baggage, doubts, and fears, and wrap our arms around Jesus and not let go. As a former offensive lineman, I know a little something about holding. I am going to latch onto Jesus like my life depended on it, because I know it really does.

The Lord stands ready to receive you, and His Holy Spirit knows nothing but victory. He will release us from the spirit of "quit." He fears nothing and neither will we any longer. Proverbs 18:10 states, *"The name of the Lord is a strong tower, the righteous run to it and are safe."* I don't know about you, but I am sprinting to the Lord this very moment. If you're with me, we will be safe together. The Lord is ready to impart to you a new and abundant life. For us, eternity begins today.

The reason you and I have likely faltered in the past is because there were likely a few areas we tried to keep hidden from God. When we give ourselves only partially to God, we fool ourselves because we haven't actually given ourselves at all. It's all in or not at all. We were disillusioned because we didn't feel His presence, power, provision, and passion. Because we were only dipping our toe in the Christian life, God's promises didn't ring true for us.

With good reason, He didn't want you and me to mistaken that halfhearted relationship for the real thing.

God saw all those sinful areas in our life all along, and He still loves us anyway. You feel the tug at your heart right now, but you think you can't completely give it up to God. What exactly is holding you back at this moment? I can promise you: whatever you have a hard time releasing is not from God. This time will be different because all of us have something to verbalize to God and give back to Him. I want us all to start by asking God to forgive us of the areas we have kept from Him. Name them specifically. Put a specific name to it and pray in Jesus's name that He take control of it.

Confess it as sin. Repent of it, which means to make a complete turn from it. And pray in Jesus's name for His Spirit to fill every area and void in your life. Welcome His Holy Spirit into your life as Master, Leader, Teacher, and Savior. Invite His presence into your life, your home, your work, your finances, your thought life, and your family's life. Ask Him to cleanse and heal your body, soul, and spirit of your sin, sickness, and any godless thoughts. Be specific if anything comes to mind. Ask Jesus to perform spiritual surgery on you to remove anything in your life that is not of Him.

Lastly, spend some time thanking Him for cleansing you and making you new. Thank Him for His faithfulness, His love, His provision, His patience, and His grace. Thank the Lord for who He is, what He's already done in your life, and for what He is going to do. Take some time to verbalize these thoughts out loud to God—don't rush it. This is a powerful spiritual act and a defining moment in your life—one that will alter eternity. The angels of the Lord are watching and rejoicing when we as men humbly seek the presence of God for our life (see Luke 15:7,10).

Begin by walking through your home with a trash bag and start filling it with anything that is not of God. Play some Christian music as you trash whatever God puts on your heart. Don't worry how much that music, book, magazine, movie, video game, artwork, or computer cost you. God can afford to replace it with something that honors Him. With a critical eye, trash or unplug anything that could be a stumbling block in following God. Then tell some other faithful believers what you've just done. Find a solid Bible-believing Christian church where you can be fed. Download a New International Version Bible app, or buy a Bible and start reading a proverb and a chapter of the New Testament every day.

No telling where God will send you. Visiting the troops in Iraq in 2008 with kicker Jason Elam (Left) and receiver Tim Dwight (right)

My brother, you are on now your way to a transformed life. We can be 100 percent assured of rejoicing together in paradise. If I get there first, I will introduce you to all of my friends and many of those whom you read about in this book. Don't worry if you don't hear the audible applause of heaven, God saw your actions and He receives you. Far better than a hot shower after a day in the mud, you have now been made clean and are seen as a new creation in Christ. We are like newborn babies in that we need to seek spiritual nourishment and care from those who can love, support, and encourage us in the things of God. I encourage you to push through the barriers the enemy throws at you, and contend for your faith like it's the most valuable possession you own.

It's Not Too Late

In football, as in life, it's not how you start the game that counts—it's how you finish. Coaches love to start fast and get up early on the opponent, but despite good intentions and preparations, it doesn't always work that way. Several of the most memorable wins in my athletic career were in games where we engineered great comebacks from as much as seventeen-point deficits. Jesus is the author of amazing comebacks. He is the redeemer, which means He restores what once was and what was intended to be. If you're reading this, then it's not too late for you. The Lord has a comeback story ready to be engineered in your life.

Two common criminals hung next to Jesus, receiving their punishment for an inglorious life of crime. One threw insults and mocked Jesus, while the other made a simple yet heartfelt proclamation:

> One of the criminals who hung there hurled insults at him: "Aren't You the Messiah? Save Yourself and us!"
>
> But the other criminal rebuked him. "Don't you fear God," he said, "since you are under the same sentence? We are punished justly, for we are getting what our deeds deserve. But this man has done nothing wrong."
>
> Then he said, "Jesus, remember me when You come into Your kingdom."
>
> Jesus answered him, "Truly I tell you, today you will be with Me in paradise" (Luke 23:39-43).

The thief was transformed in an instant from a scourge of society to a saint of God. The man went to the cross for the hell that he created, only to be saved from the hell of eternity. He met Jesus in his final minutes and gained eternal access to paradise. He still paid the penalty for his actions, but he found true freedom in the process. God can do more good in your life in one day than in all the previous years spent without Him.

My former strength coach Garret Giemont used to say, "If you're early, you're never late." It's always better to be a few minutes early to a meeting or event than a few minutes late. We can't guess the hour of our death and hope to make a salvation plea five minutes prior. I have witnessed to a friend who repeatedly tells me that is his plan. But between me and you, his plan is foolishness.

God knows our intentions and the desires of our heart, and He will not be mocked. I recently told my friend that if he does take hold of the reality of Christ in the last five minutes of his life, he would kick himself for not reaching out to Christ earlier. His spiritual eyes will have been opened to see that Christ doesn't chain us down with spiritual burdens; instead, He sets us free from them.

You may be 16 years old like I was, or 69 years old like my father was when he gave his life to the Lord; you may be early in the game or in your final hours of life and not even know it, but God has a perfect plan to be glorified in your remaining days. Are you willing to allow Him in? Are you truly ready to invite God into all areas of your life? Are you ready to be the man God intended you to be before the foundation of the world?

I wrote this simple heartfelt prayer that I myself have offered to God many times before. It may not be perfect, but neither am I. I am not a seminary graduate or theologian. I have not been a hero of faith, nor am I extremely intelligent or even articulate. What I am, however, is sincere, and that's all we need to please the Lord in our prayers.

Lord Jesus, I confess that I have sinned against You and Your Holy Word. I confess that I need You and want You to redeem my life. I ask You to forgive me of my sins, my rebellion, my disobedience, and my stubborn pride. I repent of living a life apart from You and doing things my own way for all these years. I ask that Your Spirit will come fill every part of my body, soul, spirit, and mind.

Please Lord, be my Master, my Savior, my loving Father, and my dearest Companion. I know that You are real. I believe You died to take on my sin, and I believe I can have a new life in You.

I ask You to remove everything unholy from my mind and give me a passion for the things of God. Please take mastery over every single area of my life. Spiritually, I stand naked before You. Please give me Your grace and peace as You direct my steps for Your glory. Give me boldness in my faith, conviction in my prayers, and sensitivity to be led by Your Spirit at all times. Please protect me and my loved ones from the schemes of the enemy.

My past is washed in Your sacrificial blood, my present is yielded to You, and my future is completely at Your disposal. Lord, please be glorified in my life and mold me into a righteous and godly man. Please, Lord, redeem the time I have left and allow me to be a blessing to You and others. Amen.

Endnotes

1.   Martin Luther was a German priest and scholar whose questioning of church practices led to the Protestant Reformation (1483–1546). This quote was accessed from http://thinkexist.com/quotation/i_have_held_many_things_in_my_hands-and_i_have/169725.html, accessed February 19, 2015.

2. This information was accessed from Wikipedia, http://
    en.wikipedia.org/wiki/Schindler%27s_List, accessed February
    19, 2015.

3. This information was accessed from Wikipedia, http://
    en.wikipedia.org/wiki/Battle_of_the_Alamo, accessed February
    19, 2015.

4. This information was taken from http://latinamericanhistory.
    about.com/od/TexasIndependence/p/Biography-Of-William-
    Travis.htm, accessed February 19, 2015.

ABOUT THE AUTHORS

STEVE WISNIEWSKI is a former NFL player and coach who spent fourteen seasons with the Oakland Raiders. After football, Steve volunteered as a minister for eleven years at the Well Christian Community, located in Livermore, California. Steve has recently relocated to Austin, Texas. Steve is a husband and father of three grown children. He is passionate about sharing his faith in Christ with other men, going on family adventures, and enjoying the outdoors. Through the vehicles of football and ministry, Steve has donated hundreds of hours of his time speaking, teaching, and serving the needs of others.

JEFF ROSTOCIL is a freelance author and has been a Christian motivational speaker for twenty years. He has written two books: *Unshakable: Living Your Life Anchored to God's Kingdom* and *Bulletproof: Accessing the Favor and Protection of God in the Secret Place*. He and his wife, Meljoné, founded SoleQuest International in 2002 and live in Northern California with their three children.

❤📖 LOVE to READ?

Get FREE eBooks,
Deep Discounts and New Release Updates!

Sign up now.
destinyimage.com/freebooks

📚 SHARE this BOOK!

Don't let the impact of this book end with you!

Get a discount
when you order
3 or MORE BOOKS.
CALL **1-888-987-7033**

🎤 AUTHOR INTERVIEWS

Exclusive interviews with your favorite authors!

Tune in today.

voiceofdestiny.net

 Destiny Image is a division of Nori Media Group.